VOLUME 3

BICHRI—CHRONOLOGY

The LIVING ENCYCLOPEDIA

This family library serves both adult and younger readers
It combines THE ZONDERVAN PICTORIAL BIBLE DICTIONARY
stories and narrative accounts from the KNOW YOUR BIBLE PROGRAM
a gallery of 480 paintings based on Bible themes
and the most fascinating photographs of contemporary
scenes and archaeological finds in the Holy Land

BIBLE

in Story
and
Pictures

VOLUME 3

BICHRI—CHRONOLOGY

H. S. STUTTMAN CO., INC.
New York, New York 10016

"And Jesus went about all Galilee,
teaching in their synagogues,
and preaching the gospel of the kingdom...."
(MATTHEW 4:23)

COVER ILLUSTRATION: Ruins of the synagogue at
Capernaum, which archaeologists believe is near the
site of the famous synagogue where Christ taught.
Excavations at Capernaum have yielded rich archaeological finds.

"And Cain talked with Abel his brother:
and it came to pass, when they were in the field,
that Cain rose up against Abel his brother,
and slew him."
(GENESIS 4:8)

This relief showing the struggle of the two brothers, which resulted in the first murder, comes from the palace of the Assyrian
Ashurnasirpal II who ruled in the ninth century B.C.

BICHRI (bĭk′rī, *first-born*), mentioned in II Samuel 20:1 as the father of Sheba, who made insurrection against David.

BIDKAR (bĭd′kàr), a military officer of Israel who joined Jehu in his revolt and was made his captain (II Kings 9:25).

BIGTHA (bĭg′thà), one of the seven chamberlains of Ahasuerus, i.e. Xerxes (Esth. 1:10).

BIGTHAN or **BIGTHANA** (bĭg′thăn or bĭg′thā′nà), one of the chamberlains of king Ahasuerus, i.e. Xerxes, who with another, Teresh, had plotted to slay the king. Mordecai heard of the plot, and through Esther warned the king, who had the two men hanged (Esth. 2:21-23; 6:2).

BIGVAI (bĭg′vā-ī, *fortunate*). 1. One of the 11 or 12 chief men who returned from captivity by permission of Cyrus in 536 B.C. (Ezra 2:2; Neh. 7).

2. The ancestor of a family of over 2,000 who returned with Zerubbabel from captivity (Ezra 2:14; Neh. 7:19). Some think that the slight difference of numbers in the two verses quoted is due to the possibility that Ezra's was a list made in Babylon before starting, and Nehemiah's at Jerusalem after arriving. Some few have dropped out and a few added during the migration.

3. Probably the same as 2. The ancestor of a family of which 72 men returned with Ezra in 457 B.C. (Ezra 8:14).

BILDAD (bĭl′dăd), one of Job's three "comforters" (cf. Job 2:11-13 with 42:7-10). He was evidently a descendant of Shuah (Gen. 25:2), a son of Abraham by Keturah, who became patriarch of an Arab tribe. Bildad made three speeches (Job 8,18,25), and his distinctive character as a "traditionalist" can best be seen in 8:8-10.

BILEAM (bĭl′ē-ăm), a town in the western half of the tribe of Manasseh given in Joshua's time to the Levites of the Kohathite family who were not priests (I Chron. 6:70).

BILGAH (bĭl′gà, *cheerfulness*). 1. Head of the 15th course of priests in David's time (I Chron. 24:14).

2. A priest who returned with Zerubbabel in 536 B.C. (Neh. 12:5).

BILGAI (bĭl′gā-ī), a priest in Nehemiah's time, 444 B.C. (Neh. 10:8).

BILHAH (bĭl′hà, *foolish*). 1. Maid-servant of Rachel, Jacob's beloved wife, and later given to Jacob by Rachel that she might bear children who would be credited to Rachel (Gen. 29:29; 30:1-8). She became ancestress of the two tribes, Dan and Naphtali. In the polygamous system of early Israel, she would be ranked higher than a mere concubine, but not as high as her free-born mistress.

2. A town in the tribe of Simeon. Spelled "Balah" in Joshua 19:3.

BILHAN (bĭl′hăn, *foolish*). 1. A son of Ezer, son of Seir the Horite (Gen. 36:27; I Chron. 1:42). Etymologically, the name is the same as *Bilhah,* but with the Horite ending.

2. An early Benjamite; son of Jediael, son of Benjamin (I Chron. 7:10). He had seven sons who were mighty men and heads of large families.

BILSHAN (bĭl′shăn), one of the 11 or 12 leaders of the Jews who returned from captivity in 536 B.C. (Ezra 2:2; Neh. 7:7).

BIMHAL (bĭm′hăl), one of the three sons of Japhlet of the tribe of Asher (I Chron. 7:33).

BINDING AND LOOSING. The carrying of a key or keys was a symbol of the delegated power of opening and closing. In Matthew 16:19, our Lord gave the "power of the keys" to Peter, and Peter's use of the keys is narrated in what may be called the "three stages of Pentecost." On the day of Pentecost (Acts 2:14-40) Peter preached the first Christian sermon and opened "the kingdom of heaven" to what became a Hebrew-Christian church; then with John he went to Samaria (Acts 8:14-17) and opened the same "kingdom" to the Samaritans; and still later in the house of Cornelius (Acts 10:44-48) he opened it to the Gentiles; so that the Church could become universal. The medieval teaching about Peter standing at the gate of heaven to receive or reject souls of men has no basis in the Bible teaching.

BINNUI (bĭn′ū-ī, *built*). 1. A Levite, whose son was partly in charge of the silver and gold at Ezra's return (Ezra 8:33).

2. One of the sons of Pahath-moab who had married foreign wives (Ezra 10:30).

3. A son of Bani who had been similarly guilty (Ezra 10:38).

4. One of the rebuilders of Jerusalem in 444 B.C. who also became a covenanter under Nehemiah (Neh. 3:24; 10:9).

5. Alternate spelling of Bani (cf. Ezra 2:10; Neh. 7:15) whose family returned with Zerubbabel.

6. A Levite who returned with Zerubbabel (Neh. 12:8).

BIRDS of 360 to 400 different kinds occur in Palestine, and of these, 26 are found only there. The Bible mentions about 50, using Hebrew or Greek names which can sometimes be identified with particular species of the present. Birds are mentioned in all but 21 books of the Bible and 19 times in the apocryphal books. The following birds are specifically mentioned.

Bittern, a heron-like bird of marshy environment with a mournful call. It was prophesied that it would live in a waste land which replaced the cursed Edom (Isa. 34:11). Translated as "porcupine" in ARV and RSV.

Chicken, the common domesticated barn yard fowl, descended from the wild red jungle fowl of India, Burma, and Malaya. Mentioned as the young of a hen which shows consideration for her offspring, as Christ would have comforted Jerusalem (Matt. 23:37). Perhaps the "fatted fowl" of I Kings 4:22-23. See "hen."

Cock, the male of the domestic chicken. Used as a symbol of the early part of the day because of its morning crowing (Mark 13:35), a reminder of Jesus' word to Peter that he would deny his Lord (Matt. 26:74). There is a church in Jerusalem today named Gallicante, after the cock which Peter heard.

Cormorant, a swimmer and diver with webs between all four toes. It can pursue and catch fish under water. Some orientals use it to capture fish for them. A dweller in waste places, hence a sign of a curse on land formerly inhabited, such as Edom and Nineveh. Included in list of unclean birds in Leviticus 11, probably because it is a flesh eater. Since the flesh contained blood, and Israelites were forbidden to eat blood, they were also prohibited from eating birds which were carnivorous. In Isaiah 34:11 it is "pelican" in ARV, and "hawk" in RSV. Zephaniah 2:14 replaces "cormorant" with "pelican" in ARV and "vulture" in RSV.

Crane, a long-necked, long-legged wading bird whose voice is a croak or a honk heard for several miles. Hezekiah's lament over his sickness is compared to that of a crane (Isa. 38:14). Its time of migration is well known, so that its faithful return is contrasted to Israel's faithlessness (Jer. 8:7).

Crow. No specimen is mentioned in the Bible, but the word is the symbol of the voice of the cock and other birds.

Cuckoo, an unclean bird of Leviticus 11 and Deuteronomy 14. The RSV translates this "sea gull," the ARV "sea mew," and G. R. Driver "long-eared owl." The gull and owl are flesh eaters, hence condemned for human food.

Cuckow, the KJV name for cuckoo. See cuckoo.

Dove. Probably the rock pigeon or the rock dove similar to our domestic pigeon, common in flocks in parks and around buildings. It was sent from the ark after the flood, but found no land, so returned, but did not go out until after a fortnight when firm footing was available (Gen. 8:8-12). It flies rapidly on high, as the Psalmist wishes his prayers also could. The dove is a promise of a blessed future for those in humble circumstances; for though one has lain among the pots, yet he shall be as the wings of doves covered with silver and feathers covered with gold (Ps. 68:13). The "pots" may be ash grates, as in some translations. This, then, becomes a source of the phrase, "Beauty for ashes." The dove appropriately becomes a symbol of a lover in the Song of Solomon for its soft cooing voice was well known. However, Hezekiah compares his mourning over his illness to the voice of a dove (Isa. 38:14) and both Isaiah and Ezekiel felt that sinful Israel would mourn like a dove. Like the swift flight of doves (Isa. 59:11; Ezek. 7: 16) so would help come from Zion (Isa. 60:8). Their nests "in the clefts of the rock, in the covert of a cliff" (S. of Sol. 2:14 RSV) or "in the sides of the mouth of a gorge" (Jer. 48:28 RSV) suggest peaceful retreats for lovers or from threat of judgment. Doves are among the less intelligent of birds, hence foolish Ephraim is compared to a "silly dove." Their harmlessness is mentioned in

Twice Noah sent the dove from the ark. The first time the dove found no land and returned. A fortnight later Noah again sent out the dove. In the evening the dove returned, and in her mouth was a green olive leaf. Noah knew that the waters were abated from off the earth.

Matthew 10:16. The Spirit of God descends "like a dove" (Matt. 3:16). Doves were sold in the Temple for the rites of purification, but Jesus cast out the sellers (Matt. 21:12).

Eagle, a large, hawk-like bird having powerful beak, talons, and wings, with a spread of over four feet. Israel was carried from Egypt by Jehovah on eagles' wings (Exod. 19:4; Deut. 32:11). The Lord renews the youth of the soul like the eagle (Ps. 103:5) so that it mounts up with wings as eagles (Isa. 40:31). The woman of Revelation 12 escapes the serpent by using the gift of "two wings of a great eagle." Israel will be chastised by a nation "as swift as the eagle flieth" (Deut. 28:49; Jer. 4:13). Even though Edom should be as inaccessible as an eagle's high nest, it will be destroyed (Jer. 49:16; Obad. 4). Eagles will eat the eyes of mockers (Prov. 30:17; Matt. 24:28). In these verses the KJV and ARV use the term "young eagles," while the RSV prefers "vultures." Several symbolic creatures have eagles' features (Ezek. 1:10; Ezek. 17:3). Nebuchadnezzar's kingdom was compared to a lion with eagle's wings (Dan. 7:4). In their death Saul and Jonathan were "swifter than eagles" (II Sam. 1:23), and Job's days passed away as fast as an eagle hastening to the prey (Job 9:26). Riches are not to be desired, for they fly away as eagles toward heaven (Prov. 23:5). The eagle is among the unclean birds of Leviticus 11.

Falcon, a hawk with long-pointed wings and long tail. It is an unclean bird in Leviticus 11 (KJV), translated "kite" by RSV.

Fowl, used of all flying birds (Gen. 1:20) and even includes the bat (Lev. 11:13,19) which is a mammal. Mentioned as sacrifices (Lev. 1:14), food (Deut. 14:20) and scavengers of perished sinners (Ezek. 29:5). They are wise (Job 35:11) but God possesses greater wisdom (Job 28:7). Men are worth more than many fowls (Luke 12:24).

Gier Eagle, a KJV term; called "vulture" in RSV and ARV and "osprey" by G. R. Driver. See "osprey."

Glede, a kind of vulture or hawk. An unclean bird of Deuteronomy 14:13.

Great Owl, an unclean bird of Leviticus 11. Listed as "Ibis" in RSV. See "owl."

Hawk, a fast-flying, sharp-tongued, curved-beaked predator, considered unclean in Leviticus 11 and Deuteronomy 14. It is similar to the eagle and the flight of both is mentioned as God given in Job 39:26-27.

Hen, the female of the domestic chicken, which is solicitous for its young, even as Jesus wishes to be for Jerusalem (Matt. 23:37).

Heron, a long-legged, marsh-inhabiting wading bird. Unclean in Leviticus 11 and Deuteronomy 14.

Hoopoe, see "lapwing."

Kite, see "falcon" as it is translated in ARV and RSV.

Lapwing, perhaps the woodcock, a long-billed bird living on worms. RSV and ARV translate this term "hoopoe" as does Driver. The hoopoe has a prominent crest and curved bill pictured in an Egyptian fowling scene 3800 years ago. "It probes in filth for insects and worms and this habit doubtlessly earned for it an 'unclean' classification." (Parmalee)

Little Owl, see "owl." An unclean bird of Leviticus 11.

BEDOUIN HUNTER with trained falcons. The falcon is a hawk with long, pointed wings and long tail. It is one of the unclean birds mentioned in Leviticus.

HAWK of Palestine, considered unclean in Leviticus and Deuteronomy. Its flight is mentioned as God given in Job.

Nighthawk, called the same in KJV and RSV but "short-eared owl" by Driver and "owl, swallow, cuckoo" by Young's *Analytical Concordance.* Nighthawks and whip-poor-wills are similar small-beaked, strong-flying insect-eating birds. The nighthawk is listed as unclean in Leviticus 11.

Ospray, spelled "osprey" in modern English, as in RSV. A fish-eating hawk which has roughened pads on its feet to help hold slippery fish. An unclean bird of Leviticus 11.

Ossifrage, the "bearded vulture" in Driver's dictionary account. An unclean bird of Leviticus 11. See "vulture." (Called "gier eagle" in ARV.)

Ostrich, the largest living bird, whose habits are accurately described in Job 39:13-18. With "a bounding stride of 15 feet or more, ostriches can indeed 'scour the plain,' running 40 miles an hour and easily out-distancing the fastest horse" (Parmalee). The author of Lamentations considered them cruel (4:3). Job felt that his sad state made him like a companion of the reticent ostrich (Job 30:29 ARV).

Owl, a nocturnal bird of prey, hunting rodents and other small animals. They reminded the Israelites of desolate and ruined cities (Isa. 34:15). The "great owl" is similar to the American great-horned owl, twenty-two inches long, and the "little owl" is the most common owl in Palestine. All were considered unclean (Lev. 11 where ARV and RSV have "ostrich"). All owls have mournful voices, resembling a discouraged prayer (Ps. 102:6).

Partridge, a member of the order of birds to which chickens belong. Because of their swift and sneaky running, they are excellent game birds. David compared himself to a partridge when Saul was hunting him (I Sam. 26:20). It was supposed that partridges robbed eggs from others and hatched them, a symbol of getting riches unfairly (Jer. 17:11).

Peacock, the beautiful birds brought for Solomon's courtyard, probably from India and Ceylon. The peacocks mentioned in Job 39:13 (KJV) are probably ostrich hens (ARV).

Pelican. Dr. Driver thinks the pelican in the list of unclean birds of Leviticus 11 is the scops owl, only eight inches long. Pelicans, like cormorants, have webs between all four toes, which enable them to pursue the fish they eat. Whether the Hebrew *qaath* means owl or pelican, it refers to an unclean bird on account of its flesh eating habit.

Pigeon, the common rock dove (see dove). Because pigeons do not migrate and are numerous, their young were easily obtained by the poor for sacrifice (Gen. 15:9; Luke 2:24).

Quail, a ground dweller, scratching for food and having strong flying muscles for rapid flight of short duration. Its flesh is good for food (Exod. 16:13; Ps. 105:40). Quail migrate in enormous flocks only a few feet above the ground, "two cubits high" (Num. 11:31).

Raven, similar to a large crow, with larger head and shoulders, and an omnivorous eater, hence condemned in Leviticus 11. It could live on dead bodies, so did not return when Noah sent it from the ark. Ravens fed Elijah (I Kings 17:4) and are fed by God (Job 38:41), dwell in places formerly inhabited (Isa. 34:11) and will pick out the eye of a mocker (Prov. 30:17).

Screech Owl, a small owl with penetrating voice. Parmalee mentions that many owls are found "in the rock tombs of Petra, chief city of ancient Edom," which may point to a fulfillment of Isaiah 34:13,14, although the creature mentioned here may be the ostrich (ARV).

Sea Mew, see "cuckoo."

Sparrow, a small, seed-eating bird closely akin to the American house sparrow. Noisy, active and prolific. It was protected in the Temple (Ps. 84:3). This name may also include wrens like our house wren. Sparrows were so cheap that when four were purchased a fifth was added free, but all are noticed by the heavenly Father, "Fear ye not, therefore . . ." (Matt. 10:31). Sparrows live in groups, so a sparrow "alone on a housetop" (Ps. 102:7) is an unusual sight. The Hebrew word *tsippor* in this verse may better be translated rock thrush, which haunts lonely places.

Stork, a long-legged, heron-like bird feeding in marshes but nesting in trees (Lev. 11:17). It has a regular migration time, more faithful than God's people (Jer. 8:7). Their powerful wings are referred to in Zechariah 5:9.

Swallow, probably the swift, with dashing flight and piercing repeated call. Appropriate to Hezekiah's chattering in his illness (Isa. 38:14).

Swan, member of duck and goose family but with longer neck. Called "swan" in KJV, but "water hen" in RSV, "horned owl" in ARV, and "little owl" by Driver, and Young's *Analytical Concordance.* Because it is included in the list of unclean birds it is more than likely the meat-eating owl rather than the vegetarian swan.

Turtledove, a wild pigeon of migratory habits, similar to our mourning dove, singing frequently early in the spring (S. of Sol. 2:12), abundant for sacrifices (Gen. 15:9), so that they were a godsend to the poor (Luke 2:24).

Vulture, a hawk-like bird feeding on dead animals, and the slain of Isaiah 34:15 (called "kite" in ARV). Included among unclean birds of Leviticus 11 and Deuteronomy 14. Wide ranging in its soaring, but God knows a path the vulture has not seen (Job 28:7, ARV has "falcon" here).   R.L.M.

BIRSHA (bîr'shà), king of Gomorrah who was defeated by Chedorlaomer (Gen. 14:2,10).

BIRTH, the bringing into existence of a separate life. Although this is accompanied by rending pain, there is no evidence that such pain would have occurred had not sin entered the human race. (See Genesis 3:16 where pain in child-bearing is a part of the curse upon Eve for her sin.) This pain is so uniquely severe that in nine-tenths of the forty-odd uses of the word "travail" in Scripture ("as of a woman in travail") it is used as a figure for intense suffering (Jer. 13:21; Rom. 8:22; Gal. 4:19, etc.) Apparently the ancient Hebrew women went through travail more easily than the Egyptians (Exod. 1:19).

(continued on page 309)

THE NARRATIVE ACCOUNT THAT FOLLOWS, *The Birth of Christ,* was written by Curtis Mitchell. Presented here in narrative style, it is based upon the events related in the Four Gospels.

THE
Birth of Christ

ARY AND JOSEPH of the village of Nazareth in Galilee stood close together in the doorway of her home, looking at each other with the bright expectancy that is typical of engaged couples the world over. Behind them in the shadows two other figures sat quietly, their faces soft with pride and peace. They were Mary's parents, and they had just passed a milestone of importance.

They had set a date for Mary's wedding to Joseph.

They could be proud of Joseph, their daughter's betrothed. He had shown himself to be sober and industrious. They were certain he would be good to their daughter. His income from carpentry was enough for a modest establishment. He came of a good family, of the house of David, who had been Israel's greatest king. He could read and write and had educated himself by studying the Law at the nearby synagogue.

After saying good-night to Mary's parents, he stood with her in the darkness for a few minutes. She looked up at him, anticipating the day when their betrothal would be over and he would take her to his own home. What a nuisance to be married and yet not married, but that was the custom, and perhaps it was best that the betrothal compact gave her the protection due a married woman even though she remained a virgin in her father's house. But enough of such thoughts. Their marriage would give her love in abundance, a roof, food, clothing, children.

"It is good that we've named the day," he said.

"It is very good," she said, trembling with happiness.

He touched her hand in a good-night gesture. "In all Galilee, no man will be as happy as I."

"No woman, either." Twisting about, she fled suddenly into the house and closed the door.

Joseph chuckled happily and strode into the darkness of the hillside that sloped away to the valley. Stars twinkled above the sharp horizon that was the ridge of Carmel running westward to the Mediterranean. From those heights, where he had spent many a day while his mind blazed with dreams, the eye could see the fabled Plain of Esdraelon (Es-druh-EE-lun) with its scores of battlefields and the ruined cities called Tabor (TAY-buhr), Megiddo (Muh-GIH-doh) and Gilboa (Gil-BOH-uh). Through that valley ran a web of busy roads—eastward to the Jordan River, southward to

Jerusalem and Egypt, westward to Acre (AH-ker) and the sea, and northward to fabled Damascus and Syria.

How odd that the Hebrews alone, of all the world, worshiped but one God. Athens, a decaying city since the glory of Alexander three hundred years earlier, had spawned gods by the dozens. Rome, in imitation of Greek culture, had created them by the score, even directing the populace to worship dead emperors.

But this Galilee held to the true faith as written in rock and handed to Moses on a mountaintop. These people knew that the Lord God had made a covenant, and some day He would come to help His chosen ones recover their rightful greatness. So every prophet had promised. So every true Jew believed. Why, even the whisper of His coming would move, and often had moved, those excitable Galileans to veritable tempests of sabotage against their Roman rulers.

Joseph the Carpenter

Young Mary of Nazareth believed in this forthcoming visitation as ardently as any, but she was only a hearty village girl, and neither politics nor religion were her primary interests. Instead, she was eager for marriage and her role as an adult in the community. Each day, as she visited the spring at the bottom of the hill on which she lived, she paused long enough to listen to older women telling of their own household adventures. At home, she cooked, sewed, and cleaned. Her pleasures, such as they were, came from the warm sun and fragrant breezes and an occasional taste of candy brought from distant Damascus.

"Hail, O Favored One," said the Angel

ONE NIGHT, after a day in no way extraordinary, she retired to her room and made ready for bed. As usual, she was thinking of how slowly these last months were passing. A voice interrupted her thoughts, coming from a corner of her bedchamber. The words were slow and clearly spoken. She saw that a figure like that of a man was in her room. Choking with alarm, she realized that the air was filled with a milky brightness, yet there was no source of illumination. The voice came again, comforting her.

"Do not be afraid, Mary. You have found favor with God."

She wondered what kind of favor, and with the thought her trembling ceased. "Are you an angel?" she asked.

"I am Gabriel, sent from God."

Mary searched her innocent mind for a cause of this visitation. "But what am I to you, sir?"

The angel said, "You shall conceive in your womb and bear a Son."

Mary's heart leaped, for giving birth to a man-child was the foremost duty of every Hebrew woman. Silently she rejoiced at the presence of the strange messenger.

"And you shall call His name Jesus!" he ordered.

"But why Jesus?" her mind asked swiftly. "First-born sons should have a family name."

The voice gave answer:

He will be great, and will be called the Son of the Most High;
and the Lord will give to Him the throne of His father David,
and He will reign over the house of Jacob for ever;
and of His kingdom there will be no end.

Mary tried vainly to take it all in. Not once did it occur to her to doubt her eyes and ears. Her world universally accepted the notion that angels visited people and spoke with them. But she was a practical maiden, so she asked a practical question:

"How can I have a child, since I've never known a man intimately and am not yet married but only betrothed?"

The angel replied,

The Holy Spirit will come upon you,
and the power of the Most High will overshadow you; therefore
the Child to be born will be called holy, the Son of God.

Again Mary's heart stirred. This unbelievable promise was one about which every true Hebrew had prayed for centuries. Her senses reeled. "I'm dreaming," she thought. "I must tell this messenger that I'm unworthy."

The angel, knowing her thoughts, said, "You have a cousin, Elizabeth. She also has conceived a son, even in her old age after she was called barren, and this is already her sixth month. Believe me, with God nothing is impossible."

Mary fluttered to her knees and laid clasped hands in her lap. If Elizabeth had conceived . . . well, there could be no more resistance. "Behold, I am the Lord God's obedient handmaiden," she said. "Let all this happen to me, according to your word."

Her eyes closed over tears. Were they of joy or fear? Perhaps she was wondering how much of this she should tell Joseph, and if he would believe her virtuous. Surely her visitor could give advice. She formed the question in her mind, but when it was ready for asking, the angel had vanished.

She began to tremble again, from lack of understanding. She knew nothing of nature or people beyond the limits of her home and village. But the angel had spoken of her cousin Elizabeth who was already with child.

She rose and flung together some clothing. She carefully tied the thongs by which her sandals were fastened to her feet. Her cousin's city was in Judah, which was beyond Samaria (Suh-MAHR-ee-uh) and further than she had ever walked in her life, but she must talk immediately to Elizabeth.

Of all people, why had God chosen *her* for this miraculous birth? She, a humble country girl of Nazareth had been singled out to bring into the world One who—*what had the angel said?* "He will be called the Son of the most High . . . and of His kingdom there will be no end."

This divine miracle was something far greater than the birth of a baby to Cousin Elizabeth and her husband Zacharias (Zack-uh-RYE-us) when their time for having children was long past!

Elizabeth Knows Mary's Secret

TRAVEL-STAINED and tired, she arrived presently at her cousin's modest home. No messenger had foretold her coming. No message had revealed her secret. But Elizabeth's face lighted like a lantern when Mary confronted her.

"Blessed are you among women, Mary," Elizabeth cried. "And blessed is the Child you shall bear."

"She already knows," Mary thought.

Elizabeth said, "When you entered, the babe in my own womb leaped and I felt myself filled with the Holy Spirit." Bowing her head, she made a sudden gesture of humility. "But why am I so favored that the mother of my Lord should come to visit me?"

"I saw an angel," Mary said.

Elizabeth interrupted, "O Mary, blessed are you for believing in what the Lord promised."

"My soul does magnify the Lord," Mary responded.

"Yes."

"And my spirit rejoices in God my Savior, for He has seen the humility of His handmaiden."

"Yes, yes," Elizabeth breathed, entranced.

"Behold, henceforth all generations will call me blessed, for He who is mighty has done great things for me, and holy is His name."

The words flowed sweetly from her lips, without thought or intention, bubbling up from the wellspring of her heart.

And since the day that Luke recorded them in his Gospel, the Christian church has repeated them from year to year and even does so today under the Latin title of the *Magnificat,* which means "it magnifies."

During their long talk, the two cousins came finally to the core of Mary's abiding worry. "How can I tell my Joseph?" she asked.

"God will surely show you a way," Elizabeth promised.

They were together for three months, and what a time it must have been. Elizabeth, the mother of John the Baptist, and Mary, the mother of Jesus, performing household tasks, grinding grain, preparing meals, sewing garments, just like all the other young women in the town. We do not know what messages she sent back to Joseph, but surely none could explain her disappearance to his entire satisfaction.

Then the infant John was born—and Mary returned home to tell her betrothed that she was already with child.

Disturbing News

MATTHEW is the only writer to speak of that confrontation. In essence, he says: when Mary was found to be with child before she and Joseph had come together in marriage he, being unwilling to embarrass her, resolved instead upon a quiet end to their betrothal.

Imagine the tumult of his mind as he sought sleep after that first interview. Lying awake, he must have reviewed every fact. She had kept him at arm's length when she said, "Joseph, I am with child." Her head had lifted and her eyes had looked beyond. "He is from the Most High, the Holy One, and He shall be holy also."

"What have you said, girl!" Joseph protested. "This is too much."

"Listen another moment, please."

He had flung himself back on his heels, arms akimbo, braced for the whole story. "Go on!"

Her soft voice had related each event, adding her own wonder that of all Israel she had been chosen. Then she waited.

"Have you told me all?"

"I have."

"Then I must take a night for prayer and thought," he had said. "This is a heavy concern and I must sleep on it."

Finally, he fell asleep and was visited in his slumber by an angel with folded wings whose deep voice said, "Joseph, son of David, do not fear to take the gentle Mary as your wife."

Again his mind asked the question: "But whose is this unsought Child?"

"That which is in her was conceived by the Holy Spirit," the voice stated. "She will bear a Son, whom you will call by the name of Jesus for He will save your people from their sins."

*The Angel Appears
to Joseph in a Dream*

Suddenly Joseph arose, wide awake, seeking the angel, so fresh and immediate was his experience. Of course the room was empty. Beyond the window, gray light was sweeping over the eastern hills. This was the day on which Mary expected an answer from him. He thought, "The angel said we should wed. This matter is most mysterious, but in due course it will surely become clear."

He dressed and soon began to climb the hillside to his betrothed.

The Hard Journey to Bethlehem

ALL OVER the Roman Empire, the heads of taxpayers were being counted. Once again, Rome needed money for its treasury. In Palestine, every citizen was ordered to his ancestral home for registration.

"It's an outrage," an elder stormed in the market place. "Should we leave our business to march three days and make a mark on a bit of parchment?"

The Nativity.

PETER PAUL RUBENS

JACOB JORDAENS

The Holy Family.

The Annunciation.

AELBRECHT BOUTS

Slaughter of the Innocents.

PUCCINELLI

WILHEIM ERNEST DIETRICH

Adoration of the Shepherds.

The Visitation.
JOHANN DAVID PASSAVANT

Adoration of the Magi.

MAINO

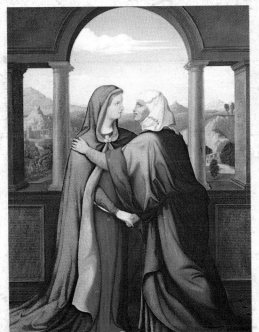

CHRISTIAN DALSGAARD

Flight into Egypt.

EDWARD VON STEINLE

Three Holy Kings.

Rest during the flight.

VAN DYCK

"Have we a choice?" Joseph asked.

"We can fight as our ancestors did. How much longer must we wait to chase these Gentiles into the sea?"

"God will lead us when the day is come," Joseph said. "In the meantime, I'm going to Bethlehem."

Walking up the hill, the village midwife joined him. "I hear of your plans," she said. "Your Mary is of David's house, too, but surely you will not take her?"

The Decree of Caesar Augustus

"She is my wife."

"She is about to have a baby, Joseph. Don't do it!"

He said, "She shall ride the gentlest of donkeys."

"It is unwise. I shall forbid it!"

"The Romans have not forbidden it."

"Curse the Romans," she said, spitting into the dust. "Take this trip and you may kill your Mary and the One she bears."

"We must go to Bethlehem, woman!"

He and Mary packed their food and clothing, and he borrowed the gentlest donkey in the valley. Slowly, they made their way to the Jordan fords, thence along the ancient caravan highway that sinks below sea level as it slopes toward the Dead Sea, thence up the mountain passes past Jericho and Jerusalem and six miles beyond to the spreading grain fields which surrounded Bethlehem. It was a distance of many miles, and they spent four days and nights on the journey, camping by the roadside at night.

On the final night, Mary said, "Joseph, we must find shelter, please. My time is near at hand."

Joseph hastened to the principal Bethlehem inn but it was jammed with earlier arrivals. Searching the neighborhood, he found that not one bed stood empty. Finally, an innkeeper's wife looked curiously at Mary and saw her great need.

"Go around to the stable quickly," she said. "You'll find a manger and some straw."

Mary and Joseph on the Way to Bethlehem

That was the night on which Jesus was born. Without even the normal conveniences and facilities of that primitive age, Mary brought forth her first-born Son and wrapped Him in swaddling cloths and placed Him in a manger.

Mary reclined on the soft, sweet hay to rest, while Joseph sat beside her on the crude stable floor.

Both were speechless with the wonderment of what had just taken place. Enrapt with joy, they gazed on the Child, and from the depth of their hearts words of worship and praise came softly from their lips.

Even in the dimness of the stable, Mary's eyes shone with quiet joy. "At last, Joseph, God's promise has come," she whispered.

The gruelling journey from distant Nazareth...the bitter disappointment at finding no lodging in the inn...Mary's ordeal in the rude surroundings of an animal stall—all was forgotten in the deep peace that had settled into the dark manger at the birth of the blessed Child Jesus.

The Remarkable Shepherds

THE SHEPHERDS of Bethlehem were of a peculiar and unique breed. Specially trained for their task, they were responsible for raising sheep to be sacrificed in the Temple. Even the priests gave them special consideration because a fat, unbruised animal was the most perfect of all sacrifices.

To say it another way, those shepherds were not country men hired to frighten off jackals. They were superb animal husbandmen. They knew the tricks of nature, had seen bolts of lightning that bounced from one crag to another, and heard the agonizing boom of thunder that often resembled mortal words.

But they were wholly unprepared for the sight that soon blinded them on their hillside above Bethlehem. A figure that resembled a man yet was something more than a man appeared in the night and stood before them. Rubbing their eyes, they saw that he was poised in the center of a gleaming ball of light so bright that it hurt their eyes.

"What is this? Who are you?" they cried in consternation.

All of the men had risen from the ground, and some of them began edging away, as if to take to their heels.

"Fear not!" said the visitor. "I bring you good news of a great joy which will come to all people."

As the shepherds waited tensely, he continued: "This day in the city of David there is born a Savior who is Christ the Lord. Go, see for yourselves. And this will be a sign: You will find a Babe wrapped in swaddling clothes and lying in a manger."

Suddenly the air around the speaker was filled with a multitude of gleaming figures so that he was no longer alone. And the voices of the multitude shook the air with hosannas of praise.

"What is it they are saying?" whispered one shepherd.

"Hush, listen!" said another.

"I can hear!" shouted a third, excitedly. "They're saying, 'Glory to God in the highest, and on earth peace among men with whom He is pleased.'" Abruptly, the choir vanished as suddenly as it had appeared.

All at once, they found their tongues. "He said we would find a sign, a Babe in a manger."

"Yes, yes! That would be in the village. Let us go down there at once." A number murmured their assent. But one man protested.

"What about our sheep?"

"Leave one of the lads, and the dogs. They'll take good care of the animals. And now come, let's waste no more time!"

In the village a lantern guided their feet to the open door of an inn. They found the owner and put their awkward question to him. The grizzled innkeeper looked dubiously from one shepherd to another.

"A Baby?" he grumbled. "I know of no new-born Baby."

"But—you have a stable, a manger?"

"Every inn has a stable," the innkeeper laughed, harshly. "What has that got to do with it?"

The youngest of the shepherds spoke up. "May we look in your stable?"

"Be off," the man ordered. "You're daft from staying so long in the fields with your sheep—"

"We must find the Babe," they said. "He's lying somewhere near here in a manger."

A slim, dark woman stopped in mid-stride through the room and flung up her head. She carried steaming towels and a pan of hot water. "What's this about a babe?"

No Room at the Inn

"We were told to find such a one," they answered.

"Follow me," she said.

They crossed a barnyard and the woman opened a door. Within, they saw Mary and Joseph, and beyond, lying in a manger, the swaddled figure of a newborn Child.

"Come in," Joseph said courteously.

They entered and fell on their knees, and the eldest said, "Sir, I can tell you things of this Child that you will not believe."

Joseph said, "Old one, I can tell you things that you will not believe."

"We were watching our sheep when the angel appeared," the old shepherd babbled. "He said that a Savior was born and we would find Him in a manger, just like we found this Son of yours."

The youngest shepherd leaned toward Joseph. "Sir, is this Baby really to be our Savior?"

Joseph answered, "Some day all things will be made clear."

The shepherds left presently, walking and talking, still bemused by their vision. Passing through the inn again, the proprietor sang out, "Did you find your party?"

"A Savior is born tonight," the old shepherd said.

"I've heard that before," the innkeeper mocked.

They recited the events of the night, from the appearance of the shining angel and the heavenly choir to the Babe in swaddling cloths. And all who heard them wondered mightily at what it meant, and their words spread throughout the country until the news was repeated in every town and village.

Mary Puts Jesus to Sleep in the Manger

A Wonder Child at the Temple

UNDER THE LAW of the Hebrews, a visit to the Temple was now required of both Mary and Jesus. According to their way, she had been defiled by the act of birth and could be purified only by making a burnt offering.

After waiting the prescribed number of days, the little family made its way to Jerusalem.

Climbing the arching trail, they came to where they could see Jerusalem's gray walls soaring above the crags and cliffs of her foundation. It was a sight dear to the heart of every Jew. For a long moment they paused to contemplate the vista. Then they trudged onward to the massive gate of the Temple area and finally ascended the worn steps to the Temple proper. Joseph went to a booth and bought two pigeons for the sacrifice.

The Child was presented to the Lord in a ceremony of dedication, and Mary offered for her cleansing the sacrifice of the pigeons, as provided by the law of Moses.

Suddenly a venerable, bearded figure came walking toward them. As his eyes fell upon the Infant Jesus, the old man raised his arms heavenward and began speaking in a voice trembling with emotion.

Entering the Temple for the Purification

"Who is this?" Joseph whispered to a priest standing nearby.

"He is old Simeon (SIM-ee-un)," replied the priest. "He tells us that the Holy Spirit has revealed to him that he will not die until he has seen the promised Redeemer of Israel."

The patriarch now placed his hands about Jesus' tiny form. With shining eyes, he murmured:

"Lord, now Your servant can die in peace—for my eyes have seen Your salvation which You have prepared in the presence of all peoples...a light for revelation to the Gentiles and for glory to Your people Israel!"

A look of benign joy lighted up the wrinkled face of the old man. Turning to Mary and Joseph, he raised his hands over them in blessing.

Again he spoke: "This Child is destined to cause the rise and fall of many in Israel. Many will oppose Him—for He will reveal men's secret thoughts." Then suddenly Simeon fixed a piercing gaze upon Mary.

"Yes, and a sword shall pierce your mother's soul," he said.

"Dear Lord, no!" murmured Mary.

Then a strange, thin voice joined Simeon's, and they saw an aged woman well-known in the Temple area. This was Anna, a prophetess, now eighty-four years of age, who had roamed the Women's Court since she was widowed after seven years of marriage. For once, however, she was not bent and cringing but stood erect and proud. Clasping Jesus, her eyes shining, she spoke in a voice that all could hear:

"This is the One, indeed! He will deliver our nation from the oppressor."

Everyone present knew how dangerously she spoke. The oppressor was Herod (HER-ud) the Great, by appointment of the Roman Senate King of the Jews, though no Jew himself. He was also a bloodthirsty, multiple murderer, so jealous of his throne that any pretenders, even his own children, were slaughtered on suspicion.

No understanding of those next few crowded months is possible without this knowledge of his character and cunning.

In brief, he was an opportunist from Edom who had married the much-loved Jewish princess named Mariamne (May-ree-AM-nee), granddaughter of a former Judean ruler. For all the thirty-odd years of his reign, his single-minded purpose was to consolidate his claim to the throne. So in almost his first official act, he chose forty-five of his principal opponents and killed them.

He murdered his wife's seventeen-year-old brother by having servants drown him in his bath.

He murdered his wife's grandfather, aged eighty.

He became so jealous of Mariamne that he falsely accused her of plotting against him and had her executed.

He married ten wives who bore him five daughters and ten sons, three of whom he slaughtered.

During his final and fatal illness, he arrested the heads of every important family in Jerusalem and locked them in an amphitheater. His death-bed order was that they should all be killed (and there were forty thousand of them) at the moment of his own death, this being his way of forcing the city to mourn on the day of his death because he knew that otherwise there would be only rejoicing. Only the mutiny of his own family frustrated his final carnage.

This was the king against whom old Anna had spoken in the Temple, and his ears burned presently with the news of an Infant who was said by some to be the promised Messiah.

Soon another rumor reached Herod's ears. Several strange officials of an Eastern land had crossed his borders and were riding toward Jerusalem. Oddly, they were also seeking a newborn Babe, for at every resting place they asked the same disturbing question.

"Where is the Infant that was born King of the Jews, for we have seen His star?" they inquired.

The Mystery of the Wise Men

MATTHEW says that the Wise Men came "from the East." Eastward beyond the Jordan River were Arabia to the southeast, Parthia (PAHR-thee-uh) to the northeast, and India far beyond. Wherever their home, they were extraordinary travelers. Their gifts, carried in saddlebags, were such that only personages of importance could afford them. Probably they were from Media (MEE-dee-uh), priestly members of some noble court where they worshiped fire, performed magic, read fortunes, and studied the stars. From tradition, we have their names: Gaspar, Melchior (MEL-kee-or), and Balthazar (Bal-THAY-zuhr). Among them it was believed that the birth of a great person was announced by the appearance of a bright, new star. Seeing such a star in their heavens, they had followed it into Judea.

The Magi Following Their Star

One night while they were resting, a courier from Herod the Great found them and summoned them to a royal conference.

So the Wise Men came before wily Herod, who had a plan by which he might discover the identity of the infant claimant to his throne. Already he had convened his sages and high priests and confirmed that the birthplace of a new Messiah would be Bethlehem.

"Go you to Bethlehem and search diligently for the Child," he now urged the Easterners. "When you have found Him, bring word back to me of His whereabouts so that I, too, may go and worship Him."

Nearing Bethlehem, one of the Wise Men said, "Look! Yonder is our bright star again. See how it hangs above the village."

So they rode through the quiet streets, made discreet inquiries of those they met, and were given directions to a certain building. Time had passed since the census, and Joseph had moved his family to a house. It was as humble as any stable, but it offered better facilities for maintaining life.

"And going into the house, they saw the Child with Mary His mother," Matthew writes, "and they fell down and worshiped Him. Then, opening their treasures, they offered Him gifts."

This was the climax of their long and dangerous journey, so they worshiped and offered up their treasures. There was sweet-smelling incense from the rosin trees of Arabia, which Matthew calls frankincense. There was a perfume called myrrh used for rites of purification and making holy oil. There was gold also, which was specially valuable because it was mined nowhere in Palestine.

The Wise Men Question a Roman Guard

So passed the climactic day, and when the Wise Men withdrew to rest for the night, they had a dream, each dreaming the same thing, which was a warning that they should not report back to Herod but return instead to their own country by a secret route.

Mary and Joseph, alone finally with their sleeping Child, clung to each other in bewilderment. In the beginning, their secret was a bond setting their Child apart in their eyes alone. Now, too much was happening. First, the shepherds who had proclaimed their discovery from the hilltops. Then

Old Simeon and Anna, who made their noisy pronouncements so that all could hear. Now, three foreigners with unbelievable gifts! In the market place, people were talking, asking what so many signs could mean. What if King Herod was wondering, too? It was a frightening thought.

Their fears were well-founded. Herod had already taken secret steps. Learning that the Wise Men had evaded him, he hit upon a fiendish scheme. If one among the children of Bethlehem was his rival, he would be one born after the appearance of the great star. From his interrogation of the Wise Men, he knew that its initial appearance was less than two years old. So he issued his infamous order:

"Soldiers, go to Bethlehem and kill every male child who is *under* two years of age."

Herod Issues His Bloody Order

How many murders would there be? Bethlehem was a small village of perhaps four thousand inhabitants. How many would die? But no matter! One of them would be the rumored Messiah and Herod's troubles would be finished. Clutching his precious crown, Herod watched his executioners march off toward the sleeping town.

Their method was neither more nor less efficient than that of official killers of more recent vintage. Pounding on doors in the middle of the night, asking unanswerable questions, and destroying humans as if they were animals—that was the technique. From door to door and street to street they slashed and stabbed until the town lay bathed in blood. Finally they wiped their broadswords and pikes clean and went home to their well-earned soldier's breakfast. Why they had to kill, they did not know. Or whom! So they reported only that their mission was accomplished, with which news the King of the Jews was well pleased.

The Dream That Warned Joseph

B UT Jesus lived, and the miracle of it became one of the pillars supporting the edifice that would be called Christianity many years later. He lived because Joseph awoke sweating from an early dream that night of the massacre, his ears echoing with an angel's voice that shouted, "Flee! Rise up and take the Baby and Mary, His mother, and go as swiftly as you can to Egypt."

"But why this unseemly hour?" Joseph asked.

"Herod is sending soldiers to destroy your Child."

"Will we be gone for a long time?"

"I will bring you word when you may return. Hurry. Go to Egypt at once."

Joseph tarried not one moment longer but aroused his sleeping family, flung their possessions onto a donkey, and hastened by a way he knew to the distant caravan tracks that led to the land of the Pharaohs.

The flight of the Holy Family has been painted by many artists and described by many writers. No words have described it better than these of Matthew:

"And he rose and took the Child and His mother by night, and departed to Egypt, and remained there until the death of Herod."

An Oasis on the Way to Egypt

Beyond that, all is conjecture. We know that two routes were available. One went through the difficult wilderness of Shur, along which Moses had once led runaway Israelites. The other traversed the territory now called the Gaza Strip. Whichever they chose, they must have been hot by day, cold by night, and hungry all of the time. Camel caravans would give them food, but the route was over two hundred treacherous miles and the pace of a donkey was slow.

Yet we know that they finally arrived safely and made their home among other countrymen who had fled long before.

Over one million Jews are said to have lived along the Nile in those days. And most of them were brighter and more progressive than those who lived in the homeland. In Alexandria they supported colleges and synagogues. Here was accomplished the first translation of the Old Testament from Hebrew to Greek. Here was one of the Seven Wonders of the World, the Great Lighthouse of Pharos, which stood where the Nile met the sea. Here was the world's greatest library and the largest scholarly assemblage of ancient times.

And here also, within one hundred years, would rise one of the strongest of early Christian churches under the missionary evangelism, according to tradition, of Mark.

Our Bible says nothing of the life of young Jesus in that community. For Mary and Joseph it was a time of watchful waiting for the command to return to the homeland. Finally, it came in a dream, as Joseph had known it would.

This time, the angel said, "Rise, take the Child and His mother, and go to the land of Israel, for those who sought the Child's life are dead."

So they went home to Israel and thence to Nazareth in Galilee. Matthew sees in this the fulfillment of an ancient promise: "Out of Egypt have I called My Son. . . . He shall be called a Nazarene."

Nor do the Gospels tell much of the years that followed in Nazareth, except that "the Child grew and became strong, filled with wisdom; and the favor of God was upon Him."

Almost certainly during those years the Boy Jesus performed the first chores of a carpenter's apprentice, learning the rudiments of sawing and planing by watching Joseph. It is equally probable that He attended the nearest synagogue school, learning Old Testament scriptures by repeating the verses over and over, as was the method.

If He was different from other boys of His age, as He must have been, we do not learn of it from the Bible. All we know is that He was obedient to Mary and Joseph, and that His mother kept in her heart the precious memories of His childhood. "And Jesus increased in wisdom and in stature, and in favor with God and man."

(continued from page 290)

The day of one's birth is, in a sense, the most important day of his life, for without it, he would not have been; and so the celebration of birthdays goes back into very ancient times (Gen. 40:20; Matt. 14:6, etc.). The Hebrew ceremonies connected with childbirth are given in Leviticus 12. The permission to the poor to offer "a pair of turtledoves or two young pigeons" in place of a lamb (Luke 2:24) gives touching testimony to the comparative poverty of Mary, the mother of Jesus. Our Lord, in John 3:3-6, makes a clear distinction between the first and second births of a regenerate person; and when this distinction is applied, it seems so to divide men as almost to make two different species; the once-born and the regenerate. The former are depraved, and unless they repent they are destined for judgment (Heb. 9:27; 10:31); while the latter are being made partakers in the divine nature (II Peter 1:4, etc.) and are destined for glory. A.B.F.

BIRTHRIGHT. From time immemorial a man's firstborn son has been given privileges above those of his younger brothers. This is illustrated today by the order of succession to the throne (in Britain for instance). Among the Israelites God had a special claim on the firstborn, at least from the time of Exodus, when He destroyed the firstborn of Egypt, and claimed those of Israel by right of redemption (Exod. 13:2,12-16). The birthright included a double portion of the inheritance (Deut. 21:15-17), and the privilege of priesthood; but in Israel God later set apart the tribe of Levi instead of the firstborn for that service. (Note Numbers 3:38-51, where the Levites are about the same in number as the firstborn of Israel). Esau lost his birthright by selling it to Jacob for a mess of pottage, and no regret could undo the loss he had brought upon himself. (See Gen. 25:27-34, Heb. 12:16 and compare the destinies of Israel and of Edom, Obad. 17,18). In Israel, Reuben lost his birthright through sin, and his next brothers Simeon and Levi lost theirs through violence; and so the blessing came to Judah (Gen. 49:3-10).

BIRZAVITH (bĭr-zā'vĭth), either a son of Malchiel of the tribe of Asher (I Chron. 7:31), or a village whose people were descendants of Malchiel.

BISHLAM (bĭsh'lăm), an officer of Cambyses ("Artaxerxes") who opposed the rebuilding of the temple (Ezra 4:7).

BISHOP (bĭsh'ŭp, Gr. epískopos, overseer), originally the principal officer of the local church, the other being the deacon or deacons (I Tim. 3: 1-7). The title "elder" or "presbyter" generally applied to the same man; "elder" referring to his age and dignity, and "bishop" to his work of superintendence. As the churches multiplied, the bishop of a larger church would often be given special honor, and so gradually there grew up a hierarchy, all the way from presiding elders to bishops (over groups of churches), then archbishops.

BITHIAH (bĭ-thī'à, daughter of Jehovah), the name suggests that she was a convert to Judaism, though she is called a daughter of Pharaoh. Mentioned only in I Chronicles 4:18 as wife of Mered of the tribe of Judah.

BITHRON (bĭth'rŏn, rough country), a region in the tribe of Gad between the Jordan and Mahanaim. Mentioned only in II Samuel 2:29.

BITHYNIA (bĭ-thĭn'ĭ-à, Gr. Bithunía), a region along the northern edge of Asia Minor fronting on the Black Sea, the Bosphorus and the Sea of Marmora. Paul and his companions desired to enter Bithynia with the Gospel (Acts 16:6-10) but the Holy Spirit was leading toward Europe, and so they could not enter. However, there were Christians there in the first century (I Pet. 1:1). The Roman governor Pliny the Younger complained to Trajan concerning the Christians and at the beginning of the second century asked how to deal with them.

Bithynia was settled very early, and its known history goes back past the sixth century B.C., when Croesus made it a part of his kingdom. A king of Bithynia in the third century B.C. invited the Gauls into Asia, so originating "Galatia." From the 13th century on, it has been Turkish, or at least ruled by the Turks.

BITTER HERBS. At the passover, the Israelites were to eat roast lamb (a lamb whose blood had been sprinkled for their salvation) with unleavened bread (because of the haste of their departure), and bitter herbs (as symbolic of the bitterness of their servitude, Exod. 12:8; Num. 9:11). Perhaps horse-radish is the nearest equivalent in our diet. See PLANTS.

BITTERN (See Birds)

BITUMEN (bĭ-tū'mĕn), a mineral pitch widely scattered over the earth, and one of the best waterproofing substances known. It was used with slime (or perhaps as "slime and pitch") to cover the ark of bulrushes (Exod. 2:3) and to waterproof Noah's ark (Gen. 6:14), for mortar in the tower of Babel (Gen. 11:3), and as a curse upon Edom (Isa. 34:9). There were great deposits near the Dead Sea, and at different places in Mesopotamia. The principal modern source is a great lake of pitch on the island of Trinidad.

BIZJOTHJAH (bĭz-jŏth'jà, contempt of Jehovah, ASV Biziothiah), a town in the south of Judah in Joshua's time (Josh. 15:28).

BIZTHAH (bĭz'thà), one of the seven chamberlains in the court of Xerxes ("Ahasuerus") who were commanded to bring out Queen Vashti for exhibition.

BLASPHEMY (blăs'fē-mē, Gr. blasphémia). To reproach or to bring a railing accusation against any one is bad enough (Jude 9), but to speak lightly or carelessly of God is a mortal sin. In Israel the punishment of blasphemy was death by stoning (see Lev. 24:10-16). The third commandment, "Thou shalt not take the name of Jehovah thy God in vain" (Exod. 20:7) was observed so meticulously by the Jews that they would not speak the sacred Jehovah name at all, and so no one knows today for certain how it was pronounced. In the Hebrew Bible the consonants of the "sacred tetragrammaton" YHWH occur more than 6,000 times, but always with the vowels for the word "LORD." As a result of this superstitious reverence, the word Jehovah is found only half a dozen times in the KJV, and the word LORD is used instead. Naboth, at Jezebel's instigation, was falsely charged with blasphemy (I Kings 21:10-13), as were our Lord (Matt. 9:3, etc.) and Stephen (Acts 6:11). What our Lord said would have been blasphemy were it not true. The Jews, with a peculiar sense of humor, sometimes used the word "to bless" meaning "to curse" or "to blaspheme" (I Kings 21:10,13; Job 1:5,11, 2:5,9).

BLASTUS (blăs'tŭs, Gr. *Blástos*), a chamberlain of King Agrippa (Acts 12:20) who apparently was easily bribed. The men of Tyre and Sidon used him in approaching the king.

BLESS, BLESSING (Heb. *bārakh*). 1. God blesses nature (Gen. 1:22), mankind (Gen. 1:28), the Sabbath (Gen. 2:3), nations (Ps. 33:12), classes of men (Ps. 1:1-3) and individuals (Gen. 24:1, etc.).

2. Godly men should "bless" God; i.e. they should adore him, worship him and praise him (Ps. 103:1,2, etc.),

3. Godly men by words and actions can bestow blessings on their fellows (Matt. 5:44; I Pet. 3:9).

4. In Bible times, godly men under inspiration bestowed prophetic blessings on their progeny, e.g. Noah blessing Japheth and Shem (Gen. 9:26,27), Isaac blessing Jacob and Esau (Gen. 27:27-29,39, 40), Jacob blessing the tribes of Israel (Gen. 49), and Moses also blessing them (Deut. 33).

5. We can bless things when we set them apart for sacred use e.g. the "communion cup" (I Cor. 10:16).

BLESSING, THE CUP OF. In the "communion" service, the church (i.e. the assembly of believers) blesses the cup when it is set apart for the Lord's Supper (I Cor. 10:16).

BLINDNESS (See Diseases)

BLOOD, the well-known fluid pumped by the heart all through the body of animals and of men. The word occurs over 400 times in the Scriptures, being especially frequent in Leviticus, which deals with Hebrew worship and the way to holiness; in Ezekiel, which has much to say about God's judgments; and in the letter to the Hebrews, which is the divine commentary on Leviticus. In 24 of the Bible books, the word does not occur, not because it is unimportant but because these books deal with other subjects.

The blood contains the vital principle or the essence of animal and human life (Gen. 9:4 — "But flesh with the life thereof which is the blood thereof, shall ye not eat"). Because of the sacredness of life, that energy which only God can give, the Israelites were enjoined from eating the blood, or even flesh from which the blood had not carefully been removed. This prohibition is at the basis of the Jewish usages referred to as "kosher," which prevents the orthodox Jews from buying or eating meat which has not been slaughtered and drained of blood under the supervision of a rabbi. Not only was the eating of blood forbidden to Israel, but also to the strangers who lived with Israel (Lev. 17:10-14), and the penalty for the breaking of this law was that the sinner should be "cut off from among his people." This meant at least exclusion from fellowship and probably death as well.

The book of Leviticus speaks of the blood nearly one hundred times. It is mentioned especially in chapter 17, which deals with the eating of flesh. In the various offerings (Lev. 1-7), except for the meal offering of chapter 2, the blood was to be sprinkled upon the altar, indicating the substitution of the victim's blood for that of the sinner.

Because of the sacredness of God's law and of His demand of holiness in His creature, man, from the beginning this principle has held — that "the wages of sin is death" (Rom. 6:23a); but "God is love," and so, in His infinite wisdom, He has provided an escape for the sinner. Though it is true that "without the shedding of blood, there is no remission" (Heb. 9:22), He has been pleased to accept the blood of our Lord Jesus Christ in lieu of ours, but only on condition of our belief in him. "Christ was once offered to bear the sins of many" (Heb. 9:28) and this could take place only once, and so the Old Testament offerings were provided, not to take away sin, but to point forward to the supreme sacrifice upon Calvary.

The prohibition of eating blood with the flesh, like the rest of the law, was no doubt "nailed to the cross" when our Lord's death fulfilled the demands of the law (Col. 2:14).   A.B.F.

BLOOD, AVENGER or **REVENGER OF.** Genesis 9:6, "Whoso sheddeth man's blood, by man shall his blood be shed," is the basis for capital punishment. In Israel of old, and among the Arabs and other primitive peoples of today, when murder or manslaughter was committed, the nearest of kin of the slain person took it upon himself to execute vengeance. In the law of Moses, it was recognized that the avenger would pursue a killer, and so cities of refuge were provided for those guilty of manslaughter, but not of murder (Num. 35:6). The Hebrew word for "avenger" is *go'el* and this word means also "kinsman" and "redeemer." This indicates that the executioner would ordinarily be a kinsman. In the book of Ruth, Boaz was the kinsman, who also performed the duty of a redeemer in Ruth's behalf (Ruth 4:1-8; Deut. 25:5-10). The word *go'el* had a twofold application to Boaz, who was both kinsman and redeemer to Ruth, but in the case of our Lord it is threefold. As Son of man he is our kinsman, he was our Redeemer (I Pet. 1:18, 19); and he will be the Avenger of blood (Isa. 63:1-6; Rev. 14:14-20; 19:11-21).   A.B.F.

BOANERGES (bō'à-nûr'jēz, *sons of thunder*), a title bestowed by our Lord upon the two brothers James and John, the sons of Zebedee (Mark 3:17), probably because of their temperamental violence (cf. Luke 9:54-56).

BOAR (See Animals)

BOAZ (bō'ăz, Heb. *bō'az*), a well-to-do Bethlehemite in the days of the judges who became an ancestor of our Lord by marrying Ruth, the Moabitess, widow of one of the sons of Elimelech, his kinsman (Ruth 2,3,4). This was in accordance with the levirate law of Deuteronomy 25:5-10; Boaz could marry Ruth only after the nearer kinsman (Ruth 3:12; 4:1-8) had refused the privilege, or the duty. The other refused because if he had married Ruth and had had a son, a portion of his property would have gone to the credit of Elimelech's posterity, instead of his own by a former marriage. It is impossible to date Boaz exactly, because the genealogy of Ruth 4:18-22 (given in Matt. 1:4-6) is almost certainly a partial list, giving ten names to cover 800 years. The list in Matthew 1 is demonstrably schematic, as it omits four names of kings, and this one in Ruth is almost as surely so. They are both true, but, like most genealogies, partial. Salmah (or Salmon) given here as the father of Boaz, lived at the time of the Conquest, for he married Rahab, but the general setting of the story is that of a later period of settled life.

BOAZ AND JACHIN (See Temple)

BOCHERU (bō'kě-roō), a distant descendant of Saul, at the time of the return from captivity (I Chron. 8:38). One of the six sons of Azel.

BOCHIM (bō'kǐm, *weepers*), a name given to the place where the Angel of Jehovah appeared and

HARVESTING in the fields which once belonged to Boaz, the wealthy Bethlehemite, kinsman to Elimelech. Boaz married Ruth, the Moabitess. Ruth was a widow of one of the sons of Elimelech. This pastoral scene is reminiscent of the story in the Book of Ruth.

rebuked the children of Israel because of their failure to drive out the heathen and to destroy their places of worship (Judg. 2:1-5).

BOHAN (bō'hăn), a descendant of Reuben after whom a stone was named (Josh. 15:6; 18:17). The stone was on the boundary between the tribes of Judah and Benjamin, and was NW of the northern end of the Dead Sea and NE of Jerusalem.

BOIL (See Diseases)

BOLSTER, a head-rest, or pillow (Gen. 28:11,18; I Sam. 19:13; 26:11,16).

BONDMAID, BONDMAN (See Occupations)

BONE. In the living body, bones form the strong framework, and the connotation is one of strength. "Bone of my bones and flesh of my flesh" (Gen. 2:23) was spoken in a literal sense of Eve; but almost the same words (Gen. 29:14), spoken by Laban to Jacob, are figurative and show only kinship. Strong chastening is thought of as a bone-breaking experience (Ps. 51:8), and the terrible writhing on the cross of Calvary literally threw bones out of joint (Ps. 22:14). Dry bones form a picture of hopeless death (Ezek. 37:1-12). The paschal lamb, without a broken bone (Exod. 12:46) was a type of the Lamb of God (John 19:36).

BOOK, generally a literary production having more or less unity of purpose. Books may be classified by their forms or subjects, but more particularly by the nature and quality of the written material within. In ancient Assyria and Babylonia much of the writing which was thought to be of value was done in wedge-shaped characters on soft clay which was then baked, and the "libraries" were, in form, almost like piles of brick.

In ancient Egypt, men early learned to press and glue thin sheets of the papyrus plant into sheets of "paper"; the writing was in narrow columns upon sheets of regular size which were then glued together and wound around two sticks, thus forming a "volumen" or roll. Still later, men learned to bind the sheets together into a "codex" very similar to our modern books. "Book" in the Bible always refers to a roll, which word occurs 14 times in Jeremiah 36. In Pergamum, in the second century B.C., due to the scarcity of paper, men learned to dress the skin of calves and of kids. This new substance was named "parchment" in honor of its origin, and almost displaced papyrus in many regions.

In ancient books made of papyrus or of parchment, the writing was generally upon one side of each sheet, but occasionally, owing to afterthoughts,

ANCIENT HEBREW SCROLLS in a synagogue in the old city of Jerusalem.

material was written also on the backside (see Rev. 5:1). When a book was sealed, the contents were made secret, and when unsealed they were open (cf. Dan. 12:4,9 and Rev. 5:1-4 on the one hand, with Rev. 5:5; 22:10 on the other). Only the Son of God was found worthy to open the seals of the book of the future which had been locked in the hands of "him that sat on the throne."

Judaism, Christianity and Islam are all "bookish" religions and their main books have greatly changed the history of the human race.

The Bible is *the* book, God's word, and it differs from all other books in that it alone is inspired (God-breathed). The Bible originally had 63 books, as the division of Samuel, Kings and Chronicles into "First" and "Second" was not originally intended. The larger books were generally written upon separate rolls (see Luke 4:17) but sometimes the "megilloth" (Ruth, Esther, Lamentations, Song of Solomon and Ecclesiastes) were bound together, as were also "The Twelve" i.e. the Minor Prophets. Many books which have been lost are mentioned in the Bible: e.g. "the book of Jasher" (Josh. 10: 13), "the Acts of Solomon" (I Kings 11:41) etc. The word "book" is also used figuratively as in "the Lamb's book of life" (Rev. 21:27). A.B.F.

BOOTH, a simple, temporary shelter generally constructed of tree-branches with the leaves left on. It was used by the guardian of a vineyard or vegetable garden when the fruit was fit to be stolen. Sometimes used for a larger enclosure (Gen. 33: 17) such as Jacob built for his cattle. (Cf. Isa. 1:8 ARV)

BOOTY, that which is taken from a defeated enemy. In the law, as given through Moses, very different arrangements were made for varying circumstances. In the case of some very wicked heathen cities, everything was to be "devoted" to the Lord; i.e. to be destroyed absolutely so as not to be used by any man, except for some metallic vessels which could be sterilized by fire (Josh. 6:18-21). Persons who were taken as prey could sometimes be enslaved (Deut. 20:14), but in other cases must be utterly destroyed (Deut. 20:16-18). The purpose here was to prevent the heathen from teaching their abominations to God's people, Israel. Cf. I Samuel 15, where Saul's hypocritical half-obedience brought ruin upon himself and his house.

The very practical question as to the division of the booty was solved partly by custom, as when Abram freely devoted a tenth of the spoil to the Lord by giving it to Melchizedek (Gen. 14:20), and partly by legislation, as when David ordered that booty be shared equally by those who because of weariness could not continue in battle (I Sam. 30:21-25).

BOOZ (See Boaz)

BORROW, BORROWING. The Semitic peoples, as a general thing, have "an eye to business," and it seems quite natural when leaving a place of service, whether as a hireling or a slave, to ask for a gift. In Exodus 3:22, 11:2, 12:35 the KJV unfortunately translates the Hebrew verb *sha'al* ("ask") by the verb "borrow," and so gives the wrong impression that the Israelites cheated the Egyptians, and worse still that the Lord encouraged this "borrowing." The fact is that the Egyptians, thoroughly cowed by the rigors of the ten plagues, were willing to give largely in order to get rid of their troublesome "guests"; and God, in His providence, allowed Israel to despoil the Egyptians (Exod. 12: 36), in order to provide gold and silver for the tabernacle which was to be constructed. "Surely the wrath of man shall praise thee" (Ps. 76:10).

The law of Moses gives careful directions concerning the responsibility of those who borrow, or who hold property in trust, or who are criminally careless in regard to the property of another (Exod. 22:1-15). Among the blessings promised Israel on condition of obedience is that they would be lenders and not borrowers (Deut. 28:12).

BOSCATH (See Bozkath)

BOSOM (bŏŏz'ŭm). Although in English the word means the part of the body between the arms, in Scripture it is generally used in an affectionate sense, e.g. "the Son, who is in the bosom of the Father" (John 1:18), carrying the lambs in his bosom (Isa. 40:11), John leaning on the bosom of Jesus (John 13:23), or Lazarus in Abraham's bosom (Luke 16:22,23). It can be almost synonymous with "heart" as the center of one's life, as in Ecclesiastes 7:9, "anger resteth in the bosom of fools," or Psalm 35:13, "my prayer returned unto mine own bosom." Quite commonly, of course, it refers to conjugal love, as in Micah 7:5, "her that lieth in thy bosom." We read also of the bosom as a place of hiding money (Prov. 17:23).

BOSOR (Same as Beor, See Balaam)

BOSSES, the convex projection in the center of a shield (Job 15:26).

BOTCH (See Diseases)

BOTTLE. 1. Container made of goat-skin, sewed up with the hair outside and used for carrying water (Gen. 21:14-19), for storing wine (Josh. 9:4,13), for fermenting milk into "leben" or "yogurt" (Judg. 4:19, etc.). The fact that fermenting wine expands and stretches its container is used by our Lord in His discourse about putting new wine into old bottles (Luke 5:37,38). A new skin bottle would be elastic enough to stretch with the pressure of the fermenting wine, whereas an old stiff wine-skin would burst. Our Lord's teaching here is that Christianity cannot be contained in Judaism, nor can grace be confined in the bonds of the law. This meaning of "bottles" is used figuratively by Elihu in Job 32:19 as indicating his feeling that he must relieve himself by speaking.

2. Container made of baked clay, and hence very fragile (Jer. 19:1-11). As Jeremiah broke the bottle, so God would deal in fury with Israel.

3. Beautifully designed glass bottles, often found in Egyptian tombs, were used originally for burying some of the tears of the mourners with the deceased. See Psalm 56:8: "Put thou my tears into thy bottle."

4. The word rendered "bottles" in Hosea 7:5 could better be translated "heat" or "fury."

5. Figuratively, the clouds as the source of rain (Job 38:37).

6. Psalm 119:83, "I am become like a bottle in the smoke" does not refer, as some think, "to a custom," but rather to careless housekeeping. In the smoke of a kitchen without windows or chimney, a leather vessel which hung there would soon become brittle and dry.   A.B.F.

BOTTOMLESS PIT (See Abyss)

BOUNDARY STONES. Our God is a God of order and not of confusion; and so in the matter of property, He not only set careful bounds to the land of His people (Josh. 13-21), but provided a curse for those who remove their neighbors' landmarks (Deut. 27:17; cf. 19:14). Figuratively, this implies a decent regard for ancient institutions (Prov. 22:28; 23:10).

WATER CARRIERS using goatskin "bottles." Jesus' simile of putting new wine into old bottles refers to goatskin bottles, which if old, would be unable to stretch with the pressure of fermenting wine.

BOW (See Arms and Armor)

BOW (See Rainbow)

BOWELS, in the KJV occurs 36 times, and in three principal senses: 1. Literally (II Chron. 21:15-19; Acts 1:18).

2. As the generative parts of our bodies whether male or female (Gen. 15:4; Ps. 71:6).

3. The seat of the emotions, as we use the word "heart." (See Lam. 1:20 [ASV "heart"]; Phil. 1:8 [ASV "tender mercies"]).

BOWL (bōl). There are a number of Heb. and Gr. words rendered "bowl" in the RV. 1. *sephel,* a large, flat earthenware dish for holding something like milk (Judg. 5:25).

2. *mizrāq,* sometimes also rendered "basin", large costly bowls, like the silver bowls presented by the princes of the congregation (Num. 7:13f).

3. *gābia',* rendered "pot" by the KJV in Jeremiah 35:5; a large silver bowl like the kind used at banquets to replenish drinking cups.

4. *gullāh,* the receptacle for oil in the candlestick of Zechariah's vision (Zech. 4:3), and the bowl-shaped capitals of Jachin and Boaz (I Kings 7:41,42; II Chron. 4:12,13).

5. *kubba'ath kôs,* RV "bowl of the cup"; KJV "dregs of the cup" (Isa. 51:41,42).

6. *phiále,* RV "bowl," KJV "vial" (Rev. 5:8, etc.).

BOX, BOX TREE (See Plants)

BOZEZ (bō'zĕz), a rocky crag near Gibeah (I Sam. 14:4). Because one of General Allenby's officers read this account, the British followed the route of Jonathan and attacked the Turks here in 1918, conquering them even as Jonathan and his armor-bearer defeated the Philistines.

BOZKATH or **BOSCATH** (bŏz'kăth), a city of Judah (Josh. 15:39), the home of the maternal grandfather of king Josiah (II Kings 22:1).

BOZRAH (bŏz'rà, Heb. *bōtsrâh, sheepfold*). 1. An important city of Edom, the residence of Jobab, one of Edom's early kings (Gen. 36:33). In Jeremiah 49:13,22, where the approaching doom of Edom is given, Bozrah is especially mentioned, and in Amos 1:12 we read of its palaces. The place is identified as the modern village of "el-Busaireh" i.e. "the little Bozrah," a few miles SE of the Dead Sea near the road toward Petra. In Micah 2:12 the word is probably "Bozrah," though it can be read as a common noun, i.e. "a sheepfold."

2. In Jeremiah 48:24 the word refers to a town in Moab. It lies about 75 miles S of Damascus, and was enlarged and beautified (c. A.D. 106) by the emperor Trajan who made it the capital of the province of Arabia.

BRACELET, properly a circlet for the wrist, but the word translates in the KJV five different Hebrew nouns. In II Samuel 1:10 the word probably means "armlet" as a mark of royalty; in Exodus 35:22 it could be "brooches," as in ASV, or "clasps"; in Genesis 38:18,25 it represents the cords about the neck from which the signet ring was suspended (see ASV in loc); in Genesis 24:22, etc., it is properly 'bracelet," from the root meaning, "something bound on," and so in Ezekiel 16:11 and 23:42, and in Isaiah 3:19, in the interesting inventory of 21 items of feminine adornment, it could be rendered "twisted chains." Bracelets and other rather showy adornments (anklets, nose-rings, armlets, etc.) were much admired in ancient days. See DRESS.

BRANCH, a word representing 18 different Hebrew and four Greek words in the Bible. The most interesting use of it is as a title applied to the Messiah as the offspring of David (Jer. 23:5; 33:15; Zech. 3:8; 6:12).

BRASS, next to silver and gold, the most frequently mentioned metal in Scripture. Today, brass is an alloy of copper and zinc, whereas bronze is an alloy of copper with tin; but the OT uses one word (or rather four words from one root) for copper (Job 28:2), bronze (II Sam. 22:35 probably), and brass (Dan. 10:6, cf. Rev. 1:15). Copper and its alloys were among the earliest metals worked by man; Tubal-cain (Gen. 4:22) being the first man mentioned as a worker in brass and iron. Most of the vessels for the courts of the tabernacle and of the temple were of "brass." In Nebuchadnezzar's vision (Dan. 2:31-39) the "belly and thighs of brass" signified the then future dominion of Greece, whose soldiers were notable for their brazen shields and weapons. The brazen cooking vessels of today in the East are mostly of copper, prevented from poisoning the food by a thin plating of tin which needs frequently to be restored by a process similar to soldering.

BRAY. 1. The ass brays when hungry (Job 6:5), and some low-grade people are described contemptuously as braying (Job 30:7).

2. To pound or "bray" as in a mortar (Prov. 27:22). This word, related to the verb "to break," is rare both in English and in Hebrew, but is easily understood by the context.

BRAZEN SEA. In II Kings 25:13, I Chronicles 18: 88, and Jeremiah 52:17, we read of the great "sea of brass," a rather exaggerated figure for the immense laver which Solomon placed in front of the temple for washing the sacrifices and the bodies of the priests.

BRAZEN SERPENT. Numbers 21:4-9 records how the people of Israel complained against Moses and against God, who in judgment sent fiery serpents against them. When the people confessed their sin, Moses made a "serpent of brass," set it upon a pole and in effect said, "Look and live"; and whosoever looked recovered. This brazen serpent later was worshipped, but Hezekiah contemptuously called it "a piece of brass" (II Kings 18:4) and destroyed it. This brazen serpent was a type of our Lord bearing our sins on the cross (John 3:14-16).

BREAD, the "staff of life," generally baked from dough made of wheat flour which has been leavened (raised by means of fermenting yeast) and made into loaves of various shapes and sizes. At the time of the Passover (Exod. 12), the Israelites ate unleavened bread because of their haste, and ever afterward they memorialized this in their annual feast of unleavened bread (Exod. 12:15-20). In times of distress and of famine, barley was used instead of wheat. It was used by the poorer classes as a general thing. In Judges 7:13, the Midianite's dream of a barley loaf, which was interpreted as "the sword of Gideon," perhaps hinted at the poverty of Israel under Midianite oppression; and in John 6:9 the boy's store of five barley loaves would suggest that he came from a family or a region which could not afford the more delicious and nutritious wheat bread.

In the more primitive parts of Syria today, there are several sorts of wheat bread. In some villages, a barrel-shaped hole in the ground is used as an oven and the women adroitly knead the bread into large thin sheets which they lay on cushions and slap against the hot wall of the oven. Though dried dung mixed with straw is used as fuel, the taste is not impaired. Ezekiel 4:9-17 gives a vivid picture of baking in famine times. In other villages of Syria, a convex sheet of iron is placed over an open fire and the bread is similarly baked; but in the larger towns and cities there are bakeries to which the people bring their loaves for baking. The long stone oven is heated for hours, then the raised loaves, about eight to ten inches in diameter and one-fourth inch thick, are placed inside by means of a long wooden paddle. The heat quickly bakes the surface, and gas forming inside splits the loaves; then they are turned and soon removed (Hos. 7:8).

"Bread," as the most universal solid food, is often used figuratively for food in general. Genesis 3:19, "in the sweat of thy face shalt thou eat bread," Matthew 6:11, "Give us this day our daily bread," and similar passages refer to all sustenance. The word "bread" is used by the Lord in a mystical, but very true and precious sense in His discourse on "the bread of life" in John 6:43-59. As important as is solid food ("bread") to our bodies, so necessary is the Lord to spiritual life. And so, in the "breaking of bread" at our "communion" services, some partake in a very real way of Christ, while others, not discerning the body, eat and drink condemnation to themselves. In the tabernacle and in the Temple, the loaves of shew-bread indicated the presence of the Lord, the "Bread of life" among His people.   A.B.F.

BREECHES (See Dress; Inner Tunic)

BRICK, building material made of clay dried in the sun. The word for "brick" in the Hebrew is derived from the verb "to be white" and is almost identical with "Lebanon," so-named for its snow-clad mountain tops. The very name would lead us to expect the oriental bricks to be whitish in color, rather than red like our more common brick. The earliest mention of brick in the Bible (Gen. 11:3) shows that the molding of clay into brick and its thorough burning were known when the tower of Babel was built, not more than a century after the Flood; and the finding of potsherds *under* the Flood deposits at Ur and Kish shows that the allied art of making clay into pottery was known before the Flood.

Owing to the prevalence of stone in Egypt, and its comparative rarity in lower Mesopotamia, the use of brick for building was much more common in Chaldea than in Egypt, though the sad record of the bondage of Israel in Egypt (Exod. 1:11-14; 5:7-19) shows that at least some cities in Egypt were built of brick rather than of stone. In fact, the ruins of Pithom have been found with the three grades of brick *in situ*: bricks with binding material of straw at the bottom; above them, brick made of stubble; and at the top, bricks of pure clay with no binding material at all. The ancient bricks were generally square instead of oblong, and were much larger than ours; something like 13 x 13 x 3½ inches, and often were stamped before baking with the name of the monarch: e.g. Sargon or Nebuchadnezzar. Much of the ancient brick-work was of bricks merely baked in the sun, especially in Egypt, but at Babylon the bricks were thoroughly burned. In Jeremiah 43:9 (KJV) we read of a "brick kiln" in Egypt in the sixth century B.C. The ASV renders the word "brickwork," but

II Samuel 12:31 clearly speaks of a brick kiln back in David's time, and Nahum, taunting the Ninevites four centuries later (Nah. 3:14) tells them to "make strong the brick kiln." In Isaiah 9:10 the "pride and stoutness of heart" of the Israelites is rebuked because they intended to replace the thrown-down bricks with stone, even as many a modern city has been rebuilt after a catastrophe. The sin was not in their desire for improvement, but in their impious and profane pride.   A.B.F.

BRIDE, BRIDEGROOM (See Wedding)

BRIDECHAMBER (See Wedding)

BRIDGE. The word "bridge" is not found in the English Bible. The idea of a bridge must have been suggested early, perhaps by a plank or fallen tree across a small stream, but Israelites seem to have been more talented commercially (Deut. 8: 17,18) than as engineers; and so they generally crossed a stream by a ford (Gen. 32:22; Josh. 2:7; Judg. 3:28) or in some cases by a ferry-boat (II Sam. 19:18). Although the principle of the arch was early known, as seen in two stones leaning against each other to bridge a small gap in Mycenaean ruins, it was not till the time of the Roman Empire that the magnificent arches, bridges and and aqueducts appeared and that the bridge may be said to have come into its own.

BRIDLE, the part of a harness that surrounds the head of the beast and connects the bit with the reins. It occurs properly, seven times in the OT and represents two words: one used in Proverbs 26:3, "a bridle for the ass," and the other in Psalm 32:9, "with bit and bridle." In Psalm 39:1 the word should be "muzzle." In the NT the word occurs once (Rev. 14:20) and the corresponding verb twice (James 1:26; 3:2). The ancient Assyrians sometimes bridled their captives. In Isaiah 37:29 God is represented as about to bridle the Assyrians in a similar way, but, of course, figuratively.

BRIER (See Plants)

BRIMSTONE, properly sulphur. The Hebrew word is related to "*gopher*," a resinous wood which was used in the construction of the ark; and so its root meaning is "resinous" or "highly combustible." It is generally connected with judgment, as when the Lord rained brimstone and fire upon Sodom and Gomorrah (Gen. 19:24; cf. Ps. 11:6), or as when the dust of Edom shall be turned into brimstone (Isa. 34:9), and in the NT, where "fire and brimstone" are principal elements in the punishment of the wicked in Gehenna, or the "lake of fire" (Rev. 20:10; 21:8). In Revelation 9:17, "fire, jacinth, brimstone" refer to colors — red, blue, yellow.

BRONZE, an alloy of copper with tin. The word is not found in Scripture, but probably the "steel" used as a material for making metallic bows (II Sam. 22:35; Job 20:24; Ps. 18:34) was really bronze. Bronze is much more elastic than brass, and so is more suitable for bows and for bells than the other alloy. Since there are so many varying proportions in which copper can be alloyed with tin, it is difficult to describe accurately "copper" (Ezra 8:27), and "brass" (Exod. 35:5, et seq.), and to be sure whether or not bronze is intended.

BROOK, a small stream. One of "the sweet words of Scripture," because the Bible was written in lands near the desert, and by men who therefore appreciated water. Many brooks are named in the Bible: Kidron (II Sam. 15:23), Besor (I Sam. 30: 9) et al. In Isaiah 19:6-8 the word rendered "brooks" in the KJV seems to refer to the Nile or its irrigating streams (see ASV). In Psalm 42: 1 the word rendered "brooks" seems to mean "channels" and is generally rendered "rivers" (S. of Sol. 5:12; Ezek. 36:4,6, etc.). The word *nahal,* rendered "brook" over 40 times in the KJV, often means "a wadi"; i.e. a torrent in winter and spring, which dries up in summer.

BROTHER. 1. A male person related to another person or other persons by having the same parents (Gen. 27:6), or the same father (Gen. 28:2), or the same mother (Judg. 8:19).

2. A man of the same country (Exod. 2:11; Acts 3:22).

3. A member of the same tribe (II Sam. 19:12).

4. An ally (Amos 1:9).

5. One of a kindred people (Num. 20:14).

6. A co-religionist (Acts 9:17; I Cor. 6:6); often, Christian disciples (Matt. 23:8; Rom. 1:13).

7. A fellow office-bearer (Ezra 3:2).

8. Someone of equal rank or office (I Kings 9: 13).

9. Any member of the human race (Matt. 7: 3-5; Heb. 2:17). Someone spiritually akin (Matt. 12:50).

BROTHERS OF OUR LORD. Were it not for the prevalence of the Roman Catholic doctrine of "the perpetual virginity of the blessed Virgin" this subject would hardly have seemed worthy of the long discussions which have been written about it. Mark 6:3, "Is not this the carpenter, the son of Mary, the brother of James, and Joses, and of Juda and Simon? and are not his sisters here with us?" (according to Protestant exegetes) testifies that when Jesus was a little more than 30 years of age he had at least six uterine brothers and sisters. If, as some have ingeniously argued, these had been sons of Joseph by a previous marriage, the whole argument of this passage would have lost its force. (Roman Catholic exegetes interpret "brothers" in the wide sense of the word, i.e., kinfolk, and refer to Gen. 11,31 and Gen. 14,14. Lot was Abraham's nephew (Gen. 11,31) but is called his brother in Gen. 14,14.)

John 7:1-10 states that the brothers of Jesus, in the midst of His ministry did not believe in Him, though it is almost a certainty that James was not only the human leader of the first church at Jerusalem by 50 A.D. (Acts 15:13, 21:18) but the writer of the epistle that bears his name; and that Jude, the author of the epistle, was the "Juda" (ASV "Judas") of Mark 6:3. The fact of their not claiming to be his brethren in the headings of their respective epistles is beautiful evidence of their Christian humility and of their reverence for His position as their Lord.

Of Joses (Tischendorf "Joseph") and of Simon, there is no further record. One would hardly expect four sons of a carpenter to have had prominent places in the early church.

The genealogists work out with much detail a list of the "kinsmen" of our Lord, making James and John His first cousins, Joseph of Arimathea the uncle of His mother, etc.; whereas the only hint of Christ's human relation in the Bible is where Elisabeth, mother of John the Baptist, is called "cousin" (ASV "kinswoman") of Mary (Luke 1:36).

BUCKET or **PAIL,** a vessel for drawing or holding water, found only in two verses of Scripture. In Isaiah 40:15 all the nations, compared with God, are but as the last drop in a bucket which has just been emptied. In Numbers 24:7 the reference is to a numerous posterity.

BUKKI (bŭk'ī). 1. A prince of the tribe of Dan chosen to help Joshua divide the land (Num. 34:22).

2. Son of Abishua, and high priest of Israel (I Chron. 6:5,51; Ezra 7:4).

BUKKIAH (bŭ-kī'à), one of the sons of Heman (I Chron. 25:4,13), who were appointed over the service of song in the time of David. Bukkiah had in his group at least 11 of his "sons and his brethren."

BUL (bōōl), the eighth month of the Jewish ecclesiastical year (I Kings 6:38), fitting into November and/or December of our calendar.

BUNNI (bŭn'ī), three Levites mentioned in Nehemiah had this name. 1. A helper of Ezra (Neh. 9:4).

2. An early dweller in Jerusalem in the fifth century B.C. (Neh. 11:15).

3. One of the chief covenanters with Nehemiah (Neh. 10:15).

BURDEN, that which is laid upon one in order to be carried. The word translates eight different words in the OT and three in the NT. When it is literally used, it is easily understood and needs no special comment. Figuratively, it is used in the sense of "responsibility" (Num. 11:11; Matt. 11:30) or of a "sorrow" (Ps. 55:22), but by far the most frequent use in the OT is "oracle" (Isa. 15:1; 19:1; 22:1, etc.). These are generally "dooms," though in Zechariah 12:1 and in Malachi 1:1 the word is used simply for a "message."

BURIAL, the act of placing a dead body in a tomb, in the earth or in the sea, generally with appropriate ceremonies; as opposed to exposure to the beasts, or abandonment or burning. Various peoples, notably the Egyptians, who believed that their dead would live and practice ordinary human occupations in "the land of the dead," often went to great lengths to preserve the bodies of their departed loved ones. They sometimes placed with the mummy tools or instruments or weapons, and occasionally slew and buried a wife or a servant to accompany the one whom they had buried.

Partly because of God's word, "Dust thou art and to dust thou shalt return" (Gen. 3:19), the people of Israel almost always buried their dead; and because the land of Canaan had so many caves, these places were very frequently used as places of burial. Probably the prevailing motive for our respect for the dead, and even for the place of burial is the sense of decency, and our feeling of love for the person, often without regarding the fact that the real person has gone and that only his former "residence" remains.

The story of the treatment of the bodies of Saul and of his sons sheds light on the whole subject. The Philistines beheaded the bodies, exhibiting the heads throughout their land and fastening Saul's body to the wall of Bethshan (I Sam. 31:8-13). The men of Israel rescued the bodies, burned them, and reverently buried the bones under a tree and mourned seven days.

It is remarkable that although God had given to Abraham the deed of the land of Canaan (Gen. 15:18-21), the only land which the patriarchs pos-sessed before Joshua's time was the burial places for the original family: a cave at Hebron, and a field at Shechem (cf. Gen. 23 — the burial of Sarah, Gen. 49:29-32 — Jacob's final request, and Josh. 25:32,33 — the burial of the mummy of Joseph and the body of Eleazar). In Canaan, in ancient times, and in the more primitive parts of the land even today, there was (and is) no embalmment in most cases, but immediate burial to avoid unpleasant odors (Acts 5:5-10) and ceremonial uncleanness (Num. 19:11-22). In the time of Christ, men's bodies were wrapped in clean linen (Matt. 27:57-60) and spices and ointments were prepared (Luke 23:56).

The strange story of the dead Moabite reviving when he touched the bones of Elisha (II Kings 13:20,21), shows not only the speedy decomposition of a body, but the informality of burials in the time of war or necessity; and the still stranger story of the disobedient prophet (I Kings 13) shows how a heathen altar could be defiled by the burning of bones upon it (13:1-3) and the desire of a prophet to be buried near another whom he honored (13:30,31). In several cases of sinful rulers, ordinary burial was denied to their bodies: the dogs ate Jezebel (II Kings 9:10); Jehoram of Judah, who died with incurable diseases, was not buried with the kings (II Chron. 21:18-20); Uzziah was buried in a field, not in the tombs of the kings (II Chron. 26:23); and Jehoiakim was buried with the burial of an ass (Jer. 22:18,19).

BURNING. God's judgments have often been accompanied with fire, e.g. Sodom and Gomorrah (Gen. 19:24-28), Nadab and Abihu (Lev. 10:1-6), the 250 rebels in the wilderness (Num. 16:2,35). The final dissolution of this present evil world is to be with fierce fire (II Pet. 3:7-10,12).

BURNING BUSH, a thorny bush which Moses saw burning and from which he heard Jehovah speak (Exod. 3:2,3; Deut. 33:16; Mark 12:26). Many attempts have been made to identify the bush, but without success. There are varied interpretations of the exact meaning of the incident as a method of revelation. There are three other theophanies with fire in the Bible: Exodus 13:21; 19:18; II Thess. 1:8 KJV (yet to be fulfilled).

BUTTER. After the milk has been churned and the "butter" (in our sense of the word) produced, it is boiled and the curds separated from the almost pure oil; this is poured into a goatskin and kept until slightly rancid (to western taste) and then is used with food, but more generally for frying eggs or vegetables. It is mentioned eleven times in the OT, of which three are figurative uses: (Job 20:17, "the brooks of honey and butter"; 29:6, "when I washed my steps with butter"; and Psalm 55:21, "the words of his mouth were smoother than butter, but war was in his heart"). In the other cases, where the word is used literally, e.g. Gen. 18:8, it implies good eating.

BUZ (bŭz). 1. A nephew of Abraham, second son of Nahor (Gen. 22:21) whose family apparently settled in Arabia. See Jeremiah 25:23, where Buz is mentioned with various districts of Arabia. The word means "contempt" and probably illustrates an eastern superstition of giving a baby an unpleasant name so as "to avert the evil eye." One belonging to this region was a "Buzite" (see Job 32:2,6).

2. Head of a family in the tribe of Gad (I Chron. 5:14) otherwise unknown.

BUZI (bū'zī), Ezekiel's father (Ezek. 1:3).

C

CAB (căb, *a hollow vessel,* ASV "kab"), a measure of capacity, a little less than two quarts; mentioned only in II Kings 6:25.

CABBON (kăb'ŏn), a town in Judah, taken by Israel from the Amorites (Josh. 15:40). It may be the same as Machbena (I Chron. 2:49).

CABUL (kā'bŭl). 1. A city of Galilee, mentioned in Joshua 19:27 as a border city of the tribe of Asher in the NE of Palestine. It lies between the hills about nine miles SE of Acre and is still inhabited.

2. A name given by Hiram of Tyre to a district in N Galilee, including twenty cities, which Solomon ceded to him (I Kings 9:13) and which probably included the original Cabul. It seems from II Chronicles 8:2 that Hiram (Huram) returned these cities and that Solomon rebuilt them.

CAESAR (sē'zêr). 1. The name of a Roman family prominent from the third century B.C., of whom Caius Julius Caesar (c. 102-—Mar. 15,44 B.C.) was by far the most prominent.

2. The title taken by each of the Roman emperors: e.g. Augustus Caesar who reigned when our Lord was born (Luke 2:1); his successor Tiberius Caesar who reigned 14-37 A.D. (Luke 3:1); Claudius Caesar, 41-54 (Acts 11:28; 18:2). Nero, under whom Peter and Paul were martyred, 54-68 (Philip. 4:22). Domitian was "Caesar" from 81-96 and it was under him that John was exiled to Patmos. "Caesar" is mentioned by our Lord (Luke 20:22-25) both literally as referring to Tiberius, and figuratively as meaning any earthly ruler. The name Caesar came to be used as a symbol of the state in general, and is often used in this sense in the NT (Matt. 22:17,21; Mark 12:14,16,17; Luke 20:22,24,25).

CAESAREA (sĕs'à-rē'à), a city built between 25-13 B.C. by Herod "the Great" at a vast cost and named in honor of his patron Augustus Caesar. It lay on the coast of the Mediterranean about 25 miles NW of Samaria which Herod had rebuilt and renamed "Sebaste," also in honor of Augusta. Herod intended it as the port of his capital, and a splendid harbor was constructed. Great stone blocks were used to top the reefs that helped to form the harbor. Being military headquarters for the Roman forces, and the residence of the procurators, it was the home of Cornelius in whose house Peter first preached to the Gentiles (Acts 10). It was the place of residence of Philip, the evangelist, with his four unmarried prophesying daughters (Acts 8:40; 21:8,9), who entertained Paul and Luke and their party on their return from the third missionary journey. Later it was the enforced residence of Paul while he was a prisoner for two years, and there Paul preached before King Agrippa (Acts 23:31-26:32). The Jewish war which Josephus described with such power and pathos, and which culminated in the destruction of Jerusalem, had its origin in a riot in Caesarea. Here Vespasian was proclaimed emperor of Rome in the year 69, while he was engaged in the Jewish war. In church history it was the birthplace of Eusebius (c. 260 A.D.) and the seat of his bishopric. Caesarea is still called Kaysārīyeh.

CAESAREA on the Mediterranean, showing the ruins of the ancient seafront from which Paul sailed for Rome. In the city of Caesarea Peter first preached to the Gentiles.

317

CAESAREA PHILIPPI on the slopes of Mt. Hermon, for centuries the center of worship of the god "Pan." Augustus Caesar gave the town and the surrounding countryside to Herod the Great. Nearby is the spot where the Lord began preparing the disciples for His sufferings.

CAESAREA PHILIPPI (sĕs'à-rē'à fĭ-lĭp'ĭ, *Caesarea of Philip*), a town at the extreme northern boundary of Palestine, about 30 miles inland from Tyre and 50 miles SW of Damascus. It lies in the beautiful hill country on the southern slopes of Mt. Hermon, and was probably very near the scene of our Lord's transfiguration. (Cf. Matt. 16:13-17: 8; Mark 8:27-9:8). The town was very ancient, being perhaps the Baal-gad of Joshua 12:7, 13:5, and for centuries it was a center of worship of the heathen god "Pan," whence it was known as "Paneas" and whence the modern name Banias (because there is no "p" in the Arabic alphabet). Augustus Caesar presented it, with the surrounding country, to Herod the Great, who built a temple there in honor of the emperor. Herod's son, Philip the tetrarch, enlarged the town and named it Caesarea Philippi to distinguish it from the other Caesarea. It lies at the easternmost of the four sources of the Jordan, and near here these streams unite to form the main river. It was at a secluded spot near here that the Lord began to prepare His disciples for His approaching sufferings and death and resurrection, and that Peter made his famous confession (Matt. 16:13-17).

CAGE, so-called when used by the fowler to keep his live birds, but "basket" when used for fruit (Jer. 5:27; Amos 8:1,2). Cf. Revelation 18:2 KJV.

CAIAPHAS, JOSEPH (kā'yà-fãs). In the century from 168 B.C. when Antiochus Epiphanes desecrated the temple, to 66 B.C. when the Romans took over, the high-priesthood was almost a political office, the priests still coming from the descendants of Aaron but being generally appointed for worldly considerations.

From 66 B.C. the Roman rulers appointed not only the civil officers (e.g. Herod) but the high-priests as well with the result that the office declined spiritually. Annas, the father-in-law of Caiaphas (John 18:13) had been high-priest by appointment of the Roman governor from 7 A.D. to 14 (see Luke 3:2) and though three of his sons succeeded for a short period, Caiaphas held the office from A.D. 18-36, with Annas still a sort of "high-priest emeritus." After our Lord had raised Lazarus from the dead (John 11) many of the Jews believed in Him (11:45,46), but some through jealousy reported the matter to the Pharisees, who with the chief priests gathered a council, fearing, or pretending to fear, that if Jesus were let alone many would accept Him, and the Romans would destroy what was left of Jewish autonomy. Then Caiaphas (John 11:41-53) declared that it would be better for Jesus to die than that the nation be destroyed. When, a little later, our Lord was betrayed into the hands of His enemies, the Roman soldiers and the Jewish officers took Him first to the house of Annas, where by night He was given the pretense of a trial (John 18:12-23). Then Annas sent Him bound to Caiaphas before whom the "trial" continued (John 18:24-27). Thence He was delivered to Pilate, because the Jews could not legally execute Him.   A.B.F.

CAIN (kān). 1. The first son of Adam and Eve, and a farmer by occupation. As an offering to God, he brought some of the fruits of the ground, while his brother brought an animal sacrifice. Angry that his offering was not received (Heb. 11:4 shows that this was because of the lack of a right disposition toward Jehovah), he slew his brother. He added to his guilt before God by denying his guilt and giving no evidence of repentance. He fled to the land of Nod and there built a city, becoming the ancestor of a line which included Jabal, forefather of tent-dwelling cattle-keepers; Jubal, forefather of musicians; Tubal-cain, forefather of smiths; and Lamech, a man of violence. His wife must have been one of his own sisters — not an impropriety in those days.
2. The progenitor of the Kenites (Josh. 15:57).
3. A village in Judah (Josh. 15:57).

CAINAN (kā-ī'năn). 1. In ASV "Kenan," the fourth from Adam in the Messianic line (Gen. 5:12-14; I Chron. 1:2; Luke 3:37).
2. A son of Arphaxad (Luke 3:36), omitted in Genesis 10:24; 11:12, but found in the LXX, from which Luke quotes.

CALAH (kā'là), a very ancient city of Assyria on the upper reaches of the Tigris, built originally by Nimrod, who is listed in Genesis 10:6-12 as a grandson of Ham, son of Noah. According to KJV, the builder was "Asshur" an eponym for Assyria, but cf. ASV. The city was apparently rebuilt by Shalmanezer I (reigned c. 1456-1436 B.C.), then later abandoned for many centuries till Ashurnasir-pal who is pictured as "Ruthlessness Incarnate" (reigned c. 926-902 B.C.) restored it. Aside from the Bible mention, the city is famous for having been the site of immense statuary in the form of winged lions and winged bulls some of which can be seen in the British Museum today. Several great palaces have been excavated there, and the place is now known as "Nimrud."

CALCOL (See Chalcol)

CALDRON, a large pot or vessel in which meat is to be boiled (Jer. 52:18,19 [ASV "pots"]; Ezek. 11:3,7,11). In Job 41:20 it is probably a mistranslation.

CALEB (kā'lĕb, *dog*). 1. The son of Jephunneh, the Kenezite; the prince of Judah who represented his tribe among the twelve chief men whom Moses sent from the wilderness to Paran to spy out the land (Num. 13:6). Most of the spies brought back a pessimistic report. Their names are almost forgotten, but two heroes of faith, Caleb and Joshua, who encouraged the people to go up and take the land are still remembered. Because Israel in cowardice adopted the majority report, God imposed upon them forty years "wandering" in the wilderness till that generation should die out. Caleb was 40 years old when the spies were sent (Josh. 14:7). At the age of 85, at the distribution of the land of Canaan, he asked for Hebron and the hill country where lived the fearful Anakim who had terrorized ten of the spies, and Joshua gave it to him. Later he became father-in-law of Othniel, the first

HOUSE OF JOSEPH CAIAPHAS on Mt. Zion, Jerusalem. Above, the approach; below, the courtyard interior.

of the "judges," by giving him Achsah his daughter (Judg. 1:12-15,20).
2. A son of Hezron, son of Judah (I Chron. 2:18,19,42) probably the same as the "Chelubai" of I Chronicles 2:9.

CALEB-EPHRATAH (kā'lĕb-ĕf'rà-tà), named in I Chronicles 2:24 as the place where Hezron died. The Hebrew and LXX texts differ here; and many scholars prefer the LXX reading, "after the death of Hezron, Caleb came unto Ephrath, the wife of Hezron, his father." When a son took his father's wife, it signified that he was claiming his father's possessions.

CALENDAR (kăl'ĕn-dȧr). Calendars are devised as a trustworthy means for recording history and determining dates in advance for social, civic and religious anniversaries, and for economic planning. Comparatively little is known of the calendar of the early Israelites from the patriarchs to the Exile, but a critical study of the Biblical records and archaeological discoveries is rewarding.

During the Bible period, time was reckoned solely on astronomical observations. The early Chaldean and Egyptian astrologers became quite learned in the movements of astronomical bodies. Their discoveries, as well as those of other Near Eastern neighbors, made their impact on the Jewish calendar. From earliest times the sun and moon were determinants of periodicity, days, months and years.

I. Days in the Biblical record of time begins with the account of creation. Various reckonings and measurements were derived from these early records. The order of the Jewish day, beginning in the evening, was based on the repeated phrase, "and there was evening, and there was morning" (Gen. 1:5b). While the Babylonian day, like that of most Near Easterners, began at sunrise, the Jewish day began at sunset (Deut. 23:11). Actually the demarcation between the end of one day and the beginning of another as observed by the ancient Israelites was that moment when three stars of the second magnitude became visible. This is confirmed in Nehemiah (4:21) "so we labored at the work, and half of them held the spears from the break of dawn till the stars came out."

Days of the week were not named by the Jews, but were designated by ordinal numbers. The term "sabbath" was not the name of the seventh day but a sacred designation.

Days were also subdivided in a manner set forth in the Creation account. And God said, "Let there be lights in the firmament of the heaven to separate the day from the night . . . the greater light to rule the day" (Gen. 1:14-16; see also Num. 9:16; Ruth 3:13).

Days were further subdivided into hours and watches. The day, as distinguished from the night, showed no exact divisions into parts in early Biblical records. It was, however, divided into periods of indefinite lengths designated by the terms "evening," "morning," "mid-day," and "the day declines" (Judg. 19:8). Dividing the day into hours was probably a later adoption. The Hebrew word for hour, *sha'ah* variously translated, is Aramaic (Dan. 3:6; 4:33), but Babylonians and Egyptians had hour-marking devices long before Daniel, and apparently Israel did, too. Babylonians divided the day by sun-watches into twelve equal parts, which were subdivided by the sexagenary system into minutes and seconds. The Egyptians divided the day plus the night into twenty-four hours, for which they had at least two calibrated measuring devices. One was a shadow clock, comprised of a horizontal piece of wood with markings to which was attached at one end a short T-like piece, toward the E in the morning and toward the W in the afternoon. A specimen, dating about 1400 B.C., is now in the Berlin Museum. Another Egyptian timepiece was the water-clock, clepsydra, the oldest known specimen of which dates from the reign of Amenhotep III, c. 1400 B.C. It is of alabaster, shaped like a flower-pot, with calibrated marks inside and a small aperture near the bottom through which the water gradually flowed out.

Whether borrowed or devised the Jews had sundials as early as the reign of Hezekiah, king of Judah, c. 715-687 B.C. When he was deathly sick, "Isaiah the prophet cried to the Lord; and he brought the shadow back ten steps, by which the sun had declined on the dial of Ahaz" (II Kings 20:11; Isa. 38:8). In the New Testament, John 11:9) records the rhetorical question of Jesus, "Are there not twelve hours in the day?" — as distinguished from night. This kind of daily reckoning is also seen in the crucifixion account which mentions the third, sixth and ninth hours (Mark 15:25; 33f), referring to 9 A.M., noon, and 3 P.M. respectively.

Early Hebrews divided the nights into three watches: "the morning watch" (Exod. 14:24); "the middle watch" (Judg. 7:19); and "at the beginning of the watches" (Lam. 2:19). The Romans divided the night into four watches, from which Jesus drew an analogy in his eschatological warning of unpredictable time — ". . . in the evening, or at midnight, or at cockcrow, or in the morning" (Mark 13:35).

II. Weeks constituted special and significant periodicity units for the "chosen people." The seven-day week is of Semitic origin, but reckoned from various reference points. The Babylonians and Assyrians bound their weeks to the lunar cycle, corresponding with the four phases, and began anew with each new moon. The Jewish week had its origin in the Creation account of seven days' duration, and ran consecutively in a free week system irrespective of lunar or solar cycles. This was out of the high esteem held for the sabbath. Conversely, the Egyptian week had ten days.

Astronomical bodies were divinely ordained in creation to be timemarkers. Days and years were measured by the sun; months by the moon; and cycles by sun, moon and stars. The week alone was not controlled by celestial bodies, but originated by divine command for man's economic, physical and spiritual welfare.

Though God placed special emphasis on the seventh day at the time of creation (Gen. 1:2f), the records are silent as to its observance during the long intervening interlude between then and Moses' day. If those of the pre-flood era or of the patriarchal period observed a "sabbath," there are no Biblical records of it. However, since it was kept alive in tradition until recorded in Genesis, it is a reasonable conjecture that it was preserved in practice also. Anyway, it was either revived or given special emphasis by Moses. The first recorded instance of the observance of "a day of solemn rest, a holy sabbath to the Lord" (Exod. 16:23) was when the Israelites were gathering manna in the wilderness. Subsequently, the sabbath became the most holy, as well as the most frequent of all the sacred days observed by the Jews.

When the fourth commandment in the Decalogue, "Remember the sabbath day, to keep it holy" (Exod. 20:8), was transmitted to Israel by Moses, it was designated as a perpetual memorial sign of the covenant between God and His chosen people. "And the Lord said to Moses, 'Say to the people of Israel, You shall keep my sabbaths, for this is a sign between me and you throughout your generations, that you may know that I, the Lord sanctify you" (Exod. 31:13). Thereafter it became a distinctive Jewish day, with successive injunctions to observe it, describing the manner of doing so, and the penalties for its desecration (Exod. 23:12;

35:2f). Emphasis on keeping "His holy sabbath" is seen in the Habakkuk (1:5) commentary of the Dead Sea Scrolls and the bitter accusations hurled at Jesus on this point (Mark 2:24). However superficial might have been the observance by some of Jesus' contemporaries, He confirmed its divine authenticity by going "to the synagogue, as his custom was," on the sabbath day to teach, preach and heal (Luke 4:16). Early Christian Jews made a habit of assembling on the first day of the week to commemorate Jesus' resurrection on that day (Luke 24:1); hence the last day became the first for worship and rest in Christendom.

III. Months, in effect, is a synonym for moons. Ancient people seemingly universally worshiped the moon and measured time by it, probably because of its conspicuousness and regular occurrence. The Arabic word for moon means "the measurer," and the Egyptian moon god, Thoth, was the god of measure. Even apostate Jews at times worshiped the moon along with other heavenly bodies (II Kings 23:5; Jer. 8:2).

"Moon" was synonymous with "month" in common parlance in Moses' day (Exod. 19:1). Later, when the responsibility of making the calendar was vested in the Sanhedrin, three of their number, including the chief, were entrusted as watchmen to report the first appearance of the new moon. A declaration of the beginning of a new month was then quickly dispatched over the country by fire signals, and later by messengers. The patriarch Hillel probably introduced the constant calendar.

The early Israelites designated their months by names which they borrowed from the Canaanites or Phoenicians. These names had seasonal connotations as implied in the four which have survived in the early Biblical records. Abib (Exod. 13:4; Deut. 16:1), corresponding to Nisan in the later calendar, means "month of the ripening ears." Ziv (I Kings 6:1), corresponding to Iyyar, means "month of flowers." Ethanim (I Kings 8:2), corresponding to Tishri, means "month of perennial streams." Bul (I Kings 6:38), corresponding to Marchesvan, means "rain or showers," being the first month in the rainy season.

About the end of the kingdom period the calendar was reformed, replacing the old names of the months with ordinal numerals, and changing the beginning of the year to spring. This is illustrated in I Kings (6:1 and 8:2), where the writer explicitly correlated the numeral month with older names, as "the month of Ziv, which is the second month." On the other hand the writer of Haggai (1:1; 2:1,10), about 520 B.C., at the time of the rebuilding of the temple, uses the numeral designation of months without any explanatory references. Yet Zechariah, a contemporary work, relates the numeral month to the Babylonian names, which came into popular use after the Exile. This is illustrated in the seventh verse of the first chapter in the expression "the eleventh month which is the month Shebat," and in chapter seven, verse one, "the ninth month, which is Chislev."

The post-exilic names of months were, as confirmed by the Talmud, adopted from the Babylonian calendar, but not used for civil and historical purposes. These, like the early Canaanite names, had their origin close to nature, as is seen from their derivations. Nisan — "move," "start," being the first month of the ecclesiastical year as

well as of the vernal equinox; Iyyar — "to be bright," "flower"; Sivan — "appoint," "mark"; Tammuz—name of an ancient Akkadian god identified with vegetation; Ab — "hostile" heat, "bulrushes" growing; Elul — "to shout for joy" at vintage; Tishri — "begin" civil year, "dedicate" to the sun-god by Babylonians, and to which the Jews might have associated the Creation and the Day of Judgment; Marchesvan — "drop," "rainy season"; Kislev — (derivation uncertain); Tebeth — "to sink," "dip"; Shebat — (unknown); Adar — "to be dark."

The Gezer Calendar, dated in the tenth century B.C., gives an interesting glimpse into the agricultural life in Palestine at that early date. This archaeological find by Macalister is a limestone plaque bearing a Hebrew inscription enumerating farm operations for eight months, mentioning sowing, flax harvest, barley harvest, and vine pruning.

IV. Years. The Jewish calendar contained two concurrent years, the sacred year, beginning in the spring with the month Nisan, and the civil year, beginning in the fall with Tishri. The sacred year was instituted by Moses following the Exodus, and consists of 12 or 13 lunar months of 29½ days each. The civil year claims a more remote antiquity, reckoning from the Creation, which traditionally took place in autumn (3760 B.C.). It came into popular use in the third century of the Christian Era. That this order of the year was kept by the ancient Hebrews is supported by the Mosaic command, "You shall keep the feast of ingathering at the end of the year, when you gather in from the field the fruit of your labor" (Exod. 23:16).

The Babylonians and Egyptians devised the intercalary month in order to reconcile the lunar and solar years. The Jewish leap years in their Metonic cycle of 19 years were fixed, adding an intercalary month to the 3rd, 6th, 9th, 11th, 14th, 17th, and 19th years. If, on the 16th of the month Nisan, the sun had not reached the vernal equinox, the month was declared to be the second Adhar and the following one Nisan.

In 46 B.C. a great advance over contemporary calendars was made by Julius Caesar, whose calendar year contained 365¼ days. It had a discrepancy of 11 minutes in excess of the solar year, and so was superseded by the Gregorian calendar in A.D. 1582, which was adopted by England in 1752. It has the infinitesimal error of gaining one day in 3,325 years.

Josephus (*Ant.* I, iii, 3) said that Moses ordered that the year of holy days and religious festivals begin with Nisan, the month in which the Exodus transpired, but that he retained the old order of year for buying and selling and secular affairs. This observation has been confirmed by critical study and subsequent Jewish custom of keeping both a sacred and a civil year.

Feasts and fasts were intricately woven into the lunar-solar sacred year. Three great historic feasts were instituted by Moses: "the feast of unleavened bread"; "the feast of harvest"; and "the feast of ingathering" (Exod. 23:14-17), corresponding roughly to Passover, Pentecost, and Thanksgiving. There were also numerous minor feasts.

Beginning in the month Nisan or Abib (Neh.

2:1; Exod. 23:15) the sacred holidays of feasts and fasts came in the following order. On the 14th of Nisan, the first month, the Passover (Exod. 12: 18f; 13:3-10) was observed in preparation for the following week's festival and in eating the paschal supper (see Matt. 26:17-29). The 15th to 21st was the Feast of Unleavened Bread (Lev. 23:6) which included, on the 15th, a sabbath, a day of holy convocation; on the 16th, Omer or presenting the first sheafs of harvest; and on the 21st another holy convocation. This is also the month of latter or spring rains when the Jordan was in flood (Josh. 3:15).

Christian Easter, fulfilling the Passover, is reckoned on solar-lunar cycles, coming on the first full moon on or after the vernal equinox (March 21).

The name of the second month, Iyyar, known formerly as Ziv (I Kings 6:1,37), does not occur in the Bible, as is also true with Tammuz, Ab, and Marchesvan. The Jews fasted on the 10th in commemoration of the death of Elijah; the 14th was the Second or Little Passover for those who could not keep the regular one (Num. 9:10,11); and on the 16th was a fast for the death of Samuel.

Pentecost or Feast of Weeks, or of Harvest, or of Firstfruits, when loaves as firstfruits of the gathered harvest were presented (Exod. 23:16; 34:22; Lev. 23:17,20; Num. 28:26; Deut. 16:9f) was celebrated on the sixth or seventh of Sivan (Esth. 8:9). (Cf. Acts 2:1.) This was the first of the two great agricultural feasts, coming at the end of seven weeks after the beginning of barley harvest, or 50 days after the Passover.

Next in annual order was the Jewish New Year (*Rosh Hashanah*), one of the most important and probably the oldest feast, observed on the first day of the civil year, in the month, Tishri, the former Ethanim or seventh month (I Kings 8:2). It was called the Feast of Trumpets, a precursor of one emblem of modern New Year's celebration. It was a day of holy convocation, of reading the law (Neh. 8:1-8), of blowing trumpets, of burnt offerings, of cereal offerings, and of profound solemnity, introducing "Ten Days of Repentance" (Num. 29: 1-16; Ezra 3:4-6). This protracted feast culminated in the Day of Atonement (*Yom Kippur*), Tishri 10th, one of the most holy days for the Jews. This is strictly a fast day and the only one commanded by law (Lev. 16:26-34; 23:27-32), called "the fast" in Acts 27:9. The Jewish Calendar makes "provision that neither *Rosh Hashanah* nor *Yom Kippur* may fall on the day before or the day after the sabbath, or the seventh day of Tabernacles on a sabbath." From the 15th to 21st of Tishri the Jews held the Feast of Ingatherings or Tabernacles or Booths (recalling the wilderness wandering), when the Firstfruits of wine and oil were offered (Exod. 23:16; Lev. 23:34-42; Deut. 16:13). It was a day of soul-searching and expiation of sins and of deep gratitude to God. It was the third of the three great feasts commanded by Moses, and the second of the two great agricultural feasts, corresponding to our modern Thanksgiving.

Winter holy days were few, though one of significance is mentioned in the Gospel of John (10: 22f): "It was the Feast of the Dedication at Jerusalem; it was winter, and Jesus was walking in the temple." Dedication of the Temple was instituted by Judas Maccabaeus in 164 B.C. This feast was held on the 25th of Chislev (Zech. 7:1), which

month was followed by the tenth month, Tebeth (Esth. 2:16), and the eleventh month, Shebat (Zech. 1:7).

Besides the one divinely ordained fast, the Day of Atonement, there were minor fasts, some temporary (Ezra 9:5; Neh. 1:4) and some annual. One fast in memory of the destruction of Jerusalem by Nebuchadnezzar (II Kings 25:1-7), instituted after the Exile, was observed on the ninth of Ab. Another, the fast of Esther, was observed on the 13th of Adar and followed the next two days by the Feast of Purim.

The lunar-solar year of Jewish feasts, fasts, and farming was fortified between the divine order of heavenly bodies "for signs and for seasons and for days and years" (Gen. 1:14), and the divine promise after the Flood that "While the earth remains, seedtime and harvest, cold and heat, summer and winter, day and night shall not cease" (Gen. 8:22).

V. Cycles. Inspired by God's hallowing the seventh day in creation, the Jews derived a special sacredness for the number seven. Religious convocations and festivals were highly regarded on the seventh day, seventh week, seventh month, seventh year, and seven times seven years.

Hence, the epitome of the sabbatical feasts, of which the perennial ones have been mentioned, may thus appear. The sabbath of seven days; Pentecost, at the end of seven weeks after Passover; the Feast of Trumpets, introducing the sacred seventh month, were all "appointed assemblies" (*mo'adhim*) of the Lord.

The sabbatical year was one of solemn rest for landlords, slaves, beasts of burden, and land, and freedom for Hebrew slaves. The volunteer produce of farm and vineyard was to be gathered and consumed by the poor alone (Exod. 23:10f; Lev. 25:20-22). The sabbatical and jubilee years were synchronized with the civil or agricultural year, beginning in autumn.

The Jubilee, every 50th year, following "seven weeks of years," was a hallowed year whose observance included family reunions, canceled mortgages, and return of lands to original owners (Lev. 25:8-17).

VI. Eras in the Bible calendar comprise the whole span of time from the Creation of the world to the consummation of the ages. Great events are terminal markers. These mountain peaks of time, in chronological sequence, are Creation, Flood, Abraham, Exodus, Exile and Birth of Jesus. Consequently the eras may be designated Antediluvian, Post-diluvian, Patriarchal, Israelite, Judean, and Christian. (Cf. Matt. 1:2-17; Luke 3: 23-37.)

Astronomically, that phenomenal star which guided the Magi divided human history. It is the pivotal point from which all history is dated, terminating the old order and initiating the new. It stands as the signal reference point of all time, the pre-eminent red-letter date in the Bible calendar. In the Jewish calendar it separates the history "Before the Christian Era" (B.C.E.) from that of the "Christian Era" (C.E.). In the Christian calendar it separates all "Before Christ" (B.C.) from that in *"Anno Domini"* (A.D.), "year of our Lord."   G.B.F.

CALF, a young bull or cow. Calves were used for food and for sacrifice. Calves used for sacrifice were usually males a year old.

CALF, GOLDEN (See Calf Worship)

CALF WORSHIP was a part of the religious worship of almost all ancient Semitic peoples. At least as early as the Exodus, living bulls were worshiped in Egypt. The Babylonians looked upon the bull as the symbol of their greatest gods. The bull was a sacred animal in Phoenicia and Syria. Among the Semitic Canaanites the bull was the symbol of Baal. It appears that the bull was in some way connected with the reproductive processes of plants and animals and with the sun. It symbolized strength, vigor, and endurance.

Aaron made a golden image of a male calf in order that the people might worship Jehovah under this form (Exod. 32:4). It is very unlikely that the Golden Calf was a representation of an Egyptian deity. The feast held in connection with this worship was a "feast of Jehovah" (Exod. 32:5).

After the division of the kingdom, Jeroboam set up two golden calves in his kingdom, one at Bethel and one at Dan (I Kings 12:28,29) because he feared that his people might desert him if they continued to worship in Jerusalem. He was not trying to make heathenism the state religion, for the bull images were erroneously supposed to represent Jehovah. In time, these images, at first recognized as symbols, came to be regarded as common idols (1 Kings 12:30; Hos. 13:2).   S.B.

CALKER, one who makes a boat waterproof whether in building or repairing (Ezek. 27:9,27). The men of Gebal (modern Jebail) were calkers for Tyre.

CALL (Gr. *klésis, calling*), one of the most common verbs in the Bible, representing over 20 words in the Hebrew and Greek text; but principally with one or another of four different meanings: 1. To speak out in the way of prayer — "Call unto me, and I will answer thee" (Jer. 33:3).

2. To summon or appoint — "I will call all the families of the kingdoms of the earth (Jer. 1:15).

3. To name a person or thing —"and God called the light Day" (Gen. 1:5).

4. To invite men to accept salvation through Christ. This last is a call by God through the Holy Spirit, and is heavenly (Heb. 3:1) and holy (II Tim. 1:9). I Corinthians 1:26 and 7:20 use tne word in a peculiar sense, as referring to that condition of life in which men were when they became Christians.

CALNEH (kăl'nĕ), one of the four cities, including also Babel, Erech (whence "Iraq"), and Akkad which were founded by Nimrod in the third generation after the Flood (Gen. 10:10). It was in the land of Shinar in the southern part of Mesopotamia. It is not identified, but Kulunu and Nippur have been suggested.

CALNO (kăl'nō), a city named in Isaiah 10:9 in a list of the Assyrians' victories. Almost certainly the same as *Calneh q.v.*

CALVARY (kăl'vȧ-rē, Lat. *calvaria, skull*), a place not far from the walls of Jerusalem where Christ was crucified and near which He was buried (Luke 23:33). The Latin *calvaria* is a rendering of the Greek *kranion,* skull, which renders the Hebrew *Gulgoleth* and the Aramaic *Gulgulta.* The common explanation is that the name was due to the cranial shape of the hill.

CHURCH OF THE HOLY SEPULCHRE, in Jerusalem. The church is said to cover the tomb where Jesus was buried. It was dedicated by Constantine in A.D. 335.

The exact site of Calvary is a matter of dispute. Two sites contend for acceptance, the Church of the Holy Sepulchre, which is within the walls of the modern city; and the Green Hill, or Gordon's Calvary, in which is Jeremiah's Grotto, a few hundred feet NE of the Damascus Gate. The first is supported by ancient tradition, while the second was suggested for the first time in 1849, although much is to be said in its favor.

CAMEL, the well-known "ship of the desert" because of its ability to go long without water and to pad safely through soft sand; and to the Arabs a prized possession. The fact that the word for "camel" is practically identical in Hebrew and in Arabic tells us that the patriarchs knew and used camels long before they used horses. They are mentioned prominently in the inventories of Abraham (Gen. 12:16), Jacob (Gen. 30:43) and of Job (Job 1:3 cf. 42:12). Though the camel was reckoned as unclean to the Hebrews (Lev. 11:4) its milk was used (Gen. 32:15). The "dromedaries"

CAMEL CARAVANS crossing the Palestine hill country. The camel is considered unclean in Leviticus.

CANA, with nearby gardens. The exact location of the "Cana of Galilee" referred to in the Gospel of St. John is not known. Although John mentions the name four times, it appears nowhere else in Scripture. At Cana, Jesus performed His first miracle, turning water into wine.

of I Kings 4:28 were probably swift horses (cf. ASV). Though some writers have described them as "docile," "stupid" would be a better word. They obey in a grumbling way and growl as loudly while being unloaded as when being loaded. Not dangerous except for a month in winter; but their bite is dangerous because of their filthy teeth. See also ANIMALS.

CAMEL'S HAIR, mentioned only in Matthew 3:4 and Mark 1:6, where we are told that John the Baptist wore a garment of camel's hair. It is probable, however, that this was not a garment made of the relatively expensive woven camel's hair, but of dressed camel's skin. Such garments are still used in the Near East. Some think that Elijah's mantle was made of camel's hair (II Kings 1:8; cf. Zech. 13:4).

CAMON or **KAMON** (kā'mŏn), a town in Gilead mentioned in Judges 10:5 as the burial place of the judge Jair.

CAMP, ENCAMPMENT (Heb. *mahăneh*), a group of tents intended for traveling or for temporary residence as in case of war — contrasted with village, town or city which are composed of houses and other more or less permanent buildings. The word *mahaneh* occurs over 200 times and is properly rendered by "camp," but 61 times it is translated "host" and four times "army," indicating the military purpose of the encampment. In Genesis 32:1,2, when the angels of God met Jacob, he exclaimed "This is God's host" (literally "camp") and he named the place "Mahanaim" or "Two Camps," referring to God's host and his own. Israel in the wilderness was given precise instructions as to the order and arrangements of its camp, both at rest and in traveling (Num. 2,3). The tabernacle in the center indicated the centrality of God in their life and worship. It was surrounded rather closely by the priests and Levites; and then further back were the 12 tribes, grouped in threes and led by Judah on the E, Reuben on the S, Ephraim on the W, and Dan on the N. In Deuteronomy 23:9-14 are given the sanitary and ceremonial observances which were used to keep the camp clean and wholesome.   A.B.F.

CAMPHIRE (kăm'fīr, Heb. *kōpher*), an Asiatic thorny shrub with fragrant white flowers (S. of Sol. 1:14; 4:13). "Henna-flowers" in ASV.

CANA of Galilee (kā'nà of găl'ĭ-lē), mentioned four times in the Gospel of John (2:1-11; 4:36-54; 21:2) and nowhere else in Scripture. It was in the highlands of Galilee, as one had to go *down* from there to Capernaum; but opinions differ as to its exact location. It may have been at "Kefr Kenna" about five miles NE of Nazareth, or at "Kana-el-Jelil" a little further N. Here Jesus performed His first miracle, graciously relieving the embarrassment caused by the shortage of wine at a marriage feast. It was here too (John 4:46) that he announced to the nobleman from Capernaum the healing of his apparently dying son; and Nathanael was of Cana (John 21:2).

CANAAN, CANAANITES (kā'năn, kā'năn-īts). 1. Canaan was the son of Ham in the genealogical lists in Genesis 9,10. His descendants occupied Canaan and took their name from that country (Gen. 9:18,22; 10:6).

2. Canaan was one of the old names for Palestine, the land of the Canaanites dispossessed by the Israelites. The etymology of the name is unknown,

as is also the earliest history of the name; but Egyptian inscriptions of c. 1800 B.C. use it for the coastland between Egypt and Asia Minor. In the Amarna letters of c. 1400 B.C. the name is applied to the Phoenician coast. According to Judges 1:9,10, Canaanites dwelt throughout the land. In Genesis 12:6; 24:3,37; Joshua 3:10 the Canaanites include the whole pre-Israelite population, even E of the Jordan. The language of Canaan (Isa. 19:18) refers to the group of West Semitic languages of which Hebrew, Phoenician, and Moabite were dialects. The Canaanites were of Semitic stock, and were part of a large migration of Semites (Phoenicians, Amorites, Canaanites) from NE Arabia in the third millennium B.C. They came under Egyptian control c. 1500 B.C. The Israelites were never able completely to exterminate them. Many were undoubtedly absorbed by their conquerors. The continued presence rendered the religious problem of the Israelites serious and difficult.   S.B.

CANAANITE, SIMON THE, so-called in Matthew 10:4 KJV, but in ASV "the Cananaean" (margin "or Zealot"); one of the original twelve apostles. He bore the epithet "Canaanite" to distinguish him from Simon Peter.

CANANAEAN (kă'nà-nē'ăn), the description of Simon "the Zealot" in Matthew 10:4 ASV, but "Canaanite" by mistake in KJV. Probably "zealot" (Luke 6:15) from an Aramaic word is the correct description.

CANDACE (kăn'dà-sē, Gr. *Kandáke*), the Queen of Ethiopia mentioned only in Acts 8:27. The name seems to have been a general designation of Ethiopian queens (like "Pharaoh" for Egyptian kings, and "Caesar" for Roman emperors). Her chief treasurer, a eunuch went to Jerusalem to worship and was led by Philip the evangelist to faith in Christ.

CANDLE. In a way, the word "candle" should not appear in the English Bible at all. The Hebrew word *nēr*, occurring 43 times, is rendered in KJV "lamp" 33 times (and this should be its rendering every time), "candle" nine times, and "light" once.

The simple fact is that in Elizabethan days in England people used candles and not lamps, whereas in ancient times in the warm climate, where the Word of God was given, men used little olive-oil lamps. Wax or tallow candles would have melted in the wilderness heat, even if they had been invented. It was the custom of the ancients to keep a house lamp burning day and night. A perennially burning lamp was a symbol of prosperity (Job 29:3; Ps. 18:28), a lamp put out, of judgment (Prov. 24:20; Jer. 25:10; Rev. 2:5).

CANDLESTICK. The Hebrew word *menôrâh*, always rendered "candlestick" in KJV, occurs 48 times in the OT, but could more accurately be rendered "lampstand," because the "lights" were not candles at all, but olive-oil lamps. The Aramaic word *nebrashta*, occurring only in Daniel 5:5, would better have been rendered "chandelier" and the Greek word *luchnia* would better be understood "lampstand." Matthew 5:15 KJV has "candle" and "candlestick," but ASV more correctly has "lamp" and "stand." In the tabernacle, as constructed in the wilderness, the lampstand (described in Exod. 25:31-40) with its seven branches holding the seven lamps of gold, stood at the left as the priests entered the Holy place. In the temple that Solomon built, there were ten lampstands of gold

(II Chron. 4:7), but they were placed in front of the Holy of Holies (I Kings 7:49; II Chron. 4:7).   A.B.F.

CANDY, a word that does not occur in the Bible, but the Jews had "confections" (Exod. 30:35) and the children chewed sugar cane when they could.

CANE, probably the sweet calamus (in KJV Isa. 43:24, Jer. 6:20 only; but cf. Exod. 30:23, where it is listed among the "chief spices").

CANKER (kăn'kêr, Gr. *gággraina, gangrene*), a word that occurs once in Scripture, II Timothy 2:17. It may mean cancer. See DISEASES.

CANKERWORM (Heb. *yeleq*), the name given to a larval stage of the locust (Joel 1:4; 2:25; Nah. 3:15,16). It was very voracious (Nah. 3:15). See INSECTS.

CANNEH (kăn'ē), mentioned only in Ezekiel 27:23 among the towns and regions with which Tyre traded. Some identify it with Calneh, *q.v.*

CANONICITY (kăn-ŏn-ĭc'ĭtē). The word "canon" originally meant "measuring rule," hence "standard." In theology its chief application is to those books received as authoritative and making up our Bible. The Protestant canon includes 39 books in the Old Testament, 27 in the New. The Roman Catholic Canon adds seven books and some additional pieces to the Old Testament (see Apocrypha). The Jews receive as authoritative the same 39 books as do Protestants.

It is commonly said that the Protestant test of canonicity is inspiration. That is, Protestants receive into their canon those books which they believe to be immediately inspired of God and therefore true, infallible, inerrant, the very Word of God. Creeds of the Reformation age often listed the books received as inspired, but the Protestant churches have received these books not because of the decision of a Church or Council, but because the books themselves were recognized as true and inspired, having God for their author. The history of the acceptance of these books and the study of the principles on which this reception occurred is an important phase of Bible introduction.

The Old Testament Canon

The Jewish Talmud of about 400 A.D. names the books of the Jewish canon in approximately the order found in our Hebrew Bibles today. By combining the 12 Minor Prophets, counting the books of Samuel, Kings, and Chronicles each as one book, etc., they arrive at the number of 24 books, divided into 5 of law, 8 of prophets, and 11 books of writings (Psalms, Proverbs, Job, Song of Solomon, Ruth, Lamentations, Ecclesiastes, Esther, Daniel, Ezra-Nehemiah, Chronicles). In earlier days they combined Ruth with Judges, Lamentations with Jeremiah and thus made 22 books equivalent to the 22 letters in the Hebrew alphabet. Origen, the Christian scholar of about A.D. 250, lists 22 OT books, but not in the order of the Talmud. Earlier, Melito of Sardis about A.D. 170 tells us that he went to Palestine to ascertain accurately the number of Old Testament books. He lists the five books of the Law first, then the others following in an order rather similar to that of our English Bible.

Before Melito, we have the vital witness of the Jewish historian Josephus. About A.D. 90 he wrote his work against Apion. In it, (i.8), he says that the Jews receive 22 books—5 of the Law of Moses,

13 of prophecy, and 4 of hymns to God and precepts for life. These books, he says, the pious Jew would rather die than to alter or deny. He says these books were written by Moses and the succeeding prophets from that time to the days of Artaxerxes (around 400 B.C.) and that their other later books, not being by prophets, were not thus regarded. It is obvious that the Talmudic order and classification of the books had not yet arisen in Josephus' day.

About A.D. 90 the Jews held the Council of Jamnia. We have only the later Talmudic reports concerning it, but apparently the canonicity of certain books was discussed, Ecclesiastes, Proverbs, etc. It should be made emphatic that this was not the time of original canonization of any book, as Josephus' witness assures us. Doubters arise in any age. But that Proverbs was already considered as canonical in the second century B.C. we can now prove by the reference in the Zadokite Documents xi. 20.

Earlier evidence on the OT canon gives us no listing, but considerable valuable information. Philo, the Egyptian Jew of the first century A.D., evidently received the 22 Hebrew books, for he quotes from many of them and from them only, as authoritative. The NT evidence is in accord. Most of the OT books are quoted and the seven apocryphal books are not. The NT gives no positive evidence on the order of the books, but it reveals in general a twofold division of the OT such as is found in Melito rather than the threefold. A dozen times the OT is referred to as the "Law and the prophets" or "Moses and the prophets," etc. As is evident from NT usage, this twofold category included all 22 books. Only once does it adopt the threefold classification, Moses and the prophets and the Psalms (Luke 24:44; but cf. vs. 27).

Pre-Christian evidence has been greatly augmented by the discovery of the Dead Sea scrolls. Previously, only the apocryphal books and other Jewish writings were available. These sources occasionally quoted books of the OT, but not with great frequency. Of special importance was the prologue to Ecclesiasticus, dated in 132 B.C. Three times it refers to the "law, and the prophets, and the other books of our fathers." One time it refers to these as already translated into Greek—the LXX. Because of the antiquity of this witness, the threefold canon was formerly held to be original. The twofold canon of the NT was not then explained. The Dead Sea Scrolls now, however, give four places (Zadokite Documents v. 21; vii. 15ff; Manual of Discipline 1,3; viii. 13ff) where the OT is referred to in two categories, the law and the prophets, as is usual in the NT. That this twofold canon included all our present books seems obvious from the fact that the Qumran Community quoted from most of the OT books, including those later classified in the third division of "writings," and has left manuscripts of all the Biblical books, except Esther. Thus the twofold canon is as early or earlier than the threefold. In line with this evidence is the fact that the LXX translation, at least in later copies, accords with the twofold, but not the threefold division.

It also appears that the critical development theory that the law was canonized in 400 B.C., the prophets in 200 B.C. and the writings in A.D. 90 is opposed to the facts. Some of the books concerning which the Council at Jamnia at A.D. 90 had

questions were already accepted in the Qumran texts (Proverbs, in the Zadokite Documents xi,20) or were in A.D. 90 actually counted among the prophets by Josephus. The view is that Daniel was not classed among the prophets because it was not written until 165 B.C. after the canon of the prophets had closed. But now it is admitted that Ecclesiastes, also among the writings in our Hebrew Bibles, was composed before 250 B.C. Josephus' testimony is also clear. Daniel *was* among the prophets in the early days.

The view of the conservative W. H. Green also is in error. He said the third division was composed by men who did not have the office of a prophet (Daniel, he claims, had the *gift* but not the *office*). But Daniel *was* among the prophets in antiquity. So were Ezra, Nehemiah, Chronicles, Ruth, etc. Furthermore, how does Green know that the author of Judges, now in the second division, was a prophet, and that the author of Chronicles, now in the third division, was not?

The fact is that those who spoke the word of God to Israel were called prophets. There is no record of any group who were inspired without being prophets. Most of the OT books were clearly written by prophets. The authors of some others, like Joshua and Proverbs, Song of Solomon, most of the Psalms, etc., were also prophets—at least they received revelations from God (Num. 12:6). For several books information on authorship is lacking, but even Green admits that Joshua, Judges, Samuel, and Kings were written by prophets. One has as much right to hold that Ruth, Job, Esther, Chronicles, etc., were by prophets as to say that Judges was. Certainly these books are included under the designation "prophets" in the Qumran scrolls and in the NT. If books of prophetic origin were to be received by Israel, this is a practical test that would check on the authority of written teaching as well as oral (cf. Deut. 13:1-5; 18:15-22). On this basis it can be explained how it was that the writings of prophets were accorded prompt acceptance by the faithful (cf. Josh. 1:7,8; Jer. 36:8-16; 26:18; Dan. 9:2, etc.). Hebrews 1:1 sums up the whole matter, "God . . . spake . . . by the prophets."

The New Testament Canon

Information on the early use of the NT books has been augmented in recent years both by the discovery of old portions of the NT and of early books quoting it.

There has been no question among the Christian churches since early times as to which books belong in the NT. All branches of Christendom have accepted as authoritative and inspired the current 27 books. They are accepted as authoritative because they are held to be true and immediately inspired of God.

Copies of the NT date from an early age. Already in the last century two remarkable old manuscripts had come to light—Sinaiticus and Vaticanus—from about AD. 325. Since then, the discovery of the Chester Beatty papyri has given portions from the previous century which cover parts of the Gospels and Acts, most of the Pauline Epistles and about half of Revelation. In 1935 an even more remarkable fragment was published. Though small —parts of five verses of John 18—it is precious as being the earliest. This Rylands papyrus is dated to the first half of the second century, or around A.D. 125. When skeptical scholars of the last century dated the fourth Gospel around 170, little did they know that there existed a piece of it coming from within 30 years of John's lifetime!

Recently the sands of Egypt have yielded new treasures. The Bodmer papyrus of John, dating from about A.D. 200, is almost complete. Another Bodmer papyrus coming from the early 200's includes I and II Peter and Jude along with a portion of the Psalms. Thus some actual NT manuscripts are now not too far removed from the days of the apostles themselves.

There was early a general agreement as to the books which the church at large accepted as canonical, but early evidence is not complete in detail for every book. Several books were accepted in some quarters but not in others. Contrary to statements sometimes made, no other books beside these 27 were ever given significant or general acceptance. The history of this acceptance of books is given very carefully by Westcott in his work on the *Canon* and the details for individual books are extensively presented in Zahn's monumental *Introduction to the NT*. One must not, however, confuse the acceptance of the books with the establishment of the canon. In a sense, the canon was established at once as soon as there were inspired books, for the NT books claim authority and recognize the authority of one another. Some churches had some of the books early, but it took time for all of the books to be distributed and for the evidence of their genuineness to be given to all and accepted by all. Fortunately for us, the early Christians were not gullible; they had learned to try the spirits. Furthermore, the Gnostic heresy rather soon began to multiply spurious writings and this made people cautious. It took time to convince everybody of every book. The history of the collection of the books traces this process.

The Period of A.D. 170

In brief survey, we may take three early periods for analysis. At about 170 the Muratorian Canon listed those books acknowledged to be apostolic and to be read in the churches. It includes the Gospels and Acts, mentions 13 Pauline epistles, warning against some forgeries, refers to two epistles of John—probably in addition to the first epistle which is quoted—and names Jude and the Revelation of John. It mentions an apocalypse of Peter "though some amongst us will not have this latter read in the churches." We now know it was a spurious writing. The Shepherd of Hermas is rejected as non-apostolic. Thus all our books are listed except Hebrews, James, I and II Peter which are not mentioned at all. Westcott thinks this was due to a break in the manuscript's archetype, for all these had been accepted earlier.

The Period of A.D. 140

This is the age of Justin Martyr who tells us how the Gospels (all four) are read in the church services along with the OT. He quotes several other books including Hebrews. From this period we now have new evidence in the "Gospel of Truth" discovered recently in Egypt. This book, written by the Gnostic Valentinus, was referred to by Irenaeus in 170 and dates from about 150. It weaves into its pantheistic composition all our NT books except James, II Peter, II, III John and Jude. Hebrews and Revelation are definitely included. One student, W. C. van Unnik, concludes that "round about 140-150 a collection of writings was known at Rome and accepted as authoritative which was virtually identical with our NT ("The Gospel of Truth and the NT," *The Jung Codex,* trans. and ed. by F. L. Cross, New York: Morehouse-Gorham, 1955, p. 124).

The Period from 95 to 118

Omitting many details, we may turn to the three great witnesses of the earliest age. Clement of Rome, Ignatius, and Polycarp all wrote between A.D. 95 and about 118. They show by quotation or clear allusion, that they knew and used all our NT books except Luke, Revelation, Colossians, Philemon, II Peter, II and III John and Jude. (See the evidence in Westcott, *General Survey of the History of the Canon of the New Testament*, pp. 22-48, and the author's *Inspiration and Canonicity of the Bible*, pp. 202-206). Moreover, these authors held the apostles in such high repute that their writings would obviously be treasured and accepted. Clement rather clearly ascribes inspiration to Paul. Actually, the omission of some of the books was not significant. Revelation and II and III John were possibly not yet written when Clement wrote in A.D. 95.

Later Problems

Although our books were accepted at an early date, yet the history of their use is discontinuous. The Gospels were never challenged until a later group of heretics questioned all the Johannine writings, claiming that they were spurious. Note that here, as usual, denial of apostolicity involved denial of authority. The book of Hebrews was continuously and from early days received and accepted as Pauline in Egypt. In Rome it was used by Clement, Justin, and Valentinus. The witness of Irenaeus (170) and Tertullian (about 200) is hardly clear. Then for a while its apostolicity was questioned and therefore its authority. Finally the views of Egypt and Palestine prevailed and it was fully accepted. II Peter had least external testimony, but here fortunately, the internal testimony is strong. Jude, which is in the Muratorian Canon and was accepted as apostolic by Tertullian, clearly quotes from II Peter 3:3. Also, if II Peter is not genuine, it is the basest of forgeries.

The New Testament Witness

And we must not forget the vital witness of the NT itself. Paul claims the authority of an apostle (I Cor. 9:1; II Cor. 12:11,12, etc.) and declares his letters are to be accepted (I Cor. 14:37; II Thess. 3:14). John in Revelation does the same (Rev. 1:3; 22:18,19). Peter insists that Paul's writings are Scripture (II Pet. 3:15; cf. 3:2). Jude quotes Peter as apostolic (Jude 18). It seems probable that I Timothy 5:18 quotes Luke 10:7 as Scripture. The fact is, as the early Church knew, that Christ had promised His apostles a special work of the Spirit, inspiring them as teachers of His revelation (John 14:26; 16:13). It is true that a few, a very few of the books were actually written by those not themselves apostles. But it is clear that the apostles used helpers in their writing (Rom. 16:22; I Pet. 5:12). The early church fathers called such men as Mark, Luke, and the author of Hebrews helpers or disciples of the apostles and accepted their work as that of the apostles with whom they labored. At least the books were all written and apparently all accepted within the period of the apostles.

Other indications combine to teach us that these 27 books are rightly in our canon. The Holy Spirit has witnessed through the generations to the saving truth therein contained. These books have brought

RUINS OF THE ANCIENT SYNAGOGUE at Capernaum. Capernaum was a town of considerable size, the headquarters of Jesus and the Apostles during the Galilean ministry, the scene of numerous miracles.

untold blessing where they have been received and obeyed. The church with one voice finds them to be the very word of God.

CAPERNAUM (kà-pûr'nā-ŭm, Gr. *Kapernaóum*, from Heb. *Kaphar-Nahum, village of Nahum*), a town on the NW shore of the Sea of Galilee where Jesus made His headquarters during His ministry in Galilee (Matt. 4:13; Mark 2:1). In Scripture it is mentioned only in the Gospels, and perhaps did not arise until after the Captivity. That it was a town of considerable size in the days of Christ is shown by a number of facts: a tax-collector had his office there (Mark 2:14); a high officer of the king (Herod Antipas) had his residence there and built a synagogue for the people there (Matt. 8: 5-13; Luke 7:1-10). Jesus performed many striking miracles there, among them the healing of the centurion's palsied servant (Matt. 8:5-13), the man sick of the palsy borne by four (Mark 2:1-13), and a nobleman's son (John 4:46-54). It was there that He called Matthew to the apostleship as he was sitting at the receipt of custom (Matt. 9:9-13). The discourse on the Bread of Life, which followed the feeding of the 5,000, and many other addresses were delivered there (Mark 9:33-50). In spite of Jesus' striking works and teachings, the people did not repent, and Jesus predicted the complete ruin of the place (Matt. 11:23,24; Luke 10:15). His prophecy was so completely fulfilled that the town has disappeared and its very site is a matter of debate. There are two main claimants, about 2½ miles apart, for the honor of being the site: Tell Hum, which is about 2½ miles SW of the mouth of the Jordan; and Khan Minyeh, which is SW of Tell Hum. The present trend of opinion is in favor of Tell Hum.   S.B.

CAPH (kàf), the 11th letter of the Hebrew alphabet corresponding to our "k." As a numeral it is eleven.

CAPHTOR (kăf'tôr, Heb. *kaphtôr*), the place from which the Philistines originally came (Amos 9:7). Jeremiah (47:4) calls it an island. There are a number of theories regarding the matter, but the one that is most widely accepted is that they came from the Isle of Crete in the Mediterranean. There is evidence of ancient connection between Crete

and Philistia (Ezek. 25:16; Zeph. 2:5, where the LXX renders Cherethites "Cretans"); and the Philistines are called Cherethites, which may mean Cretans. It is possible that Caphtor includes with Crete also the other islands in the vicinity, including Caria and Lycia.

CAPPADOCIA (kăp'à-dō'shĭ-à), a large inland region of Asia Minor which apparently was given this name by the Persians though its people were called "Syrians" by the Greeks. In the latter time of the Persian empire the region was divided into two territories of which the more northerly was later named Pontus and the southerly Cappadocia, which name it retained in New Testament times. It was bounded on the N by Pontus, on the E by Syria and Armenia, on the S by Cilicia and on the W by Lycaonia. The Romans built roads through the "Cilician gates" in the Taurus range so that Cappadocia could readily be entered from the S. The Cappadocians were Aryans. Jews from Cappadocia (Acts 2:9) were among the hearers of the first Christian sermon along with men from other Anatolian provinces; and Peter directed his first epistle (I Pet. 1:1) in part to "the elect—of the Diaspora"—dwelling in various provinces in the N. It is almost certain that many of these Cappadocian Jews were converted on the day of Pentecost and so have the honor of being among the very earliest Christians.   A.B.F.

CAPTAIN, a word that in KJV translates 16 different words in the original text (12 Hebrew, one Aramaic, three Greek), but by far the most frequent is *sar* which occurs 419 times in the OT and is rendered "prince" 208 times (cf. "Sarah" for "princess"), "captain" 126 times, "chief" and "ruler" each 33 times. All these are terms expressing leadership, and do not refer to specific grades or ranks in a military organization. The meaning is obvious. In the NT Christ is called "captain of their (our) salvation" (Heb. 2:10). "*Chiliarchos*" or "leader of a thousand" (John 18: 12) could be translated "colonel," while the "captain of the temple" (Acts 4:1, etc.) was not a military officer at all, though he had soldiers under his authority. Though the general intent is clear, the meaning is not technically definite.

CAPTIVITY. The term Captivity, when used of Israel, has reference not to the long series of oppressions and captivities of the Israelites by hostile peoples, beginning with the bondage in Egypt and ending with the domination of Rome, but to the captivity of the Ten Tribes in 722 B.C. and the captivity of Judah in 586 B.C. The practice of making wholesale deportations of people as a punishment for rebellion was introduced by Assyria, but other nations adopted it.

(continued on page 355)

THE FOLLOWING BIBLE STORY, *The Break-up of Solomon's Kingdom,* was written by Esther Kellner. It is based upon the events related in the First and Second Book of Kings and the Second Book of Chronicles.

The Breakup of Solomon's Kingdom

IT WAS a bright and beautiful day, but there was anxiety throughout the land. Solomon, the king who had ruled for forty years, was dead. And now his son Rehoboam (REE-hoe-BOE-um) would come to the throne.

Along the streets and at the crossroads, people stood close together and spoke in troubled voices. Yet there was little grief among them, for the reign of Solomon had been a bitter thing. To bring riches and glory to his own name, he had taxed the people unmercifully, had seized thousands and sent them into enforced labor. For years they had suffered such tyranny that even some of Solomon's own officers turned against him. Driven to fury by the unjust burdens upon the people, one officer, a certain Jeroboam (JAIR-oh-BOE-um), had led a revolt against the king. But his plot was discovered and his followers scattered. To save his life, Jeroboam had fled southward to Egypt and had not returned.

Now Solomon was dead, but would the lives of the people be any easier? Up one street and down another and in all the market places, murmurs of distress could be heard.

"Rehoboam is cruel and haughty, it is said. Will he then be a better king than his father?"

"Rehoboam does not worship the God of Israel alone. He sacrifices to the gods of his pagan mother also."

"No, we can expect no mercy from this arrogant prince! Only one man has shown us mercy and he is far away, in Egypt."

"Jeroboam!" Now the name was on every lip, traveling from one mouth to another, from one village to the next, in accents of rising hope. "Jeroboam will speak for us. He will know how to help us!"

A messenger was dispatched to bear their petition to Egypt. Soon the young and hardy Jeroboam was with them again. Cheers rose from the lips of the saddened people, and hope lifted their heads once more.

"Since we must know what Rehoboam intends to do," said Jeroboam, speaking before them, "let us go forth to him and ask."

And so, with Jeroboam leading them, they marched boldly upon the city of Shechem (SHEE-kum), which the new king Rehoboam had chosen as his capital.

"We wish to know," they cried out, "whether you intend to enslave and overtax us as your father did, or if you will take pity upon us. If you will make our burdens lighter, we will serve you gladly."

Rehoboam stared down at them, pale with astonishment and anger. He had not expected to see people representing the whole province of Israel standing before him demanding their rights, with his father's old enemy Jeroboam leading them. Not knowing what to say, he put them off.

"Return to me in three days for your answer," he said, and his voice was cold.

Now the young king's ministers gathered about him, some of them old and wise men who had sorrowed to see the great kingdom of David, his grandfather, become burdened and rebellious under Solomon, his father. They said to Rehoboam, "Deal kindly with them, as David would have done. Be just and merciful."

But the young princes who were his friends and relatives spoke in another way.

"Do not give up your authority for an instant. Let them know from the beginning that *you* are king, and that you will do what pleases you!"

So, on the third day, Rehoboam stepped before the waiting people and said with scorn and contempt, "My father made your yoke heavy, and I will add to that yoke. My father chastised you with whips, but I will chastise you with scorpions!"

Rebellion

NOW AT LAST the people of Israel rose up in open rebellion. They cried out that they were a free people chosen by God, and they would be slaves to Rehoboam no more. Nor would they be a part of his kingdom. David had united the lands of Israel and Judah into one kingdom but now, the people cried out, that unity was ended. They would rule their own land, have their own king! And with this declaration, they turned homeward, away from the king's capital.

Rehoboam haughtily ignored these words and refused to recognize that they had separated themselves from him. After a little while, he sent a tax collector to bring tribute from them, as usual. But when the man arrived, the people of Israel turned upon him and stoned him to death.

When word of this reached Shechem, Rehoboam sat uneasily upon his throne. Fearful rumors were brought to him. The people of Israel were marching upon him, it was said, for his capital was in their own land. They would slay him also. In terror, the king rose up and called for his chariot and fled south to the land of Judah, where he knew they would not follow.

On that day the united kingdom of Israel and Judah, ruled so long by David and then by Solomon, was broken apart forever by the arrogance of Rehoboam.

But the young king would not have it so. He cried out in a rage, "I will take my war chariots and defeat them and bring them back like dogs following their master!"

Before he could set out to fight against them, however, a holy man, a prophet by the name of Shemeiah (she-MAY-yuh), came to him and said, "The Lord has given me a message for you. The Lord says: 'Do not fight against your brethren in Israel. Send your warriors back home.' "

Reluctantly Rehoboam obeyed. But he was furious at the thought of Israel departing from his kingdom and being ruled by Jeroboam instead of himself.

Rehoboam flees south to escape the rebellion

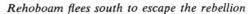

The New Kingdom of Israel

JEROBOAM set up his own capital at Shechem and ruled over the land of Israel. But his heart was troubled by doubts. The beautiful Temple of God was in Jerusalem, and Jerusalem was in Judah. When his people went up to Jerusalem to worship, they would see the men and women of Judah worshiping in the same way, and remember that they were brethren.

"Then they may wish they were reunited," he thought. "They may even turn to Rehoboam again. If that happened, I would be slain. Therefore, I must keep them from going."

331

So he built a great altar at Shechem and set up two golden calves in Bethel (BETH-ul) and Dan. Then he issued a declaration. "These are your gods, which brought your people out of Egypt long ago. It is too long a journey to go to worship in Jerusalem. Stay and worship here at Shechem, in the temple I have built for you."

Jeroboam then set up other temples and arranged the manner of worship as he pleased. Before this time, only the descendants of Levi (LEE-vye) had been made priests, for such was the Law of Moses. Now King Jeroboam made priests of anyone, even the lowliest of the people. He changed the days of the feasts and burned incense and sacrifices to the golden calves and on the high altars of pagan gods. Worship of the true God was no longer the sole faith of Israel.

Years passed in this way until the time came when the son of Jeroboam fell gravely ill. Jeroboam was frantic with anxiety, until he remembered a certain holy man who knew the ways of the future. This man, Ahijah (ah-HIGH-juh), had once told him that he would be king of Israel, and truly it had come to pass. Now Jeroboam thought, "This man can surely tell whether the lad will live."

So he said to his wife, "Take gifts, some bread and honey and cakes, and go to Shiloh (SHY-low), where the prophet dwells."

Egyptian soldiers looting the treasures of the Temple

She obeyed. Ahijah was old now and blind with age, and he could not see her. But the Lord told him who stood at his door, and he called out, "Come in, wife of Jeroboam, and hear what I have to say."

Then he delivered his message. "The Lord is angry with your husband, the king. The Lord lifted him up and made him a prince and a ruler, but Jeroboam has been false. He has worshiped, not God, but golden images and pagan shrines. Therefore, the Lord will root the people of Israel out of this rich land and scatter them beyond the river. Jeroboam shall be defeated by another, and his son shall die."

In terror, the wife fled to her home, and even as her feet touched her own doorsill, the lad died.

Jeroboam ruled Israel twenty-two years. Rehoboam ruled Judah seventeen years. Neither of them kept the Commandments of the Lord. Jeroboam led his people to the worship of idols, and Rehoboam followed the faith of his pagan mother. He built pagan shrines on every hilltop and under every green tree.

For many years the king of Egypt had looked with envy upon the land of Israel. Now suddenly he attacked and defeated Jeroboam and took away many of the treasures in the beautiful Temple of Solomon. He also seized the gold shields which adorned the palace Solomon had built.

Throughout their lives Rehoboam and Jeroboam were the bitterest enemies, each blaming the other for the misfortunes which had befallen him. In the eyes of God, both were men falsehearted and full of wickedness.

✠ ASA ✠

The True Worship Restored

WHEN Rehoboam died, his son Abijam (ah-BYE-jam) ruled in his place. It was well that this king lived only three years longer, for he did much evil. When he died, his own son Asa (AY-sah) took his place upon the throne of Judah.

Asa was David's great-great-grandson, but he ruled a much smaller region, now that David's kingdom was divided. It was full of unrest and evil. The people fought among themselves and many had ceased to worship the Lord. Shrines built to pagan gods and idols stood everywhere.

Asa, however, was a young man of great righteousness. He destroyed the altars to the false gods. He smashed the images, he cut down the groves where trees were worshiped, he shattered the pagan shrines on the high hills. And he commanded all Judah, "Seek ye the Lord God of David, do His will, keep His Commandments!"

Asa's own mother had turned to pagan worship and had an image of an evil goddess to which she prayed. Asa destroyed this image and commanded that his mother worship God. When she refused, he removed her as queen.

For years there was peace in the land. To protect his people, Asa built up a mighty army of warriors with spears, shields, bows and arrows. Afterward, when he was attacked by an Ethiopian (ee-thee-OH-pea-un) invader, he was able to defeat the foreign army, even though it was large and powerful and had three hundred chariots. For Asa called upon the Lord, crying out, "In Your name we go out against this multitude!"

Asa and his army returned victorious to Jerusalem, bearing the spoils of war, cattle and sheep and camels. As they neared the gates of the city, an old prophet came to meet them and cried out before the king, "The Lord is with you! For a long time Israel has been without the Law and the worship of God. Be strong, for your work shall be rewarded!"

Encouraged, Asa renewed the great altar in the Temple which Solomon had built long ago. For years it had been abandoned. There he offered, in gratitude to the Lord, seven hundred oxen and seven thousand sheep. He gathered about him many pious men who vowed to seek the Lord with all their heart and soul. They vowed also that anyone who refused to worship the true God would be punished.

Asa was one of the few kings of this time who possessed a gentle and God-fearing nature. His people loved and honored him. When he died, after ruling forty years, he was laid in his tomb at Jerusalem with great reverence and sorrow.

JEHOSHAPHAT

Down with the Idols

ASA'S SON, Jehoshaphat (jee-HOSH-uh-fat), was the worthy son of a worthy father, a strong and honorable king. He worshiped the Lord God and kept His Commandments and tried to lead his people in the paths of holiness.

So the Lord blessed Jehoshaphat and gave him wisdom.

The young king knew that many in his kingdom, Judah, had turned from the true God. There were places where the teachings of the holy Law had been entirely forgotten.

So he sent priests and princes through the land as missionaries to teach the word of the Lord and win back those who had strayed to false worship. His father had cast away their idols and cut down many of their sacred groves. But in spite of all that Asa had done to destroy such worship, there were still people in the land of Judah who followed it.

It was Jehoshaphat's wish that all men should have justice. To this end, he established the rule of law throughout the land and solemnly instructed his officials. "Take heed what you do, since you judge not for men, but for the Lord." It was Jehoshaphat who founded the great Hebrew "supreme court" known as the Sanhedrin (SAN-heh-drun).

He even formed a friendly alliance with Ahab (AY-hab), king of Israel, the land from which Judah had been separated for so many years. Jehoshaphat remembered that the Israelites were brethren in the eyes of God. "I am like you," he said, "and my people are like your people." He fought beside Ahab against their common enemies, even allowed his son to marry Ahab's daughter. For this, certain men were angered against him, for Ahab and his family had fallen into idol worship; but the greater number of his people continued to love Jehoshaphat dearly.

Indeed, he was honored not only in his own land, but by his neighbors. His kingdom was strong and prosperous. He built storehouses and palaces and taught the word of the Lord and made the name of Judah great.

When he died, he was buried with great honor in the tombs of the kings at Jerusalem.

AHAB

Ruled by a Woman

WHILE Jehoshaphat and his noble father, Asa, were ruling Judah, many things were happening in the northern kingdom of Israel.

The rulers who followed Jeroboam, the first king, were men of great evil. One after another, they dealt in unprovoked war, treason, murder, cruelty, and the worship of pagan gods. Finally, Ahab came to the throne, a king "who did evil in the sight of the Lord above all others that were before him."

Ahab did not take a wife from his own people. Instead he married the Princess Jezebel (JEZZ-uh-bell), daughter of a pagan king. She was a worshiper of Baal (BAY-ul), and brought this degrading faith with her. More than four hundred priests of Baal were established in Israel by the new queen and fed at the royal table. To please her, Ahab built a great altar and a magnificent temple to her heathen god. He also provided a grove in which she could worship with idolatrous pagan rites.

Through her evil power over her husband, Jezebel began to rule Israel herself. She commanded that the prophets of God be hunted down and slain. Outraged by this deed, Elijah (ee-LYE-juh), the mightiest prophet of Israel, rose up against Ahab and the new queen. She was spreading her corrupting faith throughout the land, poisoning the hearts and minds of the people against the true God.

Elijah, a righteous old man, stern, angry, defiant, spoke openly against her. When, after a time, King Ahab came face to face with this great prophet, he demanded coldly, "Are you the man who is troubling Israel?"

Elijah answered fearlessly, "It is not I, but you, who troubles Israel. You have forsaken the Commandments of God and turned to the worship of Baal!"

Elijah proved to the people that the Lord was the true God when his prayers for rain were answered, and prayers to Baal were not. This so angered Jezebel that she sent men to slay him, and he fled into the wilderness to save his life.

One of the cruelest and most vicious deeds of Jezebel was yet to come. Her husband Ahab wanted to buy a beautiful vineyard next to the palace, but Naboth (NAY-bawth), the owner, refused to sell it. Under the just laws of Israel, not even a king could seize land from its rightful owner, and so Ahab scowled and sulked.

Then Jezebel took matters into her own infamous hands. Through trickery, she had Naboth stoned to death, and his sons also. Now that there were no heirs to inherit the vineyard, according to the law it became the property of the king.

When the prophet Elijah heard of this outrage, he cried out in a voice of prophecy that the family of Ahab would come to an end as punishment for this terrible deed, that dogs would lick the king's blood and eat the flesh of the queen.

A few years later, Ahab was brought home from a fierce battle badly wounded, and died the same day. Dogs licked the blood that dripped from his chariot, and so the first part of Elijah's prophecy was fulfilled. Later the rest of it would come to pass.

Meanwhile, both Judah and Israel were gripped throughout by growing depravity. There were few men who kept or even remembered the laws of the Lord.

In Israel, Jezebel's son Joram (JOE-rum) now sat upon the throne, but Jezebel was still the true ruler of the kingdom. Joram was also a worshiper of Baal, and the influence upon the people of him and his mother was evil beyond words.

In the land of Judah, the noble Jehoshaphat had died, leaving his eldest son to rule after him. This was the same son he had allowed to marry a daughter of Ahab and Jezebel years before. The daughter's name was Athaliah (ath-uh-LYE-uh), and she was quite as vicious as her mother.

When Athaliah's husband died, her son Ahaziah (ay-huh-ZYE-uh) ruled Judah. He too had been taught cruelty and evil-doing and, like his mother and grandmother, spread the idol worship of Baal throughout his kingdom.

Those who remembered the Lord sorrowed to see the sinful ways that His Chosen People had fallen into. The mighty and wonderful kingdom of their ancestor, King David, had been shattered. Judah and Israel, its lands divided, no longer recalled the admonitions of David, nor heeded the Commandments of God.

It was in this sad time that Elijah ended his days on earth. Before his departure, however, he chose a young prophet called Elisha (ee-LYE-shuh) to serve the Lord in his place, to inherit his strength, his wisdom, his power, and his labors.

❧ JEHU ❧

Anointed by the Prophet

Now Elisha saw what wickedness was upon the kings of both Judah and Israel. He knew the people of the Lord must have a new leader, so he called to him the son of a certain prophet.

"Take this cruse of oil," he directed, "and go up to Ramah (RAY-muh), where the army is camped. When you arrive there, seek out Jehu (JEE-hew), the captain, and take him aside, away from the others. Then pour the oil upon his head. Give him this message: The Lord says, 'I have

Jezebel meets her doom.

COLOR ILLUSTRATIONS BY MAURICE BOWER

The stoning of Zechariah.

King Asa smashes his mother's
pagan idol.

Jeroboam and the Israelites
worship the golden calf.

The Israelites are marched off to captivity.

Elijah confronts Ahab with a terrible prophecy.

The fury of Athaliah when she learns her own grandson is king.

The wedding of Jehoshaphat's son
and Ahab's daughter.

At Asa's request, worshipers bring
sheep and cattle for sacrifice.

Babylonian troops burn and sack the Temple.

anointed you king over Israel — and destroyer of the house of Ahab.'
Then hurry away."

The young prophet did as he was bidden. When he and Jehu were alone,
he poured the oil upon Jehu's locks, repeated to him the words of the
Lord, and hastened away.

When Jehu reappeared, a strange look upon his face, his fellow officers
were curious. Who was the dusty young stranger who had arrived, weary
and breathless as if from a far journey, carrying a cruse and asking to
speak to the captain in secret? What word had he brought to render Jehu
dazed and staring?

At last, one of them asked, "Is all well? What did the mad young
stranger want of you?"

Then Jehu answered, telling them all that had come to pass. "The Lord
has anointed me king over Israel!" he concluded, awe and excitement
mingling in his voice.

With a shout, the men rose up and cast their garments into a heap to
form a throne for him. Trumpets blared, and the men cried aloud for all
to hear, "Jehu is king!"

Then Jehu leaped into his chariot and set off across the plain at a
furious pace, followed by his cavalry, to seize and destroy the wicked kings.

Joram, son of Jezebel, who still believed himself ruler of Israel, was at
the city of Jezreel recovering from battle wounds. Ahaziah, the cruel king
of Judah, who was Joram's nephew and the son of Athaliah, had gone down
to visit him.

When watchmen on the tower saw the warriors coming they knew by
the furious pace of the chariot that the driver was Jehu, and that he did
not come in peace. They sounded the alarm.

Both kings, even the wounded Joram, leaped into their chariots and
sought to escape, Joram crying out to his companion, "This is treachery,
Ahaziah!"

An instant later, Jehu drew his bow and sent an arrow through the air
— and through the heart of Joram. The king slumped down in his chariot,
a dying man. "Let his body be cast into the vineyard stolen from Naboth!"
Jehu commanded.

Meanwhile, King Ahaziah drove on wildly, seeking to escape. "Follow
him and slay him!" Jehu commanded his men. And they did. Yet they
brought him back to Jerusalem in a chariot and gave him an honorable
burial, because he was the son of the beloved Jehoshaphat.

The Fall of Jezebel

JEZEBEL was the last. Defiant to the end, she vowed to die in a manner
befitting a queen. She rouged her face, put on her royal garments, and
went to the window to call out bitter taunts as Jehu approached.

The new king was incensed. "Throw her down!" he cried out to her
servants.

They obeyed, and Jezebel was trampled to death by his chariot horses
as she lay upon the pavement.

Later Jehu considered the matter further. "Take care of this cursed woman and bury her honorably. After all, she is the daughter of a king." But when his men went out to do as he said, they found that nearly all her flesh had been eaten by marauding dogs — as Elijah had once foretold.

Jehu slew all that remained of the houses of Ahab and Ahaziah. Then he made a pronouncement. "Ahab served Baal a little; Jehu shall serve him much. Let all the prophets of Baal come to me, and the servants and the priests and the worshipers, that a great sacrifice may be made."

The followers of the Lord were stunned by these words, but the followers of Baal rejoiced. One and all they came to the temple for the sacrifice, so that it was crowded from one end to the other.

Jehu's command: "Kill them all!"

Then, when all were inside its walls, with not a single worshiper of the pagan god overlooked, Jehu issued a command to his men that froze the assembly of idol worshipers with terror. "Slay them all!" Afterward he destroyed the altars and images and vestments, even the great temple, thus ending Baal worship in Israel.

But he forgot one thing — to destroy the golden calves which Jeroboam had set up for the people to worship many years before.

Jehu ruled Israel for twenty-eight years, but his rule was troubled and uneasy. For a new fear had come over the land, fear of a mighty enemy to the north, the king of Assyria (uh-SEAR-ee-uh).

Israel was small and weak, Assyria vast and powerful. Eventually the expected did happen: the Assyrian king sent a demand to Jehu. "Pay us tribute, or we will conquer and destroy you."

Jehu had no choice.

To this day a famous carving has survived which shows the captive King Jehu kneeling before the king of Assyria, while the men of Israel walk like servants bearing tribute payments of gold and precious fabrics. This carving may still be seen on the Black Obelisk in the British Museum.

And so Israel, once a proud portion of the great kingdom of David and Solomon, became a slave to pagan might.

Down with the pagan temples!

❧ JOASH ❧

Victim of Evil Counsellors

FOR YEARS Athaliah, the evil queen-mother, had ruled over all the land of Judah, first through her husband and then through her sons. Then came the day when her last son, King Ahaziah, made a visit to Israel and was slain by Jehu's men. Word of this disaster was brought to Athaliah by a terrified messenger. "Behold Jehu, a captain of the army of Israel, has rebelled and made himself king!" He added that Jehu had slain all that remained in Israel of the family of Ahab, who had been Athaliah's father. Now her brother, King Joram, lay dead, along with her mother, Jezebel, and her son.

A royal murderer meets his death

Athaliah received the message without grief. Her love was not a love of family, but a love of power. For years she had directed the affairs of the kingdom as the power behind the throne. Now that her sons were dead, she would direct Judah openly. She would assume the throne.

The only heirs to the throne still alive were the young princes. Some of them were her own grandsons. Nevertheless, the ruthless and designing Athaliah commanded that they be slain.

In the same palace with the queen lived the high priest Jehoiada (jee-HOY-uh-duh) and his young wife, who was Athaliah's stepdaughter. This stepdaughter was a lovely and kindly princess called Jehosheba (jee-HOSH-eh-buh), who loved the Lord and kept His Commandments. When a servant brought her word of Athaliah's ghastly command, she cried out against the deed and fled to the chambers of the princes, hoping to save their lives.

She was too late. Every one of them, the youths, the lads, even the little ones still in their babyhood, lay lifeless upon the floor.

Jehosheba clung to the doorway, gazing in horror and anguish upon the scene, when suddenly a little cry came from one of the baby princes, little Joash (JOE-ash). His young aunt saw him stir feebly. He was not dead, as the executioners and she herself had thought. There was life in him yet!

Swiftly, Jehosheba caught him up in her arms and covered him with a fold of her robe. Then she sped to her own chambers and summoned the baby's nurse. The nurse, who had been weeping bitterly, was filled with joy to find that Joash was still alive. He had only been stunned by the executioner's blow. So she took him in her arms again, comforted and fed him, and quieted him to keep the wicked Athaliah from hearing his cries.

Trembling with fear, Jehosheba hid the little one in her bedchamber until the return of her husband, Jehoiada.

Jehoiada was a wise and resourceful man. The easiest place to hide the little one, he said, was in the Temple of the Lord. There were devout servants, priests, teachers, and watchmen in the Temple. They would conceal the little Joash and give him tender care and a prince's upbringing.

So Joash was smuggled into the beautiful Temple of the Lord built years ago by King Solomon, and the years went on. Athaliah sat upon the throne, the first and only woman ever to rule the land of Judah. Not once did she suspect that any heir to this throne still lived.

When Joash was seven years old, Jehoiada assembled the elders, the captains, and the royal guard, bringing them into the Temple. And there, before their astonished and joyful eyes, he brought out the little prince.

It was agreed, then, that they would assemble again on the Sabbath to guard Joash while he was proclaimed king and to take part in the festivities. So, armed with weapons which had been stored in the Temple, they gathered about the little prince as the high priest anointed him and placed the crown on his head.

Cries of joy broke from all the assemblage. "God save the king!" they shouted, amid the sound of trumpets and applause.

Athaliah heard the trumpets, the singing, the people calling to one another, the shouts and all the joyful tumult, and she rushed out of her palace and into the Temple to see what was happening. As soon as she realized what had happened, she tore her garments in rage and screamed, "Treason! Treason!"

Jehoiada issued orders to some members of the guard. "Let her be slain, but not in the house of the Lord."

So certain men of the guard ran after her and slew her as she was entering the horses' gate of the nearby palace. The horses trampled her as she lay upon the stones, as they had trampled Jezebel, her evil mother.

Jehoiada and the king and the people made a covenant that they would follow the teachings of God. They destroyed the temple of Baal, and all its altars and images throughout Judah.

Joash ruled forty years and walked in the paths of the Lord as long as Jehoiada was there to lead him. He restored the Temple, which had been despoiled by Athaliah. She had allowed some of it to fall into ruin, and had taken some of its loveliest and most precious vessels and ornaments to use in the temple of Baal.

At Joash's command, a chest was placed at the Temple gate. Jehoiada made a hole in the lid of this chest, so that all who entered the gate could leave money for Temple use. Much of this money was paid to the laborers who restored and strengthened the damaged structure, the masons, the carpenters, the workers in brass and iron. Some of it was used to replace the stolen vessels of gold and silver. Sacrifices were offered to the Lord each day and many people who had worshiped Baal returned to the faith of their fathers.

Then Jehoiada died, full of years and honor. He was buried in Jerusalem in the tomb of kings because he was a noble priest who had served his God and his king with great devotion. His son Zechariah (zeck-uh-RYE-uh) became the new prophet.

Without the wisdom of Jehoiada to lead him, King Joash was lost and bewildered. He began to listen to men of evil counsel, men who had worshiped idols and groves as Athaliah his mother had done. In the end, they persuaded him to turn from the Lord and worship with them.

Shocked by this sinful deed, Zechariah rebuked the king and all the others who had turned from God to heathen idols. This enraged Joash, who cried out, "Let him be slain!" And so the good prophet, son of the man who had saved Joash's life and served him so faithfully, was stoned to death before the Temple of the Lord.

The servants of the king were shocked to see how heartlessly he had put to death the son of the beloved Jehoiada. And so they conspired against the king and slew him as he lay in his bed.

So great was the crime of Joash against Jehoiada and the Lord and his own people, that none wanted him to be buried among their honored rulers. His grave was in Jerusalem, the holy city, but he was not buried in the tomb of kings.

✸ AMAZIAH ✸

"Pride Goeth before a Fall . . . "

THE NEW king of Judah was Amaziah (AM-uh-ZYE-uh), the son of Joash. He began to rule when he was twenty-five years old and remained upon the throne for almost thirty years.

Amaziah did not worship Baal, yet he allowed the people to sacrifice to various pagan gods at hilltop shrines.

Like many another king he had his enemies, among them the people who lived in the land of Edom (EE-dum), to the south. Amaziah vowed to attack and defeat the Edomites, and so gathered a large army of Judean warriors with skill at handling the spear and shield.

To make his army invincible, he increased its might by hiring one hundred thousand strong warriors from Israel to fight in its ranks.

Then a prophet of the Lord came to him and implored, "O King, do not allow the men of Israel to go with you, for they are evil. If you do this, the Lord will be displeased and you will lose the battle."

Hearing this, Amaziah protested that he had already paid the Israelite soldiers in silver coin. But the prophet declared, "The Lord can give you much more than this!"

Amaziah therefore sent the men of Israel away. This made them so angry that they plundered many Judean cities as they journeyed homeward.

With his own warriors, the king went out against the people of Edom and defeated them. This filled him with such swaggering pride that he challenged his country's old enemy, the land of Israel, to meet him on the field of war.

At this time Israel was ruled by a king named Jehoash (jee-HOE-sh) who sought to reason with the boastful Amaziah. "You have indeed defeated the Edomites," he said. "Glory in this and be content to remain at home. For if we meet you in war and you fall to defeat, Judah will fall with you."

But Amaziah would not hear these mild words. He vowed that he would fight a war with Israel. So at last the two kings and their warriors met on the field of battle. Amaziah was ingloriously defeated.

Then the king of Israel and his men broke through the wall of Jerusalem, Judah's capital, and sacked the city. They seized the gold and silver of the Temple and all the palace treasures. When they turned homeward again, they were laden with the spoils of war and had taken a large number of Judeans as captives.

Now Judah was shamed in defeat, and a slave to Israel. King Amaziah was to blame, the people said, because he had provoked the king of Israel to war. Moreover he had offended the Lord when he brought heathen idols from the land of Edom, set them up in Jerusalem, worshiped them, and burnt incense before them.

As the years passed, the people became more and more rebellious against Amaziah. At last certain men conspired to slay him. Amaziah, learning of their plot, fled to Lachish (LAY-kish), a Judean city southwest of Jerusalem, in the hope of saving his life. But the men pursued him to Lachish and slew him there.

Afterward they brought him back to Jerusalem, to bury him among the kings who had died before him.

❧ UZZIAH ❧

Judah's Shining Hour

A MAZIAH had a son named Uzziah (uh-ZYE-uh), who was made king after his father's death. He was then sixteen years old.

Uzziah was a pious lad who had a great love for the Lord. He did not follow the pagan ways of his father, but worshiped God devoutly and faithfully, according to the teachings of the prophets.

And the Lord loved Uzziah, the people said. He became strong and powerful in the eyes of his subjects, and in the eyes of his neighbors. He strengthened his army and armed his warriors well, with shields, spears, and helmets, with bows and arrows and slings which cast stones. He even devised a new and wonderful weapon which shot arrows and hurled stones from the tops of walls and buildings.

Thus was he able to defeat his enemies.

Uzziah built cities and fortresses in the land. He loved agriculture, and commanded that wells be dug in the desert to provide water for the great herds of cattle, and to water the land.

While Uzziah ruled, vast fields and orchards and beautiful vineyards prospered in the fertile regions of Judah.

Like those of his ancestors who had been godly men, Uzziah worshiped in the Jerusalem Temple. According to the Temple laws, only the priests who were descended from Aaron, the brother of Moses, could enter the holy sanctuary and burn incense upon the golden altar. But Uzziah thought *he* could perform this sacred rite, too, because he was king. He entered the forbidden sanctuary.

Horrified, the high priest Azariah (AZ-uh-RYE-uh), accompanied by eighty other priests, followed him into the holy room. Azariah spoke firmly. "It is not for you, Uzziah, but for the sons of Aaron to burn incense here. Go out of the sanctuary, for you have trespassed, and the Lord will be displeased."

This angered Uzziah greatly. He stood gazing at them stubbornly, not moving. Then suddenly a cry went up from the priests. "The Lord is punishing him even now!"

His forehead had turned white with leprosy.

In terror, Uzziah stumbled out and hastened homeward to stare into his glass. It was as the priests had said. He was a leper.

From that time until he died, Uzziah lived in a small house apart from the palace, away from everyone. His son Jotham (JOE-thum), a godly king, ruled for him. Yet Uzziah's name remained a symbol of Judean strength and glory, for it was under his rule that the land reached the pinnacle of its power.

❈ AHAZ ❈

He Trusted the Might of Kings, not God

THOUGH Ahaz (AY-haz) was the son of the good king Jotham, he himself was weak and evil.

When Ahaz came to the throne, all Judah was in great peril. The country's old enemy, Israel, had united with the land of Syria against it. It was their plan to conquer Judah and put a king of their own choice upon the throne, one who would follow their commands.

Ahaz was terror-stricken. He hurried out to sacrifice at every shrine, every grove, to all the idols and false gods, hoping to win divine favor. He even sacrificed to Moloch (MOE-lock), one of the most hideous of all the pagan gods, to whom living children were given to be burned alive.

Ahaz sacrificed his own son in this way.

The king's weakness was well known to one man of Judah, the mighty and brilliant prophet Isaiah. This great man sought to reason with Ahaz, to give him courage and strength, to lead him to the Lord. "Take heed and be calm," urged Isaiah, "not faint-hearted. Trust in the Lord. If your faith is not strong, then your throne will never be secure."

But instead of putting his trust in God, Ahaz put his trust in Assyria, the ruthless and powerful kingdom to the north. He sent a message to the king of Assyria, saying, "I am your servant. Save me from Israel and Syria, who have risen against me."

To win this king's favor, Ahaz gathered up palace treasures and some of the gold and silver vessels of the Temple and sent them to him.

The king of Assyria was won over. He marched against the Israelite and Syrian armies and took many of its people captive. When he entered the great Syrian city of Damascus as its conqueror, Ahaz hastened there to congratulate him.

In Damascus Ahaz saw a large and impressive pagan altar. It pleased him, and he had it copied in Jerusalem and set up before the Temple of the Lord. Here he worshiped in heathen rites, using some of the sacred vessels from the Temple.

His weakness and lack of faith in God horrified the priests and elders of Judah, and when he died they did not bury him in the tombs of kings.

The Fall of Israel

IT WAS while Ahaz was still ruling Judah that disaster came to the land of Israel. The mighty Assyrian army swept down and conquered it utterly. Weak King Hoshea (hoe-SHEE-uh) was taken captive and cast into prison, and the Israelites were exiled to Assyria to serve their conquerors.

In anguish and shame and sorrow and great suffering, they made their way northward, often separated from those they loved, lashed like slaves, with their beloved country in dust and ashes behind them.

Perhaps they recalled the cold and haughty Rehoboam who, generations ago, had cried out, "My father chastised you with whips, but I will chastise you with scorpions!" His arrogance and evil had brought about the first break in the great empire left to him by Solomon, his father. Because of him, Israel and Judah had separated and become two kingdoms divided, one against the other.

Once Israel had been a prosperous and honored land. Many of its people had dwelt in high houses, slept in ivory beds, ridden in handsome chariots, worn rich garments. Now, barefoot and ragged and suffering, did they remember how they had ceased to follow the Commandments of God and had turned to the easier ways of pagan worship? Did they hear again the voices of such prophets as Amos, who had implored them to love the Lord? Did they recall the men who had cried out, time and time again, that if they did not forsake evil, they would lose their beloved land and fall beneath the yoke of a conqueror?

Now it had come to pass, as the prophets had foretold. Israel had forsaken the Commandments of the Lord, and Israel had fallen through its own evil. Its ten tribes were carried off to slavery and vanished into history. From that time on, they have been known as "the lost tribes of Israel."

❦ HEZEKIAH ❦

An Angel Was His Armor

N ow, of the two kingdoms which had once been united by the wisdom and might of David and had known the glory of Solomon, Judah alone was left.

King Hezekiah (HEZ-uh-KYE-uh) was on the throne. Though he was the son of Ahaz, a weakling given to evil ways, Hezekiah was a godly king. No sooner was the crown upon his head than he called together the priests and elders and issued a moving call to repentance: all Judah should return to following the Lord.

"Our fathers have trespassed," he said, "and done evil in the eyes of the Lord. They have forsaken Him. They have closed the doors of the Temple and quenched the lights, and have offered neither incense nor sacrifices of thanksgiving."

So, by Hezekiah's command, the Temple was cleansed and made whole, the lamps lighted, the altars and vessels made bright and shining. Word was sent to the priests and elders to come together for a sacrifice before the Lord. When the sacrifice was offered, they reaffirmed their faith in God and humbly asked Him to forgive the many sins of Judah.

Then Hezekiah sent word to the people, reminding them of how Moses, their leader of long ago, had brought them out of the bondage in which they had lived in Egypt, and how the Lord had commanded that they keep the feast called the Passover in memory of that time.

Truly the Lord had commanded it, yet it had not been kept for many long years. Now Hezekiah declared that the Passover would be kept again.

Wearied by the evils of pagan worship and genuinely sorry for having taken part in it, the people came gladly and in vast numbers. For seven days they sacrificed and feasted and worshiped, singing hymns of praise amid the sound of cymbals, trumpets, and harps. They blessed the Lord and were blessed by their faith, though many made mistakes in the Passover rites, since they had not kept the feast for so long. But King Hezekiah prayed for them, saying, "May the good Lord pardon everyone who sets his heart to seek God."

Afterward the people cleansed all Judah of pagan worship, cutting down the groves where trees were venerated and destroying the pagan idols, shrines, and altars.

For a little time they rejoiced and lived in peace. Then the mighty King Sennacherib (suh-NACK-ur-ib) of Assyria set out to conquer Judah. His army descended upon the land and camped outside the walls of Jerusalem.

The people were terrified, but King Hezekiah spoke to them in words of assurance and comfort. "Be strong and courageous. Don't be afraid of the king of Assyria and the multitude with him. We have more. With us is the Lord our God, to help us and to fight our battles."

Then Sennacherib sent cunning men to speak to the Judean people in their own tongue, promising them riches and ease if they would surrender to him.

When Hezekiah heard this, he was filled with grief, fearing his people would believe these empty promises and would surrender. He garbed himself in sackcloth, the symbol of sorrow, and went to the Temple to pray. And he sent his servants to seek counsel of the great prophet and statesman Isaiah.

"Fear not," said Isaiah. "These are the words of the Lord concerning the king of Assyria: *He shall not come into the city nor shoot an arrow here.*"

The prophecy was borne out. That night an angel of the Lord spread a plague through the Assyrian army. A vast number of warriors died, and those who were still alive fled homeward. Judah and Jerusalem were saved.

Hezekiah was one of the greatest and most honorable of kings. When he died, after a reign of twenty-nine years, he was buried with great sorrow and devotion in the tombs of kings.

JOSIAH

The Lord Sends His Warning

THE YEARS which followed the death of Hezekiah were filled with injustice, terror, and evil. The later kings of Judah not only turned from the Lord and all His Commandments, but they desecrated the Temple, rebuilt the heathen shrines and altars, even persecuted the priests and prophets of God.

Then still another ruler came to the throne of Judah, a child-king named Josiah (joe-SYE-uh) who was only eight years old.

In the first years of his reign, it was of course necessary for the little king to be guided by his elders. Even then, however, he showed a deep love of God, and it appeared that he would grow up to be a wise and just man. Some scholars think that much of his goodness was due to the influence of his pious mother Jedidah (jeh-DYE-duh). Certainly he did not learn goodness from his father, who had worshiped idols instead of the Lord, and was so evil a king that his own servants slew him.

When Josiah was twelve years old, he commanded that the land of Judah be purged of pagan worship. To do this was no easy task, as vast numbers of the people had turned again to heathen rites and built countless heathen altars. Nevertheless, Josiah's orders were carried out. While he watched, his men destroyed the altars erected to Baal and other false gods, and destroyed also the ugly carved idols that stood on these altars. Groves sacred to heathen rites were cut down, hilltop shrines scattered, brass images crushed into dust.

Josiah was eighteen years old before the major cities and the countryside around them had been purged of their deep-rooted paganism.

He then summoned Shaphan (SHAY-fun), the scribe, and said to him, "Go to Hilkiah (hill-KYE-uh), the high priest, and have him gather together all the silver offerings which have been left in the Temple of God. Let the Temple be repaired, and the silver used to buy materials and pay the laborers."

And so began the work of repairing the Temple, which had been badly used by the pagan kings and was in a state wretched to behold. Sound timbers and hewn stone were bought with a portion of the silver. A great army of men worked faithfully to restore the Temple to its former beauty — carpenters, masons, hewers of stone, and others. There were overseers too, among them priests, elders, scribes, and officers. All who labored were paid from the Temple silver.

On a certain day, an astonishing thing came to pass. The high priest Hilkiah came up to the scribe Shaphan in great excitement. In his hands was a tattered and dusty scroll.

"Behold," he said, "I have found a book of the Law in a hidden place in the Temple! It may be that these are the Laws of God given to our people long ago!"

Sharing his excitement, Shaphan took the scroll and carried it up to the palace and read it aloud before the king. As he listened, Josiah was filled with dismay.

"Are these indeed the Laws of God?" he asked. "For if they are, then He must be filled with anger against us, for neither our people nor our forefathers have kept them!"

Was this the scroll of the true Law? The young king pondered. Then he summoned Hilkiah, the high priest, and certain of the scribes and elders, and said, "Go and inquire of the Lord."

So Hilkiah and the others set out for the dwelling place of Huldah (HULL-duh) the prophetess, a woman of such wisdom and goodness that the Lord often spoke through her lips.

When she had examined the scroll, Huldah said that it was indeed the book of the holy Law. And there was more that she said. The people of Judah had done much evil in the sight of the Lord and would yet do more. Evil they had sowed and evil would they reap, for doom would come upon the land. Yet because Josiah was a man of righteousness, humble and tender of heart, the Lord would take him to his grave in peace and he would never suffer the disaster to come.

When the king heard that the old and dusty scroll contained the Commandments of God, he was filled with joy. He summoned the priests and elders and people to the Temple. They formed a great gathering, and he stood by a pillar of the Temple and read the Law to them.

Then Josiah made a solemn pledge before the Lord that he and his people would walk in the paths of righteousness and keep His Commandments with all their heart and soul. And the people made the pledge with their king.

The Temple is restored

Afterward he commanded the high priest and certain lesser priests to bring out of the Temple all of the vessels that had been used in worshiping Baal and in paying homage to sacred groves. These he burned and shattered just outside Jerusalem.

He slew the idolatrous priests who had assisted the previous kings of Judah in heathen worship and who had burned incense to Baal, to the sun and the moon and the planets. He forbade human sacrifices and all other pagan rites. Throughout Judah he roamed, and even into regions which once had been a part of Israel, destroying all the sacred groves and shrines. He broke into pieces the golden calves set up in Bethel so many years before by King Jeroboam, the altar brought from Damascus by King Ahaz, and a shrine built long ago by Solomon to please one of his pagan wives.

Then he commanded the people, "Keep the Passover as it is written in the scroll of the Law."

King Josiah is wounded in battle

So that year they kept a Passover such as had not been seen since the days of King David. There were thirty thousand people coming up to Jerusalem to serve the Lord in this feast of thanksgiving and to offer animals of sacrifice before Him. So that none should lack an offering, Josiah gave them thirty thousand lambs and kids, and three thousand bullocks besides. The princes of Judah gave them sacrificial animals also, two thousand six hundred cattle and three hundred oxen. After a portion of each animal was burned upon the altar of God, the rest of the flesh was divided among the families for the feast, according to the custom.

The feast lasted seven days, and the people remembered their heritage and were thankful to God. Their hymns of praise rose up again and again amid the curling smoke and incense and the sound of harps, trumpets, psalteries, and cymbals.

At this time, Josiah was eighteen years old. For a little more than twenty years longer, this wise and good king ruled the land of Judah. He turned to the Lord with all his heart and with all his soul and with all his might, as he had promised. Never again did Judah have a king like him. For the next kings were evil beyond words, and brought the final disaster upon the land.

Before this happened, however, the prophecy of Huldah was fulfilled. When he was only thirty-nine years old, Josiah was wounded at the battle of Megiddo (meh-GID-oh). He died a little later in Jerusalem, after his servants had brought him home.

Josiah was mourned with many sorrowful tears and buried with much honor in the tombs of kings.

The Fall of Judah

THE HILL of Megiddo, where the battle was fought, has been called the grave of Judah. For the kings who followed Josiah had no love for the Lord and no reverence for His Commandments. Once more the people returned to false gods, to the worship of idols and trees. Men bowed before the lewd image of Ashtoreth (ASH-toe-reth), a goddess brought from the pagans of the north. Again children were cast into the fire and burned to death to please the hideous idol called Moloch. Baal was worshiped in the Temple of the Lord as new priests of idolatry rose up to lead the people from the ways of truth and honor. King followed king in weakness and evil, and the days of Judah were numbered.

It was not many years until Nebuchadnezzar (NEB-yew-kud-NEZ-ur), the king of Babylon (BAB-ih-lun), swept down upon Judah, besieged the capital, and captured the king.

The nation went down to defeat. The army was scattered and Jerusalem plundered. People fled in terror, driven from homes and families, dying for want of bread.

The king of Babylon sent troops into Jerusalem to burn the Temple, the king's palace, and all the great houses of Jerusalem's noble families. The troops broke up the proud pillars of brass that stood before the Temple and the beautiful reservoir known as the Sea of Solomon. They took this

ASSYRIA

Damascus

1. Dan

THE
DIVIDED
KINGDOM

KEY

1. Jeroboam sets up a golden calf.
2. "The grave of Israel."
3. Ahab's palace and Naboth's vineyard.
4. Jeroboam's first capital.
5. Home of the prophet Ahijah.
6. Elisha's disciple anoints Jehu.
7. As Isaiah prophesies, the Lord delivers Jerusalem from the invading Assyrian army.
8. Amaziah is slain.

2. Megiddo

3. Jezreel

GREAT

SEA

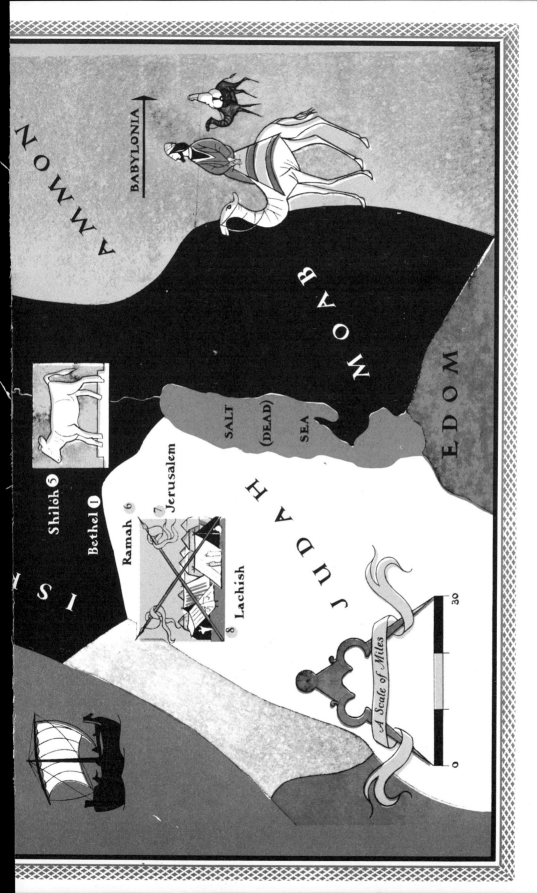

AMMON

BABYLONIA

MOAB

EDOM

ISR

SALT
(DEAD)
SEA

JUDAH

Shiloh 5

Bethel 1

Ramah 6

Jerusalem 7

8 Lachish

A Scale of Miles

0   30

brass back to Babylon, along with what treasures were left in the Temple itself. They also took the sacred vessels of silver and gold which had served the Lord, and many other lovely objects designed for Temple worship.

The walls of the city were broken down and its people led away to Babylon in shame and captivity. The poor of the land were left behind to care for the fields and vineyards. Later, however, they fled to Egypt in deathly fear of their conquerors.

The city of Jerusalem was empty and broken. The Temple that had been David's dream and Solomon's glory now lay in ashes and dust.

Israel and Judah, united in the reign of David, had under the rule of Solomon become one of the greatest, most honored, most powerful, most glorious kingdoms in all the world. Now, a little more than four hundred years later, this proud kingdom was utterly effaced from the earth.

Long ago, when he was dying, David spoke to his people in tones of farewell, saying, "Of all my sons, the Lord has chosen Solomon to sit upon the throne of the kingdom. And He said to me: *Moreover, I will establish this kingdom forever, if he keeps My Commandments.* Therefore, keep and seek for all the Commandments of the Lord, your God, that you may possess this good land and leave it for an inheritance for your children after you, forever. And you, Solomon, my son . . . if you seek the Lord, you will find Him, but if you forsake Him, He will cast you off forever."

When Men and Nations Disobey

B UT Solomon had forgotten the Lord. He had taxed and enslaved his people, had allowed them to be led into the worship of false gods by his pagan wives. His son, the haughty Rehoboam, had forsaken the Lord also, and after a few years, the same could be said of vast numbers of the people. They ceased to remember the words of David, the Commandments of God, the teachings of Moses.

They had walked, not in the paths of righteousness, but in arrogance, strife, jealousy, and greed. They had sacrificed to images and served heathen altars and broken their covenant with the Lord. Many times He had pleaded with them through the voices of their prophets, but they had been vain and heedless and unhearing. The few good and pious kings who rose among them could not stem the rising flood of evil which swept over them.

And so, as the prophets had foretold many times, the remnants of Israel, and now Judah, were taken captive and driven out of the land that they had lost through their own iniquity.

Gone were the dreams of Moses, the wisdom of David, the glory of Solomon.

The kingdom of the Chosen People was no more.

(continued from page 328)

1. *The Captivity of the Northern Kingdom.* Assyria first made contact with the Northern Kingdom when Shalmaneser II (860-825 B.C.) routed in the battle of Karkar (854 B.C.) the combined forces of Damascus, Hamath, Israel, and other states who had united to stop his westward progress. In another campaign Shalmaneser received tribute from Jehu, king of Israel. Not many years later, Rimmon-nirari III (810-781) compelled Syria to let go her hold of Israel. Tiglath-pileser III (745-727 B.C.), one of the greatest monarchs of antiquity, after capturing Samaria, put on the throne as his vassal Hoshea, who had slain Pekah, king of Israel. With the death of Tiglath-pileser III, Hoshea decided to strike a blow for independence. Help was promised by the king of Egypt, but it did not come. Hoshea was made a prisoner, and the capital doomed to destruction, as the prophets had foretold (Hos. 10:7,8; Isa. 28:1; Mic. 1:5,6). It was, however, only after a three years' siege that the city was captured. Before it fell, Shalmaneser had abdicated or died, and Sargon, who succeeded him, completed the conquest of the city and deported the inhabitants to Assyria (II Kings 17:6,7; 18:11,12). Some time later, Sargon's grandson Esarhaddon, and his great-grandson Ashur-banipal, imported to the region of Samaria some conquered peoples from the East (Ezra 4:2,10). Not all of the inhabitants of the Northern Kingdom were taken into captivity. The very poor, who could cause no trouble in the future, were left (II Kings 25:12). Intermarriage with the imported peoples resulted in the hybrid stock later known as the Samaritans. The Ten Tribes taken into captivity, sometimes called the Lost Tribes of Israel, must not be thought of as being absorbed by the peoples among whom they settled. Some undoubtedly were, but many others retained their Israelitish religion and traditions. Some became part of the Jewish dispersion, and others very likely returned with the exiles of Judah who had been carried off by Nebuchadnezzar in 536 B.C.

2. *The Captivity of the Southern Kingdom.* The captivity of Judah was predicted 150 years before it occurred (Isa. 6:11,12; 11:12). Isaiah (11:11; 39:6) and Micah (4:10) foretold that the place of the captivity was to be Babylonia; and Jeremiah announced that it would be for 70 years (Jer. 25:1,11,12). The Southern Kingdom rested on a firmer religious foundation than the Northern Kingdom, and was therefore able to survive longer, but it too had in it the seeds of moral and spiritual decay that caused its eventual disintegration.

Sargon was followed by a number of brilliant rulers, but by 625 B.C. the hold of Assyria over its tributary peoples had greatly slackened. Revolts broke out everywhere, and bands of Scythians swept through the empire as far as Egypt. Nineveh fell to the Babylonians in 606 B.C., never to rise again. A great new Babylonian empire was built up by Nebuchadnezar (604-562 B.C.). Judah became a vassal of Nebuchadnezzar, but Jehoiakim the king, although warned by the Prophet Jeremiah, turned and rebelled against him. Nebuchadnezzar thereupon came into Jerusalem in 605 B.C. and carried off to Babylon the vessels of the house of God and members of the nobility of Judah, among them Daniel the prophet (II Chron. 36:2-7; Jer. 45:1; Dan. 1:1-3). Jehoiakim was taken in chains to Babylon (II Chron. 36:6). In 597 B.C. Nebuchadnezzar carried off Jehoiachin, his mother, his wives, 3,000 princes, 7,000 men of

WITH HIGH HEARTS the Jews left Babylon. The exiles numbered over 40,000, and their caravans stretched for miles. An entire city was on the move, on route to rebuild the City of God. With them they carried the Temple treasures that Cyrus king of Persia had returned to them.

355

might, and 1,000 artisans (II Kings 24:14-16). Among them was the prophet Ezekiel. This was the first large-scale deportation of the Southern Kingdom into Babylonia. Eleven years later (586) Nebuchadnezzar burned the temple, destroyed the city of Jerusalem, and deported into Babylonia all but the poorest of the land (II Kings 25:2-21). A third group was taken into Babylonia five years after the destruction of the city (Jer. 52:30).

The exiled Jews were not heavily oppressed by their conquerors. They engaged in business, built houses (Jer. 29:5-7; Ezra 2:65), and even held high positions in the state (Dan. 2:48; Neh. 1:11). They could not continue their system of sacrifices, but they had with them their priests and teachers (Jer. 29:1; Ezra 1:5); and Ezekiel gave them constant encouragement (Ezek. 1:1). In 539 B.C. Babylon fell to Cyrus king of Persia, who issued a decree permitting the return of the Jews to Jerusalem to rebuild the temple (Ezra 1:1-4). The next year about 43,000 returned with Zerubbabel (Ezra 2:64), the rest preferring to remain in Mesopotamia (Zech. 6:10). In 458 B.C. 1,800 returned with Ezra.   S.B.

CARAVAN, a group of travelers united together for a common purpose or for mutual protection and generally equipped for a long journey, especially in desert country, or through foreign and presumably hostile territory. Jacob's "company" (Gen. 32,33) is a good example of a caravan organized to carry a clan to a new home; and the host of the Amalekites whom David destroyed (I Sam. 30:1-20) is another caravan, organized for raiding purposes. In the trackless desert where oases are few and far between and where savage beasts and more savage men are found, it was essential to go in caravans for protection's sake. The word does not occur in KJV, but "company" and "troop" could often have been "caravan."

CARBUNCLE, a word occurring four times in KJV but rendering three different Hebrew words, all representing something bright and glittering. Both ruby and emerald have been suggested as equivalents. Used in the high priest's breastplate (Exod. 28:17; 39:10). See Minerals.

CARCAS (kàr'kăs), a eunuch in the service of Xerxes ("Ahasuerus"). (Esth. 1:10.)

CARCASE (ASV and modern English, *carcass*), the dead body of a man or beast. The word is a translation of six different words in Scripture with root ideas of something fallen, exhausted; or just the bare idea of body, as in Judges 14:8,9. The law of Moses, probably partly for sanitary reasons, required that carcasses of "unclean" beasts should be considered abominable. Read Leviticus 11:8-40.

CARCHEMISH (kàr'kē-mĭsh), an ancient city of the Hittites located on the W bank of the Euphrates 63 miles NE of Aleppo. It was important commercially and militarily. For many years it paid tribute to the kings of Assyria. When Sargon captured it in 717 B.C., the Hittite empire fell with it (Isa. 10:9). It was the scene of a great victory by Nebuchadnezzar over Pharaoh Necho in 605 B.C. (Jer. 48:2; II Chron. 35:20). Its site is called Jerabis or Jerablus.

CAREAH (kà-rē'à), or generally and more properly Kareah. The father of Johanan and Jonathan who tried to save Gedaliah from assassination (Jer. 40:8-43:7), but later wickedly went to Egypt to dwell there.

CARMEL (kàr'mĕl, *garden*). 1. The mountainous promontory jutting into the Mediterranean Sea just S of the modern city Haifa and straight W of the Sea of Galilee. On the map of Palestine, it forms the principal deviation from a comparatively straight coastline, and it forms the southern wall of the magnificent bay (or gulf) of Acre, the best natural harbor south of Beirut. When the word occurs with the definite article it generally refers to Mt. Carmel and is often used as an illustration of a beautiful and fruitful place (Isa. 35:2; but contrast 33:9, which pictures God's judgment). South of Carmel lies the fruitful plain of Sharon and NE of it flows the river Kishon through the plain of Esdraelon. At Carmel Elijah stood against 850 heathen prophets and defeated them (I Kings 18). Carmel was visited by Elisha (II Kings 2:25; 4:25).

2. A very ancient town of Judah about seven miles nearly S of Hebron. First mentioned in Joshua 15:55, it is best known as the residence of the very churlish Nabal who refused kindness to David (I Sam. 25:2-40) and whose life was saved by the tact of his beautiful wife Abigail, who later became a wife of David.

CARMELITE (kàr'mĕl-īt), a native of Judaean Carmel: applied to David's wife Abigail who had first married Nabal (I Sam. 27:3, etc.) and to Hezro, one of David's mighty men (I Chron. 11:37, etc.).

CARMI (kàr'mē). 1. One of the sons of Reuben, eldest son of Jacob; and head of the family of the "Carmites" (Gen. 46:9; Num. 26:6, etc.).

2. An early descendant of Judah (probably great-grandson) and father of Achan (Josh. 7:1), mentioned in I Chronicles 4:1 as "son" i.e. descendant of Judah.

TYPICAL CARAVAN of Bedouin nomads crossing the desert, reminiscent of "Jacob's company."

MOUNT CARMEL, sunset scene. Mount Carmel, part of the inheritance of the tribe of Asher, was the site which the prophet Elijah chose for the trial of strength between the Lord and the heathen god Baal. Elisha received the visit from the bereaved mother at Mount Carmel.

CARNAL (kår'nål). Fleshly, of or pertaining to the body as the seat of the desires and appetites; usually employed in Scripture in the bad sense, as opposed to spiritual. In I Corinthians 2:14-3:4, Paul first divides mankind practically into two classes—the natural and the spiritual. This corresponds to the classification of men as once-born and twice-born. Then he classifies Christians as "carnal" and "spiritual" and lists the marks of carnality as "envying, strife, divisions" (KJV) and undue emphasis of personalities: "I am of Paul—I am of Apollos." "Carnal" does not necessarily imply active and conscious sin, but is opposed to "spiritual" (Rom. 7:14; II Cor. 10:4; Heb. 7:16; 9:10, etc.), the dominance of the lower side of man as apart from the divine influence.

The Old Testament uses the expression "lying carnally" to describe adultery (Lev. 18:20) and fornication (Lev. 19:20), but these ugly words are used far more often figuratively and refer to idolatry. To take the love that belongs to husband or wife and give it to another is adultery; and to take the love that belongs to God and give it to another is idolatry (Hos. 1-3; Rev. 17:18).   A.B.F.

CARPENTER (See Occupations, Professions)

CARPUS (kår'pŭs), a Christian brother living at Troas mentioned only in II Timothy 4:13. He had evidently been the host of Paul while he was in Troas.

CARRIAGE, occurs five times in the KJV and in each case refers to that which is carried; baggage (I Sam. 17:22; Isa. 10:28).

CARSHENA (kår'shē-nà), one of the seven princes of the Medo-Persian kingdom in the days of the great Xerxes, husband of Vashti, and later of Esther (Esth. 1:14).

CARTS, and wagons, are very ancient. In Genesis 45:19-21 Pharaoh provided carts for the wives and children of Jacob at the descent into Egypt. In the days of Eli the Philistines took the ark of God, and finding it a most unwelcome guest, they put it upon a cart and let it go back to Israel (I Sam. 6); but when David later desired to bring the same ark to his city, he used a cart, and the result was disastrous (See II Sam. 6:1-11).

CASIPHIA (kà-sĭf'ĭ-à), a place near the river Ahava, a tributary of the Euphrates, twice mentioned in Ezra 8:17 as a place where exiled Levites lived.

CASLUHIM (kăs'lū-hĭm), one of the seven tribes listed in Genesis 10:13,14 and its parallel passage I Chronicles 1:11,12 as descended from "Mizraim," which is the name for Egypt. The Philistines are said to have come out from this tribe.

CASSIA (See Plants)

".... So the men sat down, in number about five thousand.
And Jesus took the loaves; and when he had given thanks,
he distributed to the disciples, and the disciples to them that were set down;
and likewise of the fishes as much as they would."
(JOHN 6:10, 11)

The ancient synagogue at Capernaum, the town where Jesus
made His headquarters during the ministry in Galilee. It was
here that Jesus delivered His discourse on the Bread of Life,
which followed the feeding of the five thousand.

"And when Jesus was entered into Capernaum, there came unto him a centurion, beseeching him, And saying, Lord, my servant lieth at home sick of the palsy, grievously tormented."
(MATTHEW 8:5, 6)

It was at Capernaum that Jesus healed the Roman centurion's palsied servant and performed many striking miracles. A centurion in the Roman army commanded a hundred soldiers.

KRAK DE CHEVALIERS, the famous ancient Crusaders' Castle, in Lebanon.

CASTLE, a large fortified building or set of buildings, as that of a prince or nobleman. David took the Jebusite castle in Jerusalem and made it into his residence (I Chron. 11:5,7). Castles were built in the cities of Judah by Jehoshaphat (II Chron. 17:12) and in its forests by Jotham (II Chron. 27: 4). Where the KJV uses "castles," the RV sometimes, more correctly, uses encampments (I Chron. 6:54). Nehemiah erected a castle in Jerusalem which later became the Tower of Antonia, where Paul was confined.

CASTOR AND POLLUX (kăs′têr, pŏl′ŭks; Gr. *Dióskuroi, sons of Zeus*). In Greek mythology, they were sons of Zeus by Leda, one of his numerous mistresses. Castor was a horseman, and Pollux an adept boxer. They were later put in the sky in the constellation known as "Gemini," "the Twins," and were considered as tutelary deities favorable to sailors, which explains why the ship mentioned in Acts 28:11, in which Paul sailed, was named in their honor. St. Elmo's fire used to be credited to Castor and Pollux.

CATACOMBS are subterranean burial places used by the early Church. The principal catacombs are outside Rome, where the galleries in the tufa rock extend for six hundred miles, according to one estimate, and so surround the city that they even act as a cushion against earthquake shocks. The lowest estimate of the graves contained in the catacombs is 1,750,000, the highest 4,000,000, covering ten generations. This permits minimum and maximum estimates of 175,000 and 400,000 Christians in each generation, not allowing for the upward curve in the numbers of those connected with the Church over the period named. Since the population of Rome was about 1,000,000 it will be seen that the catacomb figures make nonsense of Gib-

bon's once accepted estimates of the Christian population of the capital. Family burial places in the catacombs provide striking evidence for the vertical spread of the faith.

CATERPILLAR (See Insects)

CATHOLIC EPISTLES, a term applied to the Epistles of James, Peter, John, and Jude. It goes back to the early church Fathers, but how it arose is unknown. The most commonly accepted explanation is that the Epistles were addressed not to individual churches or persons, but to a number of churches. They were addressed to the Church at large, i.e., the universal Church. The seeming exceptions, II and III John, were probably included as properly belonging with I John and of value to the general reader.

CATTLE (See Animals)

CAUDA (kow′dà), a small island lying about 25 miles to the S of Crete (Acts 27:16 in KJV "Clauda") and now called Gavdo. Here Paul and his companions were almost wrecked on their journey toward Rome.

CAUL. 1. The chief meaning is a deep fold above the liver, the omentum which is loaded with fat and which with the kidneys was used in several of the Levitical offerings (Lev. 3:4; 4:9, etc.).

2. The pericardium or the breast as a whole (Hos. 13:8).

3. Bag or purse (Isa. 3:18). See also DRESS.

CASTLE TOWER of Antonia, connected with the Temple at Jerusalem. After Paul was seized in the Temple, he addressed the people from the stairs of this castle, in which a Roman legion was stationed.

CAVE, a hollowed-out place in the earth, whether formed by nature or by man. In a mountainous land such as Palestine, where there is much limestone, caves are likely to be quite numerous. Caves were often used for regular human habitation, for hiding from the law or from enemies in warfare, for securing precious treasure (such as the recently discovered Dead Sea scrolls), for storehouses and cisterns, for stables for cattle, and for burial (Gen. 19:30; I Kings 19:9, etc.).

CEDAR (See Plants)

CEDRON (sē'drŏn, in ASV more properly "Kidron"), a ravine which in winter contains the brook of the same name, flowing southward between Jerusalem and Mt. of Olives on the E of the city. It is mentioned by this name only in John 18:1. It is loved for the sacred memories connected with it and the Garden of Gethsemane which lay beside it.

CEILING (KJV and ERV "cieling"), appears only in I Kings 6:15, where it says that Solomon built the walls of the ceiling with cedar. The reference here is not to the upper surface of a room, but to the inner walls. The word "ceiled" appears several times, but it usually means to panel the walls of a building.

CELLAR, a place for storage of wine (I Chron. 27:27) or oil (v. 28). The root idea here is not that of a room under a house, but that of a place of storage.

CENCHREA (sĕn'krē-à, Cenchreae in ASV), the eastern harbor of Corinth, and the little town on the harbor. Paul in Romans 16:1 commends to the Roman church, Phoebe, a deaconess of the church at Cenchrea, which Paul may have founded on his second missionary journey. Paul stopped here to have his head shaved in fulfillment of a vow (Acts 18:18).

CENSER, a vessel, probably shaped like a saucepan, for holding incense while it is being burned (Num. 16:6,7,39). The Hebrew word rendered "censer" is generally translated "censer," sometimes "firepan," and in three cases "snuffdish" (Exod. 25:38; 37:23; Num. 4:9).

CENSUS, a numbering and registration of a people. The OT tells of three different occasions when a formal census was taken. The first was at Mount Sinai, soon after the Israelites left Egypt (Num. 1). The second was taken at Shittim near the end of the 40 years' wilderness wandering. The third was made by David. The exiles who returned from Babylonia with Zerubbabel were also numbered (Ezra 2). Shortly before the birth of Christ, the Emperor Augustus ordered an enrollment in his empire (Luke 2:1).

CENTURION (cĕn-tū'rĭ-ŏn, Lat. centum, 100), a commander of a hundred soldiers in the Roman army. The word, of course, does not appear in the OT. The one first mentioned is the centurion of Capernaum whose beloved servant was sick unto death (Matt. 8:5-13; Luke 7:2-10). This officer had gone so far as to build a synagogue for the Jews, so that the Jews appreciated him and begged Jesus to heal the servant. The centurion showed real reverence to Jesus when he said "I am not worthy that thou shouldest come under my roof," and Jesus said "I have not found so great faith, no, not in Israel." The next is Cornelius (Acts 10) "a devout man, and one that feared God with all his house." It was to him that Peter was sent, and going almost unwillingly, Peter "used the keys" to open up salvation to the Gentiles, as he had at Jerusalem for the Jews (Acts 2) and at Samaria for its people (Acts 8:14-17). Another was Julius, of the Augustan band (Acts 27:1-43) whose duty it was to take Paul to Rome. He saved Paul's life when the soldiers wished to kill all the prisoners, and Paul, by his presence and counsel, saved the centurion with all the ship's company. Other centurions are mentioned elsewhere (Matt. 27:54; Acts 22:25; 23:17).   A.B.F.

CEPHAS (sē'fās, Gr. Kephás, from Aram. Kepha, rock, or stone). A name given by Jesus to the Apostle Peter (John 1:42). See PETER.

CHAFF, the refuse of the grain which has been threshed and winnowed. This is partly dust and dirt, but the real chaff is the hard and inedible coat of the grain. By threshing, most of this is separated, and then on a windy day the grain is tossed into the air and the chaff and the shorter pieces of straw are blown away. In Isaiah 5:24 and 33:11 the word properly means "dry hay" fit for burning. The more common word (Heb. mots) is generally used as a figure for worthless or godless men (Ps. 1:4; "The ungodly are not so: but are like the chaff which the wind driveth away"). It is used also for godless nations (Isa. 17:13). The evanescence of the wicked is likened in Hosea 13:3 to the morning cloud, the early dew, the chaff driven by the whirlwind, and the smoke out of the window (KJV "chimney"!). In Daniel 2:35, the Aramaic word rendered chaff signifies the small chaff that can get into the eye and irritate it. The word in Jeremiah 23:28 means the broken straw. In the preaching of John the Baptist (Matt. 3:12; Luke 3:17) our Lord is to save the righteous (gather the wheat into His garner) but the wicked ("the chaff") He will burn with unquenchable fire.

CHAIN. The English word represents many Hebrew words, meaning chain, necklace, band, bracelet, clasp, hook, ring and rope. All OT references are given without distinguishing the Hebrew originals. Chains were used: 1. As marks of distinction, in the case of Joseph (Gen. 41:42), and Daniel (Dan. 5:7,16,29).

2. For ornaments (Exod. 28:14,22; 39:15,17, 18) in the tabernacle. Chains were among the atonement offerings (Num. 31:50). Some had lunettes attached, such as the Midianites used to adorn their camels' necks (Judg. 8:21,26). Wreaths of chain work ornamented the tops of the pillars (I Kings 7:17; II Chron. 3:16) and elsewhere in Solomon's Temple (I Kings 6:21; II Chron. 3:5). As jewelry, chains are referred to in Psalm 73:6; Proverbs 1:9; Song of Solomon 1:10; 4:9; Isaiah 3:19; 40:19 (idols); Ezekiel 16:11.

3. For fetters (Ps. 68:6; 149:8; Isa. 45:14; Jer. 39:7; 40:1; 52:11; Lam. 3:7; Ezek. 7:23; 19:4, 9; Nah. 3:10). In the NT most of the references represent the Greek hálusis, chain. In Mark 5:3,4; Luke 8:29, chains are used to bind a demoniac; in Acts 12:6,7, Peter in prison was bound with two chains to the guards who slept on either side of him; in Acts 21:33, Paul was bound with two chains, but quickly released; in Acts 28:20, Paul was bound by a chain on his right hand to a soldier's left; to which he refers also in II Timothy 1:16; a circumstance which offers one explanation of why Paul dictated his letters to an amanuensis. An angel binds Satan with a chain (Rev. 20:1). In Jude 6 chain translates desmós, anything for tying or fastening; in II Peter 2:4, seirá, cord, rope. See also DRESS.   E.R.

CHALCEDONY (kăl-sĕd′ō-nē, kăl-sĕ-dō′nē, Gr. *chalkedón*), the precious stone adorning the third foundation of the New Jerusalem (Rev. 21:19). The modern meaning of the term cannot be traced earlier than the 15th century A.D. Pliny writes of a Chalcedonian emerald, also of a Chalcedonian jasper. Chalcedon, modern Kadikoy near Scutari on the Bosporus opposite Istanbul, was probably the place of origin. RSV translates "agate" without explanation.

CHALCOL (kăl′kŏl), a son (or descendant) of Mahol (I Kings 4:31). Solomon was wiser than he. Calcol, a son (or descendant) of Zerah (I Chron. 2:6). Since four of the same names occur in both passages as brothers, Chalcol and Calcol are probably the same person. ASV, RSV have Calcol in both places.

CHALDAEA or **CHALDEA** (kăl-dē′à), the country of which Babylon was the capital, and which conquered Judah and carried its inhabitants into captivity. The name occurs in KJV only in Jeremiah 50:10; 51:24,35; Ezekiel 11:24; 16:29; 23:15,16.

CHALDEAN (kăl-dē′ăn), an adjective referring to things pertaining to Chaldaea; or a noun referring to a man of Chaldaea.

CHALDEAN ASTROLOGERS (See Wise Men)

CHALDEES (kăl-dēz, kăl′dēz), the people of Chaldea; the Chaldeans.

CHAMBERING (chăm′bêr-ĭng), repeated or habitual acts of illicit intercourse (Rom. 13:13).

CHAMBERLAIN (chăm′bêr-lĭn). In the OT the eunuch in charge of a king's harem, especially

JEWISH MONEY-CHANGER in Jerusalem. Money-changers performed a necessary function. Not their trade, but the place they chose to ply it led Jesus to drive them from the Temple court.

in Persia (Esth. 1:10,12,15; 2:3,14,15,21; 4:4,5; 6:2,14; 7:9), called "eunuch" in RSV. In II Kings 23:11 RSV retains "chamberlain" for the same Hebrew word. In Acts 12:20 the chamberlain is "one who is over the king's bedchamber," an intimate and confidential position. In Romans 16:23 the word used is often translated "steward." ASV, RSV have "treasurer," which is accurate in this connection.

CHAMBERS OF IMAGERY, rooms in the temple where seventy elders of Israel worshiped idols with incense. RSV has "room of pictures" (Ezek. 8:12). Verse 10 indicates what the pictures or images represented.

CHAMELEON (See Animals)

CHAMOIS (See Animals)

CHANAAN (See Canaan)

CHANCELLOR (chàn′sĕ-lêr, RSV *commander*), a Persian official in Palestine (Ezra 4:8,9,17).

CHANGERS OF MONEY, men who exchanged one currency for another at a premium. Coins issued by many governments circulated in Palestine; also Jews must convert their currency into shekels for the temple-tax. It was not the trade but the place where they plied it which led Christ to drive them out of the temple court (Matt. 21:12; Mark 11:15; John 2:14,15). All three Gospels use the Greek *kollybistés, a changer of small coins.* John 2:14 has *kermatistés,* with identical meaning. "Exchangers" (Matt. 25:27) translates *trapezítes,* better rendered (RSV) "banker," lender of money at interest. Both used tables (*trapezas*) and often combined the two functions.

CHAPMAN (chăp′măn), a traveling trader or merchant (II Chron. 9:14).

CHARASHIM (kăr′ă-shĭm, Heb. *hărāshîm, craftsmen*), Valley of, E of Joppa between Ono to the N and Lod (Lydda) to the S; settled by one Joab, apparently of Judah (I Chron. 4:14). It received its name because artificers or craftsmen dwelt there (Neh. 11:35).

CHARCHEMISH, CARCHEMISH (kàr′kē-mĭsh, kàr-kē′mĭsh), Hittite capital on the Euphrates, focus for invasions between Egypt, Assyria and Europe. See CARCHEMISH.

CHARGER, a dish or platter given as an offering for the tabernacle (Num. 7:13-85); called "dishes" in Exodus 25:29; 37:16. Another word (Ezra 1:9) refers to baskets or dishes belonging to the temple service. The NT word means a wooden dish or platter (Matt. 14:8,11; Mark 6:25,28).

CHARIOT (chăr′ĭ-ŭt, Heb. *rekhev* and derivatives, from a root meaning *mount and ride*), a two-wheeled vehicle drawn by two horses. In Egypt, Joseph rides in Pharaoh's second chariot (Gen. 41:43). Chariots were in Jacob's funeral procession (Gen. 50:9). Pharaoh pursued the children of Israel into the Red Sea with chariots (Exod. 14:7-15:19). The Canaanites used chariots studded with iron, or covered with plates of iron, which kept the Israelites from conquering the plains (Judg. 1:19). The Philistines mustered mighty hosts of chariots against Israel (I Sam. 13:5). David hocked the chariot-horses of his enemies (II Sam. 8:4). Adonijah prepared chariots when he plotted to overthrow his father David (I Kings 1:5). Solomon built establishments to house many chariots (I Kings 9:19). He imported chariots from Egypt at 600 shekels each (I Kings 10:28,29). Both divided kingdoms used chariots in war (I Kings 16:9; 22: 34; II Kings 23:30). Some parts of a chariot are referred to in I Kings 7:33. There was a pole to which the two horses were yoked; an axle; wheels with six or eight spokes; and a body fastened to the axle and pole.

Often only two men rode in the chariot; a driver and a warrior (I Kings 22:34), but sometimes the Hittite practice of adding a shield-bearer was followed. The Assyrian chariot was heavier than the Egyptian or Hebrew, and carried three or four men. Nahum 2:3,4 is a vivid picture of such chariots. Elijah was honored by being escorted up to heaven by a chariot of fire (II Kings 2:11), and his manner of going became a proverb (II Kings 2:12; 13:14). God is represented as having thousands of chariots, showing His power (Ps. 68:17). Trust in chariots is vain compared with trust in God (Ps. 20:7). Habakkuk 3:8 sees God riding upon the chariots of salvation. The chariots of the sun (II Kings 23:11) were used in sun-worship (verse 5). Chariots were used for riding (S. of Sol. 1:9; 6:12), especially by royalty. Other Hebrew words are used for chariot: in Song of Solomon 3:9,10, a *litter* is meant; in Ezekiel 23:24 a *war-chariot*; Psalm 46:9, a *wheeled vehicle*. In the NT, Greek *hárma*, a *war-chariot* (Rev. 9:9) drawn by horses, used also for riding (Acts 8:28,29,38). In Revelation 18:13 the word is *rhéda*, a Gallic wagon with four wheels.   E.R.

CHARITY (chăr'ĭ-tē), the KJV rendering of Greek *agápe* in 28 places. *Agápe* is translated "love" in 87 places; "dear," once (Col. 1:13). Charity represents Latin *caritas*, but *caritas* also stands in the Vulgate in passages where KJV has "love." Charity in the Bible never means giving to the poor, but always a God-inspired love which includes respect for, and concern for the welfare of the loved one. The inspired description is found in I Cor. 13.

CHARRAN (See Haran)

CHASTE, CHASTITY (chāst, chăs'tĭ-tē, Gr. *hagnós*), originally meaning *pure* in a ritual sense, *tabu, consecrated*; it developed a moral sense as the Greeks gained higher conceptions of deity. In the Bible, where the highest conception of God always prevailed, the moral and the religious are never separated. *Hagnós* is translated "chaste" in I Peter 3:2, Titus 2:5, regarding Christian women; II Corinthians 11:2, referring to the Corinthian Christians as a "chaste virgin" bride for Christ. It is translated "clear" (II Cor. 7:11), "pure" (I John 3:3; Phil. 4:8, etc.). Derivatives are translated "pure," "pureness," "purity," "purify," "purification," "sincerely," and in the LXX they are used for Heb. words of kindred meanings. Chastity in the relations of men and women is the NT norm; the standard for all forms of purity.

CHASTISEMENT (chăs'tĭz-mĕnt, Heb. *mûsār*, from verb *yāsar, discipline* [the moral nature], *chasten, admonish, correct*; Gr. *paideía, child-training, the formation of manhood*). Both are translated by many English words, exhibiting shades of meaning derived from the central concept: the widest sense (Deut. 11:2); *punishment* (Jer. 30:14); *discipline* (Heb. 12:8); in Isaiah 53:5 the whole range of meaning is exhibited in the substitution of the sinless Servant of Jehovah for His guilty people. When *mûsār* is translated "chastening," discipline rather than punishment is meant (Job 5:17; Prov. 3:11,12, whence Heb. 12:5-11 is drawn; Isa. 26:16); *retribution* (Lev. 26:28); *instruction in*

wisdom is prominent in Proverbs; *unjust chastisement* (I Kings 12:11); the prayer of Psalm 6:1 is answered (Ps. 94:12). The Greek word in Acts 7:22; 22:3; II Timothy 3:16 (*learn, teach, instruction*) refers to education. Heb. *yākah* occurs of child-training (II Sam. 7:14); of the meaning and value of suffering (Job 33:19; Ps. 73:14). Daniel has chastened himself by humility (Dan. 10:12, Heb. *'ānāh*). Chastisement is the process by which God provides a Substitute to bear our sins, brings men to put their trust in Him, trains those whom He has received till they reach maturity.   E.R.

CHEBAR (kē'bär), a river or canal beside which Ezekiel saw visions (Ezek. 1:1; 3:23; 10:15,20,22; 43:3); in Babylonia ("the land of the Chaldeans," Ezek. 1:3); at Tel-abib (Ezek. 3:15); not yet identified.

CHECKER WORK (chĕk'ĕr-wûrk), ornamentation for the capitals of two pillars in Solomon's temple (I Kings 7:17). ASV, RSV have "coats of checker work" in Exodus 28:4. The root means "interweave."

CHEDORLAOMER (kĕd'ŏr-lā-ō'mûr), king (Gen. 14:1,4,5,9,17) of Elam, S of Media and E of Babylonia; named by Semites (Gen. 10:22), but inhabited chiefly by Indo-Europeans; later part of Persia, modern Iran. Chedorlaomer, with Amraphel king of Shinar (Babylonia), Arioch king of Ellasar and Tidal king of nations or of Goiim (so ASV, RSV), made war with Bera king of Sodom, Birsha king of Gomorrah, Shinab king of Admah, Shemeber king of Zeboiim, and the king of Bela or Zoar, all near the Dead or Salt Sea. Chedorlaomer held sway over the five cities for 12 years. In the 13th year they rebelled. In the 14th year Chedorlaomer and his allies conquered the country they traversed, and met the king of Sodom and his allies on the same battleground (the vale of Siddim or the Salt Sea) where Chedorlaomer had defeated them 14 years earlier. The bitumen pits of the region were the undoing of the local defenders. But Abram the Hebrew in a swift night raid with 318 retainers recovered the spoil of Sodom, and pursued the invaders to a point near Damascus. The story is told fully (Gen. 14) because it involved Abram and his brother's son Lot.

CHEESE, once Heb. *gevînâh* (Job 10:10) *curd, cheese*, from a root meaning "coagulate"; once Heb. *shāphāh* (II Sam. 17:29) *cream*, because skimmed off; once Heb. *hărîtsî hehālāv* (I Sam. 17:18) *cuts of milk, i.e., cheese*. Milk of kine, goats or sheep was stored in skins. In a warm climate, without refrigeration, it would soon curdle. The process of cheese-making employed can only be guessed from the practices current in the Near East today.

CHELAL (kē'lăl), a man of Palath-moab who put away his foreign wife (Ezra 10:30).

CHELLUH (kĕl'ū), one of the sons of Bani who married a foreign wife (Ezra 10:35).

CHELUB (kē'lŭb, Heb. *kelûv*, another form of *Caleb*). 1. A brother of Shuah, a Judahite (I Chron. 4:11).

2. Father of Ezri, and superintendent of the tillers of the ground in David's time (I Chron. 27: 26).

CHELUBAI (kē-loo'bī), son of Hezron, elsewhere called Caleb (I Chron. 2:9).

CHEMARIM (kĕm'à-rĭm, Heb. *kemārîm*), probably from a root meaning "prostrate oneself"

(Zeph. 1:4). The Heb. word occurs also in II Kings 23:5; Hosea 10:5, and always refers to idolatrous priests.

CHEMOSH (kē'mŏsh), the god of Moab, so named in an ancient Israelite song (Num. 21:29, alluded to in Jer. 48:7,13,46). Jephthah refers to Chemosh as god of the Ammonites (Judg. 11:24), either by mistake or because Ammon also worshiped Chemosh in addition to Molech. Solomon introduced the worship of Chemosh into Jerusalem to please a foreign wife, though thereby he displeased his God (I Kings 11:7,33). Josiah defiled this high place of Chemosh (II Kings 23:13), putting an end to its use as a place of worship. Mesha, king of Moab, suffered a great disaster in his rebellion against Israel, in consequence of which he offered his son, the heir to the throne of Moab, as a burnt offering (II Kings 3:4-27). The inscription on the Moabite stone shows that this sacrifice was made to Chemosh, and describes (in terms whose similarity in style to the terms employed by the Israelites of the true God only accentuates the contrast between the two) the help which Mesha believed Chemosh had given his people in war, and the chastisement which Chemosh meted out to them when they were unfaithful.

CHENAANAH (kē-nā'ȧ-nȧ). 1. The father of the false prophet Zedekiah who smote Micaiah (I Kings 22:11,24; II Chron. 18:10,23).

2. The brother of Ehud, son of Bilham, a Benjamite (I Chron. 7:10).

CHENANI (kē-nā'nī, kĕn'ȧ-nī), a Levite who helped bring the returned exiles into agreement about the covenant worship of God (Neh. 9:4).

CHENANIAH (kĕn'ȧ-nī'ȧ). 1. A chief Levite when David brought up the ark from the house of Obededom (I Chron. 15:22,27).

2. An Izharite, an officer of David's (I Chron. 26:29). Some identify the two as one.

CHEPHAR-HAAMMONI (kē'fȧr-hă-ăm'ō-nī, ASV, RSV Chephar-ammoni, Josh. 18:24), an Ammonite town in the territory of Benjamin, site unknown.

CHEPHIRAH (kē-fī'rȧ), a Hivite town which, with Gibeon, by deceit gained the protection of the Israelites (Josh. 9:17); in the territory of Benjamin (Josh. 18:26); some of whose citizens returned after the Exile (Ezra 2:25; Neh. 7:29); modern Tell Kefireh between Aijalon and Gibeon.

CHERAN (kē'răn), son of Dishon, the son of Seir the Horite (Gen. 36:26; I Chron. 1:41).

CHERETHIM, CHERETHITES (kĕr'ĕ-thĭm, kĕr'ĕ-thīts), a Philistine tribe in southern Palestine (I Sam. 30:14; Ezek. 25:16; Zeph. 2:5), from whom David drew his bodyguard, commanded by Benaiah (II Sam. 8:18; 15:18; 20:7,23; I Kings 1:38,44; I Chron. 18:17). The Heb. name may be from a root kareth, to cut down, indicating that the Cherethite guards were executioners, or at least swordsmen. Twice LXX translates "Cretans" (Ezek. 25:16; Zeph. 2:5), indicating their belief that the Cherethites came from Crete; and indeed the Philistines originated there. Elsewhere LXX has Cheleththi or Chereththi (except I Sam. 30:14, Cholthi). David's guard was probably recruited from foreign mercenaries.

CHERITH (kē'rĭth), the brook where, at God's command, Elijah hid himself during the first part of the famine he had predicted (I Kings 17:1-5). It was "before Jordan," a Heb. expression ('al-penê), which means "toward the face of"; of loca-

tion, "in front of"; usually "east of" (so RSV); but not always so; hence is no conclusive help in identifying the brook. Perhaps it was as obscure in Elijah's day as now; therefore a secure hiding place.

CHERUB (chĕr'ŭb), pl., **CHERUBIM** (chĕr'ŭ-bĭm), which KJV treats as singular, with a plural, cherubims. In other than Biblical usage, the English plural is cherubs. The cherubim and a flaming sword were placed at the E of Eden to keep the way of the tree of life, after Adam and Eve were expelled from the garden (Gen. 3:24). God directs Moses to place two cherubim of beaten gold on the mercy seat above the ark, where God would commune with Moses in the tabernacle (Exod. 25:18-22; 37:7-9). The curtains of the tabernacle were embroidered with cherubim (Exod. 26:1). God dwelt between the cherubim (Num. 7:89; I Sam. 4:4; II Sam. 6:2; II Kings 19:15; Ps. 80:1; 99:1; Isa. 37:16), both in the tabernacle and the temple. The cherubim in the temple were huge figures newly made for the purpose (I Kings 6:23-28; II Chron. 3:10-13; 5:7,8). Carved cherubim also ornamented the walls of the house (I Kings 6:29). Hebrews 9:5 mentions the cherubim in the tabernacle. David sings of God riding on a cherub (II Sam. 22:11; Ps. 18:10). Psalm 18 pictures a storm, God riding upon and speaking from the clouds. His glory rested between the cherubim above the mercy seat in the tabernacle.

That the cherubim were more than clouds or statues is plain from the description Ezekiel gives (Ezek. 10:1-22; 9:3), which shows that they are the "living creatures" of the first chapter. They were winged creatures with features both animal and human. Each had four faces; of a man, a lion on the right side; of an ox on the left side; also of an eagle (Ezek. 1:10). In Ezekiel 10:14 the faces are of a cherub, a man, a lion and an eagle, wherein "cherub" substitutes for "ox." The etymology is doubtful; possibly from Heb. root karah, give a feast. A connection with Greek glyps, griffin, is not established. There is no corresponding word for similar winged animal-human representations in Assyria or Egypt. The Heb. conception is original.

Primarily the cherubim are the living chariot or carriers of God when appearing to men; His throne or the bearers of it. Their earliest recorded employment was as guardians of Eden. Figures of these living beings were used symbolically in both tabernacle and temple. In the new temple of Ezekiel's vision the only cherubim are those decorating the walls (Ezek. 41:17-25); and those show two faces; of a man and a young lion.

The seraphim of Isaiah 6:2-8 are similar beings. Four constellations of the zodiac were given the same names as the four faces of the cherubim, and in ancient times they marked the solstices and the equinoxes. Rabbinical tradition assigns them to the standards of the divisions in the camp of Israel; the lion, Judah, on the E; the ox, Ephraim, W; a man, Reuben, S; the eagle, Dan, N. Thus the standards, leading the Israelites, would indicate Israel as the earthly counterpart of the heavenly host, led by the cherubim. Early church fathers equated the four faces with the four Evangelists; Matthew, the lion; Mark, the ox; Luke, the man; John, the eagle. In Revelation 4:6-9; 5:6-14; 6:1-8; 7-11; 14:3; 15:7; 19:4 are four "beasts" (Greek zôa, living creatures; so ASV, RSV; to be distinguished from the beasts, Greek thería, wild beasts mentioned in Rev. 13:1, etc.). They are described in terms identifying them with Ezekiel's living creatures or cherubim. The first living creature was like a lion; the second like a calf; the third had a face as a man; the fourth was like a flying eagle (Rev. 4: 7). They are the bearers of the judgments which follow the breaking of the first four seals.

To sum up: the cherubim are living heavenly creatures, servants of God in theophany and judgment, appearing in winged human-animal form with the faces of lion, ox, man, and eagle. Their representations in tabernacle and temple as statues and in embroidery and carving are not a breach of the commandment (Exod. 20:4). They are significant in prophecy (Ezek.), and in the Apocalypse (Rev.). Their service is rendered immediately to God. They never come closer to man than when one took fire in his hand and gave it into the hands of "the man clothed with linen" (Ezek. 10: 7). Yet it is "between the cherubim" that lay the mercy seat on which the blood of atonement was sprinkled: nothing can more nearly touch our salvation. In the OT sanctuary, where everything was done and taught by visible, tangible types and symbols, physical representations of the living heavenly cherubim were essential. In Ezekiel's new temple, and in the heavenly sanctuary of Hebrews and Revelation, they are no longer needed, for redeemed man there stands in the presence of the living cherubim themselves. The carvings in Ezekiel 41:18 are memorial only.   E.R.

CHERUB (kē'rŭb), an unidentified place in Babylonian territory whence exiles returned to Judea (Ezra 2:59; Neh. 7:61).

CHESALON (kĕs'à-lŏn), a place identified (Josh. 15:10) with Mount Jearim. It lay on the northern border of Judah, W of Jerusalem, NE of Bethshemesh. Modern Kesla.

CHESED (kē'sĕd, kĕs'ĕd), the fourth son of Nahor, and nephew of Abraham (Gen. 22:22).

CHESIL (kē'sĭl, kĕs'ĭl), a town in the S of Judah, near Hormah and Ziklag (Josh. 15:30). Its place in the lists is taken by Bethul in Joshua 19:4; by Bethuel in I Chronicles 4:30.

CHEST. 1. Receptacles for money to repair the temple (II Kings 12:9,10; II Chron. 24:8,10,11). Heb. '*ārôn* is translated "coffin" once (Gen. 50: 26); elsewhere the "ark" in tabernacle and temple. 2. "Chests of rich apparel, bound with cords, and made of cedar," of the merchandise of Tyre (Ezek. 27:24). RSV, on no better lexical authority, translates "carpets of colored stuff, bound with cords and made secure." Heb. *genāzîm* is rendered "treasuries" in Esther 3:9; 4:7.

CHESTNUT TREE (See Plants)

CHESULLOTH (kē-sŭl'ŏth), a town in Issachar (Josh. 19:18). In NT times Exaloth or Xaloth, modern Iksâl, SE of Nazareth.

CHEZIB (kē'zĭb), the town where Shelah was born to Judah and Shuah (Gen. 38:5). It may be the same as Achzib.

CHICKEN (See Birds)

CHIDON (kĭ'dŏn), threshing floor of, (I Chron. 13:9), where Uzza died for touching the ark. Called Nachon's in II Samuel 6:6. Near Jerusalem; site unknown.

CHILD, CHILDREN (chĭld, chĭl'drĕn). Among the people of the Bible, both OT and NT, as in most other cultures, children, especially male, were greatly desired (Gen. 15:2; 30:1; I Sam. 1:11,20; Ps. 127:3; 128:3; Luke 1:7,28). Among the Hebrews all the firstborn belonged to God and must be redeemed (Num. 3:40-51). Children were sometimes dedicated to God for special service (Judg. 13:2-7; I Sam. 1:11; Luke 1:13-17,76-79). Male descendants of Abraham were circumcised on the eighth day (Gen. 17:12; 21:4; Luke 1:59; 2:21), when the name was given. Weaning often was delayed, and celebrated (Gen. 21:8) with a feast. Education was primarily in the home and was the duty of parents (Exod. 12:26,27; Deut. 6:7; Josh. 4:21-24; Prov. 22:6; Eph. 6:4; Col. 3:21; II Tim. 3:15). Discipline was to be firm, with corporal punishment (Prov. 22:15; 23:13; 29:15). Much was expected of children (Prov. 20:11). Obedience and respect to parents were commanded (Exod. 21:17; Eph. 6:1-3; Col. 3:20; I Tim. 3:4,12; Tit. 1:6). Favoritism was sometimes shown (Gen. 25: 28; 37:3). Affection for children is strikingly portrayed in many instances, as in David's love for a child who died (II Sam. 12:15-23); and in the raising of children to life by Elijah (I Kings 17: 17-24), by Elisha (II Kings 4:18-37) and by Jesus (Matt. 9:23-26; Mark 5:35-43; Luke 8:49-56). Jesus' love and concern for children is seen in Matthew 18:1-14; 19:13-15; Mark 9:35-37; 10: 13-16; Luke 9:46-48; 18:15-17. Jesus recognized children's play (Matt. 11:16). Many attractive pictures of childhood occur; e.g. Moses (Exod. 2:1-10), Samuel (I Sam. 1:20-3:19), Jesus (Luke 2:7-40), Timothy (II Tim. 1:5; 3:14,15).

"Children" is an affectionate address, as in I John, of an old man to adults, who are, nevertheless, expected to act their age (I Cor. 13:11; 14: 20). The attention given to the childhood of the Messiah in prophecy (Isa. 7:14; 9:6) prepares us for the infancy narratives in Matthew 2 and Luke 2. The Savior came as a helpless babe, and grew up through a normal childhood. A return to childlike receptiveness and trust is required of those who would enter the kingdom of heaven (Matt. 18: 1-14; 19:13-15; Mark 9:35-37; 10:13-16; Luke 9: 46-48; 18:15-17).   E.R.

CHILDBEARING. The word occurs (I Tim. 2:15) in a passage relating to the proper sphere and conduct of woman. "She shall be saved in childbearing" cannot refer to salvation from sin, which is by grace through faith, but to safe-keeping through the pain which became incident to childbirth through the Fall (Gen. 3:16). Hebrew mothers had the assistance of midwives (Exod. 1:15-21). Newborn babies had the navel cut, were washed with water, salted and wrapped in swaddling clothes (Ezek. 16:4; Luke 2:7,12). Purification rites were prescribed after childbirth (Lev. 12; Luke 2:22-24).

CHILDREN OF GOD, or sons and daughters of God. 1. Angelic beings (Gen. 6:1-4; Job 1:6; 2:1; 38:7), though at least the first of these may be godly men.
2. Men, by creation (Luke 3:38; Isa. 64:8; "his offspring" Acts 17:28).
3. Israel in covenant relation to God (Exod. 4: 22; though rebellious Isa. 1:2-4).
4. Individual Israelites (Hos. 1:10).
5. The inclusion of Gentiles is intimated (Isa. 19:25).
6. Jesus (Matt. 3:17; 17:5; Luke 1:35).
7. Through Jesus men may become redeemed children of God (John 1:12; 14:6; by a new birth, John 3:3) in full moral and spiritual sonship (Rom. 8:14-17; Phil. 2:15; I John 3:10) with final likeness to God (I John 3:1-3).

RUINS OF CHORAZIN, north of Capernaum, near the Sea of Galilee. The town is mentioned only in Christ's condemnation of it as one of the several towns committed to destruction.

CHILDREN OF ISRAEL (See Israel)

CHILEAB (kĭl'ē-ăb), the second son of David (the first by Abigail) born at Hebron (II Sam. 3:3). Called Daniel in I Chronicles 3:1.

CHILION (kĭl'ĭ-ŏn), one of the two sons of Elimelech and Naomi, who married Orpah in Moab and died there (Ruth 1:2-5; 4:9,10).

CHILMAD (kĭl'măd), a place which traded with Tyre; associated with Asshur (Ezek. 27:23); site unknown, perhaps modern Kalwâdha near Bagdad. Other readings of the text give "all Media," or "Asshur was as thine apprentice in trading."

CHIMHAM (kĭm'hăm), presumably a son of Barzillai the Gileadite, whom David took to Jerusalem in his service at the request of Barzillai and in his place (II Sam. 19:37-40). "The habitation of Chimham" (Jer. 41:17) retained his name for centuries after his time.

CHINNERETH, CHINNEROTH (kĭn'ē-rĕth, -rŏth). 1. A fortified city on the NW shore of the Sea of Galilee (Josh. 19:35)); modern Tel Oreimeh, meaning *Harp Hill.* Chinnereth means "harp," and the hill on which it stood is harpshaped.
2. A district in Galilee; "All Chinnereth, with all the land of Naphtali" (I Kings 15:20).
3. The sea later known as Gennesaret or Galilee (Num. 34:11; Deut. 3:17; Josh. 11:2; 12:3; 13:27). The sea also is harpshaped.

CHIOS (kī'ŏs), an island in the Mediterranean Sea 12 miles W of Smyrna, past which (between Mitylene and Samos) Paul sailed on his voyage to Rome (Acts 20:15).

CHISLEV (kĭz'lĕv, KJV Chisleu), the ninth month of the Hebrew ritual year (Neh. 1:1; Zech. 7:1).

CHISLON (kĭz'lŏn), the father of Elidad, the prince of Benjamin in Moses' time who assisted in the division of the land (Num. 34:21).

CHISLOTH-TABOR (kĭs'lŏth-tā'bêr), the same place as Chesulloth (Josh. 19:12).

CHITTIM, KITTIM (kĭt'ĭm), descendants of Javan (Gen. 10:4; I Chron. 1:7, Kittim); Cyprus and its inhabitants. Balaam prophesies that ships from Chittim (KJV), Kittim (ASV, RSV) will afflict Asher (Num. 24:24). In Isaiah 23:1,12; Jeremiah 2:10; Ezekiel 27:6, KJV has Chittim, ASV Kittim, RSV Cyprus. In Daniel 11:30 KJV has Chittim, ASV, RSV Kittim. The Heb. *kittîm* came to apply not only to Cyprus, but also to the islands and coasts of the Mediterranean.

CHIUN (kī'ŭn), Saturn as a god (Amos 5:26). KJV has, "the tabernacle of your Molech and Chiun your images, the star of your god"; ASV, "the tabernacle of your king and the shrine of your images, the star of your god"; RSV, "Sakkuth your king, and Kaiwan your star-god, your images."

CHLOE (klō'ē), a woman whose people informed Paul of contentions in the Corinthian church. Where she lived and how her people gained their information is not told. She was well-known to the Corinthian Christians by her personal name.

CHORASHAN (kŏr'ăsh'ăn), a place in the S of Judah to which David sent some of the spoil of the Philistines (I Sam. 30:30). ASV, RSV Borashan. The same as Ashan.

CHORAZIN (kō-rā'zĭn), modern *Khirbet Kerâzeh,* ruins about two miles N of *Tell Hûm,* the site of Capernaum. Chorazin is mentioned only in the woes Christ pronounced upon it (Matt. 11:21; Luke 10:13). His condemnation of it, in conjunction with Bethsaida and Capernaum, indicates that Chorazin must have been an important city. It ceased to be inhabited by the time of Eusebius (latter half of the third century). Only a few carved stones remain today.

CHOZEBA (kō-zē'bà), a town of Judah; ASV, RSV, Cozeba (I Chron. 4:22). "Then men of Chozeba" are notable, among others, because "the records are ancient" (ASV, RSV).

CHRIST, JESUS (krīst, jē'zŭs, Gr. *Iesoús,* for Heb. *Jeshua, Jehoshua, Joshua, Jehovah is salvation;* Heb. *māshîah,* Gr. *Christós, anointed*).

I. Comprehensive Life and Work. Though the life of Christ, as ordinarily understood, embraces the years our Lord spent on this earth, as described in the four Gospels, His full career spans the ages and invites reflection on its several aspects. Fundamental to the various "I Am" sayings of Jesus is His assertion of absolute existence (John 8:58). Therefore it is reasonable to think of Him as belonging to eternity. Scripture, in fact, affirms His *pre-existence,* and does so in terms of fellowship with the Father (John 1:1); glory (John 17:5) and designation in advance as the Saviour of the world (I Pet. 1:20). His more immediate relation to the realm of men and things belongs to His activity in *creation.* All things came into being through Him (John 1:3; I Cor. 8:6; Heb. 1:2) and in Him continue to have their cohesive principle (Col. 1:17). Evidence is not lacking for His presence, too, in the OT. The manifestations of God in this period are apparently connected with the pre-incarnate Christ. When Isaiah glimpsed the glory of God he was seeing Christ (John 12:41).

Moses and the prophets spoke of Him (John 5: 46; Luke 24:27,44) with special reference to His sufferings and the glories that should follow (I Pet. 1:11). Some of the more important passages of a predictive nature are Genesis 3:15; Deuteronomy 18:15,18; Psalms 2,16,22,110; Isaiah 7:14; 9:6-7; 11; 42:1-4; 52:13-53:12; 61:1-2; Jeremiah 23: 5-6; Micah 5:2. In addition there are covenantal statements which do not speak of the Messiah directly and personally, but which involve Him in crucial ways (Gen. 12:3; II Sam. 7:12-16). As though in anticipation of the incarnation, the Son of God showed Himself at times to the faithful in visible form as the Angel of the Lord or the Angel of the covenant (Gen. 18:1-19:1; Judg. 13). Before His Advent Christ had thoroughly identified Himself with His people, so that when He came, He came unto His own (John 1:11).

By the *incarnation,* the Christ of God took on Himself human nature in order to reveal God to men in a way they could grasp (John 1:14,18), to become their Saviour by ransoming them from their sins (Mark 10:45) and to deal sympathetically with their needs (Heb. 2:17-18). Today, in glory, He is still the God-man. The incarnation persists.

The *present ministry* of Christ is being carried on in heaven, where He represents the saints before the throne of God (I John 2:1; Heb. 7:25). By the successful completion of His work on earth He is exalted to be the head of the church (Eph. 1:22; 4:15), and by the Spirit directs the life and service of His saints on earth (Matt. 28:20).

One purpose of the incarnation was not achieved during the earthly ministry of our Lord, but is reserved for His *second coming.* His kingly rule will then be introduced following His work as judge (Matt. 25:31-34). This future coming is one of the major truths set forth in the Epistles (Phil. 3:20-21; II Thess. 1:7-10) and is the leading theme of the Book of Revelation. After the millennial kingdom, Christ will enter with His people upon the blessedness of the *eternal state* which will be unmarred by the inroads of sin or death.

II. The Earthly Ministry. The long-heralded Christ came in the fulness of time (Gal. 4:4). God providentially supplied the proper *background* for His appearing and mission. The world had become to a great extent homogeneous through the spread of the Greek language and culture and through the organizing genius of Rome. The means were thus provided for the spread of the gospel once it had been forged out in the career of the Son of God. His Advent occurred at a point in human history when the law of Moses had done its work of demonstrating the sinfulness of man and the impossibility of achieving righteousness by human effort. Men here and there were looking with longing for spiritual deliverance.

Entirely in keeping with this divine control of the circumstances surrounding the incarnation is the careful selection of the Virgin Mary as the mother of Jesus. The *birth* of the Saviour was natural, but His conception was supernatural, by the power of the Holy Spirit (Matt. 1:18; Luke 1:35). Augustus, too, was drawn into the circle of the instruments chosen of God, when he was constrained to order a universal enrollment for taxation, not realizing that thereby he would make possible the birth of Jesus in the place appointed by prophetic announcement (Luke 2:1-7; Mic. 5:2). The shepherds, by their readiness to seek out the babe

in the manger and by their joy at seeing Him, became prototypes of the humble souls in Jewry who in coming days would recognize in Jesus their Saviour. An intimation of Gentile desire to participate in the Christ may be seen in the coming of the Magi from the East. In darker perspective appears the figure of Herod, emblematic of the hatred and opposition which would meet Jesus of Nazareth and work for His death. In the scribes who are conversant with the Scriptures but apathetic about seeking the One who fulfilled them we see the shape of things to come—the leaders of a nation receiving Him not when He came unto His own.

In more theological terms the Christ-event is an incarnation. God was manifest in flesh. The one who was in the form of God took the form of a servant and was made in the likeness of men (Phil. 2:6-7). Therefore, when the Scriptures assert from time to time that God sent His Son into the world, this affirmation is not to be treated as though Christ is merely a messenger of God such as the prophets of old. Rather, He is the eternal Son of God now clothing Himself with human nature to accomplish the salvation of men. Though the expression God-man is not found in the sacred records, it faithfully expresses the truth regarding the person of Jesus Christ. God did not appropriate a man who already existed and make of him an automaton for the working out of the divine purposes. He took what is common to us all, our human nature, yet free from any taint of sin, and combined it with deity to become an actual person with His own individuality. This is the mystery of the incarnation. The gulf between the Creator and the creature is bridged, first by the person and then by the mediatorial work of Christ.

The *boyhood* of Jesus should be approached from the standpoint of the truth revealed about the incarnation. Deity did not eclipse humanity so

BETHLEHEM in Judea, the town that was "little among the thousands of Judah."

NAZARETH, in lower Galilee, the home town of Mary and Joseph. Here Jesus was reared. This view is from the ancient road leading east to the Sea of Galilee.

as to render the process of learning unnecessary. Christ grew in body and advanced in knowledge and in the wisdom which enabled Him to make proper use of what He knew. He did not command His parents but rather obeyed them, fulfilling the law in this matter as in all others. The scriptural accounts have none of the fanciful extravagances of the Apocryphal Gospels which present the boy Jesus as a worker of wonders during His early years. They emphasize His progress in the understanding of the OT and affirm His consciousness of a special relation to His Father in heaven (Luke 2:49).

At His *baptism* Jesus received divine confirmation of the mission now opening out before Him and also the anointing of the Holy Spirit for the fulfillment of it. The days of preparation were definitely at an end, so that retirement was put aside and contact begun with His people Israel. By the baptism He was fulfilling all righteousness (Matt. 3:15) in the sense that He was identifying Himself with those He came to redeem.

Closely related to the baptism is the *temptation*, for it partakes likewise of this representative character. The first man Adam failed when put to the test; the last Adam succeeded, though weakened by hunger and harried by the desolation of the wilderness. In essence, the temptation was the effort of Satan to break Christ's dependence on the Father, so that He would desert the standpoint of man and rely upon special consideration as the Son of God. But Christ refused to be moved from His determined place of chosen identification with the race. "Man shall not live by bread alone . . ." is His first line of defense, and He maintains it in the two

following episodes, quoting the obligation of Israel in relation to God as His own reason for refusing to be moved from a place of trustful dependence upon the Almighty (Matt. 4:7,10).

Only when equipped by the baptism and seasoned by the ordeal of temptation was Jesus ready for His life work. No word of teaching and no work of power is attributed to Him prior to these events, but immediately thereafter He began moving in the power of the Spirit to undertake the work the Father had given Him to do (Luke 4:14).

The public ministry of Jesus was brief. Its length has to be estimated from the materials recorded in the Gospels. John gives more information on this point than the other Evangelists. Judging from the number of Passovers mentioned there (John 2:23; 5:1 [?]; 6:4; 13:1) the period was at least somewhat in excess of two years and possibly more than three.

John supplements the Synoptic Gospels also in the description of the place of ministry, for whereas they lay chief stress upon Galilee, plus notices of a visit to the regions of Tyre and Sidon (Matt. 15:21-28); Caesarea-Philippi (Matt. 16:13ff); the Gentile cities of the Decapolis (Mark 7:31; cf. also Mark 5:1-20); Samaria (Luke 9:51-56; 17:11); and the region east of the Jordan River known as Perea (Mark 10:1), John reports several visits to Jerusalem. In fact, most of his record is taken up with accounts of Jesus' ministry in Judea. The Synoptists hint at such a ministry (e.g., Matt. 23:37; Luke 10:38-42), but give little information.

For the conduct of His Galilean mission, Jesus made the city of Capernaum His headquarters. From this center He went forth, usually in the

MOUNT OF TEMPTATION, the traditional site of Satan's temptation of Jesus. "Man shall not live by bread alone . . ." was Jesus' first line of defense against the ordeal of the temptation. The building barely visible on the hillside is a Greek monastery.

company of His disciples, to challenge the people in city and town and village with His message. Several such tours are indicated in the sacred text (Mark 1:38; 6:6; Luke 8:1). A part of His ministry consisted in healings and exorcisms, for many had diseases of various sorts and many were afflicted with demon possession. These miracles were not only tokens of divine compassion but also signs that in the person of Jesus of Nazareth the Promised One had come (cf. Matt. 11:2-6; Luke 4:16-19). They were revelations of the mercy and power of God at work in God's Anointed. Jesus found fault with the cities of Galilee for rejecting Him despite the occurrence of so many mighty works in their midst (Matt. 11:20-24).

The message proclaimed by Jesus during these itinerating journeys was epitomized in the phrase, "the kingdom of God." Fundamentally, this means the rule of God in human life and history. The phrase may have a more concrete significance at times, for Jesus speaks now and again about entering into the kingdom. In certain passages He makes the kingdom to be future (Matt. 25:31ff) but in others it is present (Luke 11:20). This last reference is of special importance, for it connects the kingdom with the activity of Jesus in casting out demons. To the degree that Jesus invades the kingdom of Satan in this fashion, to that degree the kingdom of God has already come. But in the more spiritual and positive aspects of kingdom teaching, where the individual life is concerned, the emphasis does not fall upon invasion of personality or compulsive surrender to the power of God. The laws of discipleship are demanding indeed, but for their application they await the consent of the individual. No disciple is a monument to force but rather to the persuasive power of love and grace.

If we inquire more definitely into the relation of Jesus Himself to the kingdom, we are obliged to conclude that He not only introduces the kingdom (in a sense John the Baptist did that also) but was its perfect embodiment. The appropriate response to the preaching of the kingdom is committal to the will of God (Matt. 6:10), and it is crystal clear that the doing of the will of God was the mainspring of Jesus' ministry (Matt. 12:50; John 4:34; Mark 14:36). It is evident, of course, that Jesus will also inaugurate the final phase of the kingdom when He comes again in power and glory. Entrance into the present aspect of the kingdom comes through faith in the Son of God and the successful completion of His mission. This could be done during His earthly ministry by anticipation of His redeeming work and thereafter by acceptance of the Gospel message.

Much of our Lord's teaching was conveyed through the instrumentality of parables. These were usually comparisons taken from various phases of nature or human life. "The kingdom of God is like . . ." This method of teaching preserved the interest of the hearers until the spiritual application could be made. If the truth so taught was somewhat veiled by this method, this served to seal the spiritual blindness of the unrepentant and at the same time created a wholesome curiosity on the part of those who were disposed to believe, so that they could be led on to firm faith by more direct teaching.

The ministry of the Saviour was predominantly to the multitudes during its earlier phase, as He sought out the people where they were, whether in the synagogue or on the city street or by the lakeside. "He went about doing good" is the way Peter described it later on (Acts 10:38). But much of the last year of ministry was given over to instruction of the twelve disciples whom He had chosen (for the two phases see Matt. 4:17 and 16:21). This shift of emphasis was not due primarily to the lack of response on the part of the multitudes, although His following faded at times (John 6:15,66), but principally to His desire to instruct His disciples concerning Himself and His mission. These men, nearly all Galileans and many of them fishermen, had been able to learn much through hearing Jesus address the crowds and through watching Him heal the sick and relieve the distressed, and especially through being sent out by Him to minister in His name (Luke 9:1-6), but they needed more direct teaching to prepare them for the part they would play in the life of the church after the ascension.

What they saw and heard during those early days confirmed them in their understanding of the person of Jesus as the Messiah and the Son of God (Matt. 16:16), but they were quite unprepared to receive His teaching on the issue of His earthly life as involving suffering and death (Matt. 16:21-23). Although this prospect was a "must" for Jesus (vs. 21), for Peter it was something that the Lord could dismiss from consideration if He would (vs. 22). If the most prominent one of the apostolic circle felt this way about it, no doubt the others were of the same mind. Their thoughts were so taken up with the prospect of a kingdom of external power and glory that they were perplexed and disturbed to find that their Master anticipated quite a different experience. His prediction of a rising again from the dead fell on deaf ears, for the blow of the announcement about the forthcoming death had been too heavy. Even the lessons of the transfiguration scene, where the death was the theme under discussion and the glory beyond was presented to their sight, did not completely effect the orientation of the disciples to the teaching of Jesus. He had to repeat it more than once (Mark 10:34-45). Their sorrow in the garden of Gethsemane shows that they had reluctantly adjusted to it but could not look beyond it to resurrection nor could they realize how much that death itself could mean to their spiritual welfare. After the resurrection they were much more open to the Lord's instruction, and He used the occasion of His appearances to them for enlightenment from the OT as to the divine purpose pre-written there concerning Himself (Luke 24:26-27,44).

Christ's investment of time and patience with these men was well rewarded, for when the Spirit took up the work of instruction begun by Him and gave them His own power for witness, they became effective instruments for the declaring of the Word of God and for the leadership of the Christian Church. The record of the Book of Acts vindicates the wisdom of Christ and His understanding of the future.

Standing over against the Twelve in their attitude to Jesus are the scribes and Pharisees. The former were experts in the law and the traditions which had grown up around it, and the latter were men dedicated to a meticulous devotion to this heritage of Judaism. These groups usually worked together, and they collided with Jesus on many occasions over many issues. It was shocking to them that He would declare men's sins forgiven and claim a special relation to God as Son which others did not have. They resented His rejection of the traditions which they kept so carefully, and stood aghast at His willingness to break the sabbath (in their way of thinking) by doing deeds of mercy on that day. It was tragic that men who held to the Scriptures as God's Word should fail to see in Jesus Christ the One of whom that Word spoke. They refused to put their trust in Him despite all His miracles and the matchless perfection of His personal life. Because tradition meant more to them than truth, they stumbled in their apprehension of the Christ of God. In the end they made common cause with their opponents, the Sadducees, in order to do away with Jesus.

Even as Christ was engaged in teaching His disciples, from the days of the transfiguration on, He was ever moving toward Jerusalem to fulfill His course at the cross (Luke 9:51). In those latter days some stirring events were unfolded—the triumphal entry into Jerusalem, the cleansing of the temple, the institution of the Lord's Supper, the soul conflict in the garden of Gethsemane, the arrest and trial, the crucifixion, the resurrection, the appearances, the ascension into heaven. In all of them Jesus remains the central figure. In all of them He receives testimony to Himself or gives it. Nothing is unimportant. All contribute to the working out of the plan of God. The cross is man's decision respecting Christ, but it had already been His own decision and that of the Father. It underscored the sins of some men even as it removed the sins of others. In the cross man's day erupted in violence and blasphemy. In the resurrection God's day began to dawn. It was His answer to the world and to the powers of darkness. In it Christ was justified and His claims illuminated.

III. Names, Titles and Offices. Considerable help in understanding the person and work of Christ may be gleaned from a consideration of the terms used to designate Him, especially as these are employed by Himself and His close associates. *Jesus* is used mostly in the narratives of the Gospels, and only rarely does it appear in direct address. It means Saviour (Matt. 1:21), being related philologically to the Hebrew name Joshua. In the KJV of Hebrews 4:8, Jesus actually stands in the text instead of Joshua. For the most part the name Jesus is joined with other terms when used in the Epistles, but occasionally it stands alone, especially in Hebrews, and doubtless for the purpose of emphasizing His humanity as a continuing element of His being. Therefore it is legitimate for us today to use the simple name in unadorned fashion, but to do so exclusively could indicate a lack of appreciation of the rounded presentation which the Scriptures give of Him.

Christ, meaning "anointed one," is the Greek equivalent of the Hebrew word *Messiah*. Its function as a title is emphasized by the fact that often it occurs with the definite article, which gives it the force of "the promised Christ," the one who fulfills the concept of Messiah as set forth in the Old Testament Scriptures. Our Lord uses it thus of Himself in Luke 24:46, for example: "And he said to them, Thus it stands written that the Christ should suffer and rise from the dead the third day." By extension of meaning the same form is used by Paul as a synonym for the Church (I Cor. 12:12), thus emphasizing the intimate bond between Christ and His people. Of special interest is the development which led to the use of Christ as a personal name. It must have taken place early in the life of the Church, for we find it reflected, for example, in the opening verse of Mark's Gospel—"The beginning of the gospel of Jesus Christ, the Son of God." Possibly our Lord Himself is responsible for this usage (John 17:3). In the Epistles there are numerous occurrences of Christ alone as a name (I Cor. 15:3, e.g.).

A circumstance which may strike the reader of the Gospels as odd is the prohibition against making Jesus known as the Christ during the days of His ministry. He imposed this restriction on the disciples (Matt. 16:20) and somewhat similarly choked off any possible testimony from demons (Luke 4:41). If this title should be used freely of Him among the Jews, it would excite the populace to expect in Him a political Messiah who would gain for them their national freedom and many accompanying benefits. Since this was not the purpose of Jesus, He did what He could do to suppress the use of the term Messiah with regard to Himself, though He welcomed it in the circle of the apostles (Matt. 16:16).

Only once does the name *Emmanuel* occur, and then in connection with the conception of Jesus (Matt. 1:23). It is a Hebrew word meaning "God with us," and is peculiarly appropriate as an explanation of the significance of the birth of Jesus as involving the incarnation. For some reason the name did not gain currency in the Church, perhaps because it was crowded out by Jesus and Christ.

Among the ancients it was common to distinguish a man not only by name but also by place of residence. Consequently Jesus was often called the Nazarene because of his years spent in the village of Nazareth (Luke 24:19). As used of Jesus' followers by the Jews the term took on an element of reproach which it did not possess in any recognizable way during His life on earth.

When Jesus referred to Himself His most usual method of identification was to use the title *Son of Man*. It was more than a means of identification, however, for it linked Him to a conception of majesty which had gathered around the term since its use in Daniel 7:13. Although it is possible that occasionally the title stresses Jesus' humanity, in the main it serves to point to His transcendence as a heavenly figure. Certainly the widespread notion that Son of Man expresses the humanity of Jesus, as Son of God expresses His deity, is quite misleading (cf. Luke 22:69-70). By using this title publicly rather than Messiah, Jesus was able to avoid suggesting that His mission was political in nature, and instead could put into the title by His own use of it the content which He wanted to give to it. The Church recognized the Lord's right to exclusive use of the term and did not employ it, out of deference to Him (the one exception is Stephen in Acts 7:56).

One of the most familiar designations for Jesus is *Son of God*. Only in John's Gospel does He use it of Himself (John 5:25; 10:36; 11:4). But elsewhere He uses its equivalent, the Son (Matt. 11:27), which is especially appropriate when used opposite the Father, and which in such a passage clearly sets off the uniqueness of this particular Son. In the Synoptic Gospels considerable care is needed in order to impute to the term Son of God the exact nuance of meaning proper to its every occurrence. Geerhardus Vos discerned four meanings: the nativistic, which stresses the divine orig-

ination of the person of Jesus as a human figure; the ethico-religious, which points to the filial relation which Christ sustained to the Father within the context of His human life, similar to that which any child of God has; the Messianic, which has to do with His appointment as the anointed of God to execute His mission as the one sent of the Father, in fulfillment of OT prophecy; the trinitarian or ontological, in which the unique relation of Christ to the Father as the only Son is expressed. This latter, of course, represents the highest level of sonship (see G. Vos, *The Self-Disclosure of Jesus*, pp. 141ff).

Rather frequently in the course of His ministry Jesus was addressed as *Son of David* (Matt. 21:9; Luke 18:38), which is distinctly a Messianic title pointing to Him as the one who fulfilled the Davidic covenant, the one who was expected to establish the kingdom and bring Israel to freedom, peace, and glory (cf. Matt. 1:1; Luke 1:32-33).

A few passages proclaim outright that Jesus is *God* (John 1:1 in a pre-incarnate setting; John 1:18 according to the strongest manuscript evidence; John 20:28; Rom. 9:5 according to the most natural construction of the verse; Titus 2:13; Heb. 1:8). That the passages are relatively few in number is probably due to the fact that Jesus Christ, as known to men, was in a position of subordination to the heavenly Father, His deity veiled by His humanity, so that it was much more natural to assign to Him the predicates of deity than to refer to Him directly as God. Semitic monotheism as the background for the early Hebrew Christians doubtlessly exercised a restraining influence also. Some moderns about whose orthodoxy there is no question have nevertheless confessed to a feeling of restraint in referring to Jesus as God, though they do not doubt His essential deity (e.g., James Denney in a letter to W. Robertson Nicoll included in the life of Nicoll by T. H. Darlow, New York: Doran Co., 1925, p. 361).

No term is more expressive of the faith of early believers in Jesus than *Lord* (Acts 2:36; 10:36; Rom. 10:9; I Cor. 8:6; 12:3; Phil. 2:11). It denotes the sovereignty of Christ, His headship over the individual believer, the church as a body, and all things. For those who were strangers, it was merely a title of respect (John 4:11), but for those who were deeply attached to the Saviour it had the highest import, calling alike for homage and obedience (John 20:28; Acts 22:10). Used sparingly during the period of the earthly ministry prior to the resurrection, it takes on an increased use and heightened significance as a result of that tremendous event.

Some titles pertain to the mission of Christ more than to His person. One of these is *Word* (John 1:1,14; I John 1:1). As such Christ is essentially the revealer of God, the one who opens to the understanding of men the nature and purposes of the Almighty and discloses that higher wisdom which stands in contrast to the wisdom of men. In keeping with such a title is the designation *Teacher*, by which our Lord was customarily addressed in the days of His flesh. This attests the impact of His instruction and the authority which lay behind it. Despite the fact that Jesus lacked rabbinic training, He could not be denied the recognition of the wisdom which shone through His spoken word.

The classic designation of Christ as *Servant* is given by Paul in Philippians 2:7, but it was widely recognized in the early church that our Lord fulfilled the Servant of Jehovah role in Himself (see Matt. 12:17-21). That it dominated the thinking of Christ Himself may be safely affirmed in the light of such a passage as Mark 10:45.

Central to the mission of Christ was His work as *Saviour*. We have already seen that the name Jesus has this meaning, the name suggesting the reason for His coming into the world. Luke 2:11 and John 4:42 are among the passages which herald Christ under the aspect of His Saviourhood. The idea in the word is not merely deliverance from sin and all the other woes which afflict man, but the provision of a state of wholeness and blessedness in which man realizes the purpose of God for him. In reports of the healings of Jesus, the verb form denotes the state of soundness which results from the healing touch of the Saviour.

Jesus' saving mission is declared also in the expression, *Lamb of God* (John 1:29,36; cf. Rev. 5:6). Peter likewise uses the word "lamb" of Jesus, with special reference to His qualification of sinlessness (I Pet. 1:19).

The reference to Jesus as *High Priest* is confined to the Epistle to the Hebrews, where it occurs some ten times, His work being described as taking place in the heavenly sanctuary, in the presence of God, where the fruits of His death for sinners on the earth are conserved in His work of intercession (Heb. 9:11-12).

More general is the characterization of our Lord as the *Mediator* between God and men (I Tim. 2:5). This term takes account of the barrier which sin erected between the Creator and the creature, which Christ alone was qualified to remove. For the concept in the OT, see Job 9:33.

Paul uses the title *Last Adam* (I Cor. 15:45) in contrast to the first Adam, suggesting the undoing of the consequences of sin brought on by Adam's transgression (cf. Rom. 5:12-21), and the realization of new creation life which is to be communicated to all believers in resurrection glory even as it is already their portion in Christ in a spiritual sense.

This list of names and titles of Christ is not exhaustive. The resources of languages are taxed in the sacred record to set forth the full excellence and worth of the Son of God. When His work is considered in its broad sweep, the most satisfying analysis divides it in accordance with the offices which He fulfills—*prophet, priest* and *king*. The prophetic ministry relates especially to the testimony borne in the days of His flesh as He heralded the kingdom of God, warned of coming judgment, and encouraged the people of God. He is still the faithful and true witness as He speaks to the church through the Spirit. As priest our Lord made the one sacrifice of Himself which brought to an end animal sacrifices and put away sin for ever (Heb. 9:26). Faithful and merciful, He ministers before God on behalf of His people who are compassed by sin and infirmity (Heb. 2:17; 4:15-16). The term *king* relates especially to the future activity of our Lord as He comes again to supplant the kingdom of the world with His own gracious and sovereign rule (Rev. 11:15). He shall be no ordinary ruler, but King of kings, without a peer.

IV. Character. "What manner of man is this?" Such was the amazed observation of the disciples of Jesus as they beheld Him in action and felt the strength and mystery of His personality as they companied with Him. Certain ingredients of character deserve special mention, but it cannot be said

that He was noted for some things above others, for this would involve disproportion and would reflect upon the perfection of His being. He had *integrity*. After all, this is the kernel of character. The Gospel appeal consisting in the challenge to lodge faith in Christ would be impossible if He were not trustworthy. No taint of duplicity marred His dealings with others, for there was no mixture of motives within His heart. He could not deceive, for He was Truth incarnate. The claims of Jesus in areas where we have no means of testing them can be cordially received for the reason that in areas where His affirmations can be judged they stand the test.

Christ had *courage*. When Aristotle advanced his famous doctrine of the mean, he illustrated it by courage, which lies midway between cowardice and recklessness. Judged by this standard, the character of Jesus appears in a most favorable light, for in Him one can detect no wild instability even in the most intense activity, nor any supineness in His passivity. Christ had physical courage. Without it He could never have cleared the temple singlehandedly. He had the courage of conviction. Peter was probably His boldest disciple, yet he denied his Lord under pressure, whereas Jesus confessed His own person and mission before the Sanhedrin even though it meant His death. The stamina of men is often attributable, at least in part, to the help and sympathy of their fellows, but Jesus stood alone as He faced His final ordeal.

Our Lord showed great *compassion* as He dealt with people. This is the word used in the Gospels. In the Epistles it is called love. The sight of multitudes forlorn and forsaken by those who should have been their spiritual shepherds stirred Christ to the depths of His being. Out of His compassion He ministered to their physical need for food and health, and went on to tell them the secrets of the life of true godliness. Compassion was more than an emotion with Jesus. It was a call to action, to selfless ministry on behalf of the needy. He gave Himself to one with the same intensity that He showed in dealing with the many. Virtue went out of Him and He did not regret the loss, for it is the nature of love to give. To love the loveless and love them to the end and to the uttermost — this is the love that Paul describes as passing knowledge (Eph. 3:19). It is a love that proved itself through death—He loved me and gave Himself for me (Gal. 2:20), and yet remains deathless.

Jesus clothed Himself with *humility*. He could talk about this as His own possession without affectation (Matt. 11:29). Christ wrought a revolution in ethics by dignifying humility in a world which despised it as weakness. Though the universe was His creation and though He was equal with the Father, though every knee would one day bow before Him, yet He was not lifted up with pride

(continued on page 403)

THE FOLLOWING NARRATIVE ACCOUNT, *The Personality of Jesus,* was written by Dr. Chad Walsh. It is based upon the events related in the Four Gospels.

372

The Personality
of JESUS

O NE NAME above all others haunts the memory and imagination of mankind.

That name is Jesus.

He lived in one of the most obscure provinces of the Roman Empire; He was probably in His early thirties when He was put to death; the Crucifixion seemed to mark the absolute and final failure of everything He stood for.

But His apparent failure was His permanent success. His name is one that the human race cannot forget. We are haunted by His memory — and His meaning. The centuries go by in slow succession, but the ultimate question still confronting each man is: *"What do you think of Christ?"*

There are other names that refuse to die. Some of them were great and noble-hearted teachers, like Socrates (SOCK-ruh-teez) in Greece. We see in him a purity and integrity of life, and we can imagine what it would have been like to talk with him face to face and have him teach us. Or we daydream about how exciting it would have been to know Julius Caesar and Alexander the Great, and converse with them about military strategy and political events. Those who love literature would willingly journey back in a time machine to the age of Shakespeare, to ask him why Hamlet delayed his task of vengeance so long, or simply to talk with a man who saw with such depth and sober compassion into the human spirit.

Mankind Is Haunted

A LL THIS IS TRUE, but mankind is haunted by Jesus in an additional way. Our desire is not simply to know Him as a man, to ask Him questions, to receive His teachings by direct communication. We have a feeling, a conviction, hard to put into words. We sense that if we could have wandered with Him day after day in Palestine, listening to His words, talking with Him over the leisurely evening meals, sharing His sorrows and His joys — *something would have happened to us.* This something would be more than a matter of learning His teachings and trying to follow them. The very presence of Jesus would make us into *new persons.*

In short the man, Jesus Himself, is as important as His teachings. We are not content to know merely the way of life that He proclaimed. We want to know Jesus. We are certain that if we could truly *know* Him, our very nature would be transformed and we would become different people. He came into the world not simply to teach a higher way of life, but to remake quite ordinary men and women — remake them into children of God. A caterpillar changed into a butterfly or a shapeless block of stone carved into a statue is not a greater transformation!

We are haunted. Our hearts and minds yearn to know not merely the teachings of Jesus, but what kind of man He was, what His personality was like, from what source He drew His strange power over human lives.

His Early Life

B UT when we start to learn more about Jesus, we run into difficulties. The four Gospels, which are what we have to go on, are not ordinary biographies. They do not pretend to give a systematic life of Jesus. From them we learn of His ancestry and the remarkable circumstances of His birth. But then there is a gap of thirty years, except for the story about the boy Jesus lingering behind in the Temple. We can assume that Jesus was busy in Joseph's workshop, learning the trade of a carpenter. Like other Jewish boys of His time, He would have learned to read, and would have known the Old Testament thoroughly.

But the curtain does not really rise on His life until He is about thirty years old. And then we see Him not in all his daily activities but only in those that have some relation to His special mission. Our hearts still cry out for the small, human-interest details that make a person real to us.

Artists and writers have worked with the known facts and given us their portraits and interpretations. Dorothy L. Sayers, in her cycle of radio plays, *The Man Born to Be King,* has achieved, I think, the best job of any author in presenting a living and believable Jesus. Often the work of inferior writers and artists has been a hindrance rather than a help. Sometimes we are given a pallid picture of a slender and effeminate Jesus which suggests a man of compassion and gentleness but misses the towering strength, the capacity for unashamed anger that the Jesus of the Gospels demonstrated.

What we want to see is the *whole* Jesus, as far as we can. And the whole Jesus is not simply a "meek and mild" teacher. If He had been merely that, He would never have drawn the fearful and hostile attention of the men who controlled the life of Palestine.

Back to the Gospels

A LWAYS we are driven back to the Gospels, to read them with as much imagination and insight as we can. We have to read between the lines, so to speak. We must try to discern the personality of the man who speaks certain words and performs certain deeds. That is what I have tried to do here. Jesus is so inexhaustible a personality that no one can claim to have seen Him completely or with total accuracy of vision. If my attempt to recognize the personality of the Man who moves through the Gospels seems unreal or distorted to any reader, I hope the latter will forget this little book and turn instead to the Gospels, where he will find the basic information out of which his own portrait of Jesus will emerge.

And yet, that is not quite all. It was the unshakable conviction of the first Christians that, though Jesus genuinely died, He did not *stay* dead. They saw Him afterwards in the flesh, and throughout their lives they perceived Him spiritually, as vibrantly alive and close to them as ever. Their experience has been repeated through the centuries. Jesus is not just a fact of ancient history. He is a living and contemporary experience to anyone who will commit himself to Him. Thus it is that the Gospel accounts are not the only way we come to know the personality of Jesus. The man who genuinely commits himself to Jesus will find out what kind of Person he is following. He will *know* Jesus.

Joseph taught young Jesus the carpenter's trade

But back to the Gospels, our basic source of written information. What we find there is that the man Jesus is sufficiently complex and many-sided so that, while no man's portrait of Him can be completely accurate, few portraits are likely to be completely false. Take the "gentle Jesus meek and mild." It is not the whole picture, but it is an important part of the picture. We catch glimpses of *this* Jesus in a number of events.

The very night that He was arrested and brought to trial something happened that must have puzzled His disciples. They had met together to celebrate the great Jewish festival of the Passover. Judas had already secretly made plans to turn Jesus over to His enemies, and Jesus foresaw what was coming. But the other disciples were in happy ignorance. To them, the time must have seemed very close at hand when Jesus would reveal Himself completely and begin reigning as the Messiah (meh-SIGH-uh), God's special representative over all the Jewish nation. He would rule in splendor, and they would share His glory. Such must have been the secret dreams that many held, for few of them yet understood very clearly who He was and what His real mission would prove to be. The cheers of the great Jerusalem crowds on Palm Sunday still rang in their ears, and the moment of triumph appeared to be almost upon them.

Jesus the Servant

During the supper, however, Jesus did a strange thing — a thing one could not imagine a king ever doing! Quietly He arose and laid aside His cloak. "Can I give You a hand, Master?" asked big, burly Peter, always eager to help, even when he didn't know what Jesus was planning to do.

"No, thank you," Jesus smiled gently. "I'll do this Myself."

Judas looked up uneasily. Everything made him nervous that evening. Meanwhile, the other disciples were watching Jesus intently. What was their teacher planning to do? Serenely and swiftly, Jesus picked up a towel from the nearby table and tucked it in His belt. He filled a basin with water, and knelt down before John. One at a time, He carefully washed John's feet, then expertly dried them with the towel. The other disciples watched with mounting bewilderment. Was this the way God's Messiah would behave? Was this a kingly act?

But Jesus proceeded around the table, washing each man's feet in turn. Peter waited nervously. When Jesus reached the big fisherman, the latter shook his head. "No, sir, You don't wash my feet," Peter sputtered. "Look here, it isn't proper for You to go around washing *my* feet."

Jesus smiled quietly. "You don't understand now. You will later."

"No, sir," Peter insisted. "You're not going to wash my feet. I won't have it. It isn't proper for You to do that for the likes of me."

There was a little pause while Jesus gently began washing Peter's big right foot. "If I don't wash you," He said, "you cannot share My lot." He washed the other foot and began drying them one at a time.

Peter was speechless a moment, a rare condition for him. Suddenly the words tumbled out. "All right, Master," he said. "And, while You're about it, wash my hands and head, too. They need it."

A ripple of laughter went around the table. Jesus chuckled, remembering how impulsive Peter was, and how he always spoke first and thought afterward. The tension was broken. Jesus soon finished drying Peter's feet. "There," He said, "if anybody has bathed, it's enough to wash his feet. You're clean now." And Jesus moved on to the next disciple.

The Avalanche of Children

THE GENTLE SIDE of Jesus comes out especially in His attitude toward children. No matter how busy He was, He had time for them. One day, earlier in His mission, He was teaching a huge crowd that seemed to press in upon Him from all the compass points of Judea (jou-DEE-uh). The Pharisees were there, not so much to learn as to trap Him by trick inquiries. They had just asked Him some very difficult questions about divorce, hoping that they could catch Him in a contradiction. It was the kind of discussion that the great scholars loved to carry on in the Temple at Jerusalem.

In the very midst of the debate, there was an interruption. A woman carrying a small baby moved sideways through the crowd and put her child on Jesus' lap. The little girl sat there, looking up at Him with big, solemn eyes. Another mother suddenly appeared, and plunked her one-year-old son on His other knee. The little boy stared briefly at the tiny girl, lost interest, and began chewing at Jesus' sleeve.

"Now about this question of eternal life," an earnest young Pharisee asked Him. "What must I do to inherit it?"

Jesus looked thoughtful. He remained in silence a moment, idly tousling the hair of the two children. A sudden commotion developed just a few feet away.

"They're coming by the dozens!" one of the disciples whispered to his companion. And indeed, it looked as though all the mothers of Judea were converging on Jesus, each with at least one baby or small child. "Look here!" the disciple yelled at the advancing mothers. "Don't you see the Master is busy? This is a serious discussion. Take those children away!"

Jesus gave him a quick look and turned toward the mothers. "Do nothing of the sort," He called out. "Bring your children here. We can talk about religion later on." He put His hand on the head of the tiny girl and murmured a blessing, then gently handed her back to her mother. He blessed the little boy, and returned him. Soon the other mothers were lined up, bringing their children to Him for His blessing.

In the midst of blessing them, Jesus looked up and said, "Let the children come to Me. If you want to know what the kingdom of God is like, look at these children." The line of mothers and small children did not seem to be getting any shorter. The disciple who had tried to keep them away smiled wryly, and the Pharisees looked on impatiently. It was some time before they had a chance to pose any more questions. . . .

Another time Jesus made the same point about children. One of His disciples asked Him, "Who is the greatest in the kingdom of Heaven?"

Instead of answering directly, Jesus called a child to Him and said simply, "There is your answer. Unless you become like this child, you will never get inside the kingdom of Heaven. You must be humble like a child, if you want to be great in the kingdom of Heaven." His tone grew sterner. "Remember this," He said. "You see how these little ones trust Me. If anyone causes one of them to sin — well, it would be better for him to have a millstone fastened around his neck and be thrown into the deepest part of the sea!"

The Wrong Kind of People

JESUS loved the innocence, trustfulness, and spontaneity of children, and He always had time for them. But He also had a particular love for people who were not innocent at all. His heart went out to sinners — provided only that they did not try to deceive themselves. If they knew that they were sinners, He was quick to accept them as His own and give them His love and understanding. This was something that the sternly righteous people found difficult to understand. He seemed to be condoning bad conduct.

Jesus' attitude toward sinful people bothered the Pharisees in particular. They were men who took their religion very seriously. They tried to live up to the Ten Commandments and all the other teachings of Moses, as these had been understood and explained by many generations of rabbis. They were the "pillars of the church" — earnest, often humorless, but desirous of living up to all the externals of a godly life and setting themselves up as good examples to other people. No wonder they were puzzled by Jesus. He

seemed to make the strangest friends. He associated with tax-collectors, who were regarded as accomplices of the hated Roman rulers, and He was often with dubious men and women who made no real effort to keep the Ten Commandments, much less the detailed provisions for ritual purity. In fact, people of this sort appeared to feel a special pull toward Him.

One day a Pharisee named Simon invited Jesus to dinner. He had been moved by Jesus' teaching, and vaguely disturbed; he wanted to find out more about this man who could say such strange and uncomfortable things.

While they were sitting at the dinner table, an odd thing happened. The door quietly opened and a haggard woman — though still with traces of beauty in her face — entered so quietly that her footsteps made no sound.

"What are you doing here?" Simon demanded angrily. He knew the woman. Everyone in town knew her. Her reputation was notorious.

The woman made no answer. She was intent on a small bottle of ointment in her hand. Removing the cap, she knelt down before Jesus and began weeping uncontrollably. Her tears fell on His feet as she knelt there. When her sobs began to slacken a little, she took her long hair and wiped His feet dry. Then, with infinite care, she rubbed the ointment on His feet.

"A fine prophet this is!" Simon thought to himself, observing the scene in stony silence. "If this man were a prophet, He'd know that this woman is no good and wouldn't let her paw Him like this."

Jesus looked up straight into Simon's eyes. "I have something to say to you."

Simon was a little taken aback. "What is it, Teacher?" he stammered.

"For of such is the kingdom of God"

Forgiveness and Gratitude

"I 'LL TELL YOU A STORY," Jesus said. "A wealthy person once lent five dollars to one man and fifty to another. Neither one was able to repay him. So he decided to forgive them both and not ask for the money back. Which of the two men do you think would love him more?"

"Why, the one who borrowed fifty dollars," Simon said. "Fifty dollars is ten times as much as five dollars."

"Exactly," Jesus nodded. Then he glanced at the woman and added, "You see her? When I came to your house, you didn't bring out a basin of water for My feet. But this woman has washed My feet with her tears and dried them with her hair. You didn't give Me a kiss of welcome, but from the time she came in she hasn't stopped kissing My feet. You didn't anoint My head with oil, but she has anointed My feet with ointment. You are right — she's guilty of many sins, and they are serious ones. But she also knows how to love."

Friend of sinners, foe of the Pharisees

Jesus turned and faced the woman directly, as she still covered His feet with kisses. "Stand up," He said kindly, taking her hand. "Your sins are forgiven. Your faith has saved you. Go in peace."

The woman stumbled to her feet, tried to say something, then dashed from the room as suddenly as she had entered.

Jesus looked at Simon and the other guests. "If anyone is forgiven only a little," he remarked in a low voice, "he will love only a little."

Simon, for his part, shook his head in bewilderment. At least the unwelcome visitor had disappeared into the night out of which she had come. He still felt upset. This episode had troubled him more than it ought to.

The kind of people who turned most readily to Jesus were like this woman. They had no illusions about themselves. They did not pretend to be moral examples. They knew how far short they fell from the ideal. They were precisely the sort of people that many of the Pharisees scorned and carefully avoided.

But something about Jesus gave these people a kind of boldness. They felt in Him an understanding, a love, a willingness to meet them where they were. It was as though His very presence made it possible for them to love, and to be sorry for the way they had lived their lives.

"The Company He Keeps!"

IT MUST HAVE SEEMED to the Pharisees, who were so earnestly trying to set a good example by being religious and keeping company only with moral people, that Jesus went out of His way to be shocking. They kept harping on His habit of picking up very questionable followers — people who didn't even go through the motions of observing the Law of Moses. Or take the tax-collectors. At that time, tax-collectors were really agents of the Roman government. The job of collecting taxes was farmed out to them by the Romans, and they had a way of demanding enough so that plenty was left over for their own pockets. They were regarded as racketeers, or as collaborators with the Roman enemy. Yet these unpatriotic social outcasts turned to Jesus, somehow drawn by His compassion and understanding.

One day Jesus was walking past the office where Matthew was collecting taxes, and He simply said to him, "Follow Me." Matthew left his tax books lying where they were and followed.

Then there was the time when Jesus was at dinner with a large assortment of tax-collectors and other shady characters. Some Pharisees, checking up on Him, asked His disciples, "What is your Teacher doing, eating with people like that?" The very thought made them shiver in disgust.

When Jesus heard of their question, He spoke pointedly. "People who are well don't need a doctor. Sick people do. I was not sent on earth to look after the good people, but after the bad ones."

If the Pharisees took this to mean they were already good and needed no help from Jesus, it was because they could not recognize the subdued but unmistakable sense of humor that Jesus frequently showed. This is a side of Him that is often overlooked, but if you read the Gospels carefully, you will see that He had a dry, ironic sense of humor, which He could use with powerful effect in the heat of debate.

The Uses of Wit

OFTEN His sense of humor served Him well when His enemies wanted to trap Him in a discussion. One time — He was preaching in the Temple — the usual group of priests and scribes came up to Him, eager to lead Him into some damaging statement on which they might pin charges against Him. If they could lure Him into saying something that would be considered blasphemy in court, it would simplify their plans to get rid of Him. One of the listeners came up close to Him, rubbing his hands together in apparent deference. "Would You be so kind as to tell us," he said with exaggerated politeness, "what the source of Your strange authority is? We have heard of all the wonderful things You do. Where do You get Your authority? Who gave it to You?"

If Jesus had answered the plain truth, that His authority came from God, they might have taken and twisted His words to suit their hostile purposes. It was a loaded question, full of danger. The time had not quite come when He would put aside all reticence and proclaim His special mission in all its fulness. He knew why they were asking — to get Him into trouble. But two could play at this game. He spoke slowly. "I'll tell you if you let Me ask you a question."

"Yes, yes," the man said, as one of his companions secretly drew out a little writing tablet and prepared to record everything Jesus said. "What is Your question?"

The trapper had walked into a trap. "My question," said Jesus, "is this: When John baptized people, was the baptism from Heaven, or was it just an idea of John's?"

The questioner's face fell. "Let me think that one over," he stammered, and went into a huddle with several of his friends. "He's got us there," the man with the writing tablet whispered. "If we say, 'From Heaven,' He'll say, 'Then why didn't you believe John and follow him?' But if we say that John was just doing a purely human thing—"

"We don't dare say *that*," the questioner hissed. "This Temple is full of people who followed John. First thing we know they'll start throwing stones at us. They're dead sure John was a prophet, straight from God, and they won't stand for anyone casting doubts on him."

"Well?" asked Jesus. "I'm waiting."

The man who had first questioned Him cleared his throat. "Well, sir," he said, "I'll have to admit it — I don't know the answer."

Jesus smiled. "You didn't answer My question. I don't have to answer yours. Now let Me tell you a story. . . ."

The Unreasonable Children

THUS Jesus could use quick wit and ironic humor to turn aside the plots of His enemies. But His humor also comes out in other ways. A great deal is revealed in the parables, those simple stories from daily life that Jesus often told to illustrate religious truths.

For instance, one thing that apparently irritated Him was the *inconsistency* in the objections that people made. John the Baptist had been severely criticized for being too strict, and Jesus was denounced for being too lenient. "I'll tell you what the people of this generation are like," Jesus said one day. "They are like a big group of children in the market place. One minute the children yell, 'What's the matter with you? We play music for you, but you won't dance. Come on and have a good time!' The next minute you see their faces drop and the tears begin to form, and they sob out, 'We cry, but you won't cry with us!' Children, you can't have it both ways. John the Baptist was as strict as they come. He didn't drink wine; he wouldn't even eat bread. And what did you say? You said, 'Aha, he's got a demon in him.' Then I came along, and you see Me eating bread and drinking wine. And what do you say? 'Look at that glutton and drunkard.' Take your choice, children — you can't have it both ways," He smiled.

Some of the parables have the dry humor one associates with men swapping stories around the traditional cracker barrel in a country store. It is a humor based on common sense and a canny understanding of human nature.

"Let Me tell you about a farmer," Jesus once said. "He owned a big vineyard, so early one morning he went into town to hire some day laborers. They agreed to work for a dollar a day. He put them to work in his vineyard, but around nine o'clock he saw he was going to need some more hands, so he went into town again, and there was the usual cluster of men, idling in the market place, having a drink or just passing the time of day. 'Come on,' he said, 'I can use some hands in my vineyard. I'll settle up with you at the end of the day — I'll make it right with you.'

"So they went back with him and set to work. The day was getting pretty hot by now. Several times more he went to the market place and hired people. The last time it was almost sunset. But each time he said he would pay them what was right.

The Payment

"AT LAST the sun set. 'Time to knock off,' the farmer said. He called to his foreman. 'Line the men up and give them their pay. Start with the last ones first.'

"The men lined up and the foreman passed down the line, handing out the money. 'A dollar!' exclaimed one of the men hired just before sunset. This farmer was more stupid than he had taken him for!

"The men who had been hired at sunrise craned their necks. If the fellows who were hired *last* were going to get a dollar — let's see, we early birds had worked about ten times as long — that ought to come to ten dollars!

"The foreman moved down the line as though he had all evening to do it. Finally he reached the men who were the dirtiest and sweatiest. 'Here's your dollar,' the foreman said.

" 'Look here,' one of the men protested.

" 'Talk to the boss,' the foreman said wearily.

"The man turned to the farmer. 'Look here, mister, we've been working all day long till our backs are fit to break, pruning these grapes of yours, and these johnny-come-latelies get the same pay as we do! It's not right, I tell you, not fair!'

"The farmer looked him in the eye: 'How much did I promise to pay you? A dollar, wasn't it? What have you got in your hand? Looks like a dollar to me. It isn't counterfeit — it's good money. Now, if I choose to pay everybody the same wages, is that any business of yours? It's my money, isn't it?' "

Jesus added, as He smiled at His disciples, "That's what the kingdom of Heaven is like. You're not going to like it unless you get used to seeing people at the end of the line served first."

Surprised by Joy

I F JESUS had a deep well of humor, He was also a man who could experience sudden transports of joy, though they were always tempered by the overwhelming responsibility to God and man that rested upon Him. One of these sudden flashes of sheer joy occurred after He had made the great experiment of sending forth seventy of His disciples, two by two, to stop in towns and villages and prepare the people for a visit by Him. There was no way of telling what reception they would get, or indeed how well the partially trained disciples would stand up to the daily challenges of their work.

At last the day came when the seventy returned, and they were bubbling over with delight. "Master," one of them shouted from far off, "Master, even the demons obey us when we just speak Your name!"

A moment of blinding happiness and exultant joy filled Jesus. His disciples had not failed. They had indeed prepared the way for Him. He looked up, as though He perceived something in the sky that no one else could see. "I see Satan falling like lightning from Heaven," He said, a note of joyful awe in His voice.

But now He was surrounded by His disciples, all babbling at once of the cures they had performed and the miracles that had flowed from their fingertips. "Yes," said Jesus, looking more serious now, "I have given you authority so that wild beasts won't harm you and enemies can't hurt you. But don't rejoice in that. Rejoice because *your names are written in Heaven.*"

Thus it was that temporary joys always led Him to see joy in perspective. The final joy — and He never lost sight of this — was to be in the loving presence of God, now and forever.

But there is one time in the Gospel accounts when we see Him wholeheartedly giving Himself to the joy of a purely human occasion. This was when He went to a marriage feast in Cana (KAY-nuh).

"The wine has run out," Mary whispered in her son's ear when she was able to get Him aside in a corner.

Jesus looked across the room — at the bride, as radiant as all brides are and looking very young; at the groom; at the great crowd of relatives and friends — all laughing and singing and getting in a mood for dancing. Evidently the caterer had underestimated their capacity for wine. Wine — a trivial thing, in a way, but not trivial this evening, Jesus thought. This was

AUGUST JERNDORFF

The Sermon on the Mount.

Head of Christ.

Behold the man.

The Saviour.

GIOVANNI BARBIERI

Behold the man.

Christ gives His blessing.   *Christ.*

HANS HOLBEIN THE ELDER   TITIAN

HEINRICH HOFMANN

Christ at the age of twelve.

GIOVANNI BELLINI

Christ Crucified.

Christ and the repentant woman.

PETER PAUL RUBENS

the only marriage feast these two young people would ever have, and the memory of it ought to be as perfect as it could be.

Mary turned to the servants. "Do whatever He tells you to," she said.

There were six stone jars, big ones, standing nearby. "Fill the jars up with water," Jesus said. The servants scurried about, and brought back buckets of water to fill the jars. "Now draw some out and take it to the caterer," Jesus said. The servants shrugged their shoulders in bewilderment, but did as they were told. They filled a pitcher from one of the jars and carried it away.

Jesus instructing His disciples

A moment later the caterer took the groom aside and said in a tone of respect, almost of awe, "This takes the prize! I've managed a lot of these wedding parties. Usually people serve the best wine first, and then bring out the cheap stuff when nobody is paying much attention. But you've kept the best wine till now."

"Who wants to dance?" someone called out.

"Let's have some of that wine first," another voice shouted.

The evening was still young. The bride's eyes were bright with mounting excitement. She smiled at the groom and he smiled back. The party was a success, and they would both remember it all their lives. Jesus, looking on, felt His own heart beat with the simple joy that surged and danced and shouted all about Him.

The Lord's Sense of Beauty

IT HAS sometimes been said that, though Jesus inspired much of the world's greatest literature, painting, and music, He Himself showed little interest in beauty and the arts. Certainly the Gospels do not say much about all this. Jesus gives no advice on literary and artistic standards, and His ethical teaching concerns sober duties of the most practical sort, rather than artistic self-expression. Does this mean that He was insensitive to beauty?

Here again one must read between the lines. Jesus had a particular mission, the salvation of mankind. A bridge was needed between God and man, and He was that bridge. Those sides of His character that bear upon this mission are revealed in the Gospels, but for the most part, *only* those aspects. The Gospels are rigidly selective in what they report. If Jesus had ever painted a picture or wrote the words for a song, it might not have been mentioned. Yet, despite this, a sharply defined sense of beauty breaks through in some places, united always with a purpose that goes beyond beauty. . . .

One day Jesus and the disciples had slipped away from the crowd that was always pressing in upon Him. They were on top of a lonely mountain, and the familiar landscape of Galilee receded into the distance wherever the eye could see. The cluster of disciples gathered around Him. It was time now to teach them the heart of the Christian life, so that they could live it and teach it to others.

Thus Jesus began the immortal Sermon on the Mount, saying, "Blessed are the poor in spirit, for theirs is the kingdom of Heaven." The circling faces watched Him intently, as He quietly went on: "Blessed are those who mourn, for they shall be comforted." He continued through the series of blessings, each exploring the depth of the redeemed life. Then He challenged His disciples: "You are the salt of the earth. Now if salt loses its taste, how can it become salty again?" After this, He touched briefly on the Mosaic (mo-ZAY-ick) Law and made it clear that the new era He was bringing into existence did not mean the destruction of the Law but the fulfillment of its inner spirit. On and on He spoke, describing a way of life more demanding than anything the Pharisees had dreamed of. His disciples must live by love and forgiveness, loving and forgiving those who were loveless and unforgiving. And their religion must be inward rather than outward. Above all, He told them, they must avoid a religion of show and make-believe.

Two Kinds of Treasure

THE CIRCLING FACES were all turned to Him, listening as though life depended on each word from His lips. John had a look of serenity and quiet understanding. Big Peter was fidgeting as though he wanted to leap up and find an enemy to love without further delay. Jesus now began to talk about the things that last, and those that pass away. "Don't pile up treasures here on earth," He pleaded. "If you do, moths and rust and thieves will do away with them. If you want to accumulate treasures, store them in *Heaven,* where they will be safe. I tell you, wherever you put your treasures, that is where your heart will really be. You can't serve two masters. Choose between God and the dollar sign. You can't have it both ways."

When He paused, a ripple of uneasiness went through the crowd that had been gathering all the while Jesus was talking. Very few of them ever had enough money to be sure of tomorrow's dinner. A bad crop year, a migration of fish to another part of the lake, a fire in some small house — any one of these would mean catastrophe to them and their families. Their concern was not to pile up great riches in the bank but to feed and clothe their families day by day. But *that* concern was a constant one, and their days were often anxious and fearful.

"Master," one of the disciples on the outer edge of the circle spoke up, "what you say is true, but a man must eat and have some clothes to wear."

Jesus looked his way and thoughtfully met his eye. Since Jesus had left Joseph's home, He had shared the uncertainties of the very poor. Food was something to eat when it happened to be available. A bed was something to sleep in when one happened to be offered at the end of day. He knew what the man was talking about. But as He remained silent, pondering His answer, memories raced vividly through His mind. He was back in Nazareth, a boy again. He remembered the meadows, turned into a sea of brightness by the blossoming lilies. There was the morning He and His brothers had romped through them, and watched the free birds flying high overhead.

"A fellow has got to look out for himself and his wife and children," the man repeated in a low voice.

The Carefree Birds and Lilies

"YES," Jesus said. "Someone has to look out for them. But don't worry about your daily life. You spend too much time wondering how you will get something to eat or clothes to wear. Look at that bird flying over us now. It doesn't sow grain or get out the sickle at harvest time and store up wheat in the barn. But it still eats. Your Heavenly Father takes care of it. Now, don't *you* outrank a bird in God's eyes?

"And don't worry about clothes, either. Solomon was our richest king, and he dressed in beauty and majesty. But I tell you, he couldn't match the wild lilies in the field for beauty and splendor. Yet those lilies aren't industrious. They don't work; you never see them spinning cloth and sewing clothes for themselves. God is their dressmaker. He takes care of clothing them. And do you think He loves *you* less than He loves the lilies? Put first things first. Love God, enter His kingdom, and He will see that you are fed and clothed."

Jesus' sure sense of the artistic form comes out most sharply in the parables, which are often miniature literary masterpieces — amazingly compressed, filled with exact detail, and conveying an incredible impact for all their brevity. Some of them are as tightly constructed as a sonnet. The parable of the Prodigal Son (*Luke* 15) is less than a page long, but in it are three convincing and lifelike character sketches of the two sons and the father. And the relationship among the three is more plausibly drawn than in many full-length novels. In addition, there are touches that only literary genius can produce, such as the ultimate horror endured by the younger son when, as a Jew, he found himself taking care of *pigs*. To the audience this must have brought home, more sharply than volumes of description, the depths to which the young man had sunk.

When the Prodigal Son returns home, the selection of details to express the father's joy is made with a sure eye for what would most vividly symbolize the overpowering happiness: the best robe, a ring, shoes, the fatted calf, music, dancing. Any poet or novelist can envy the absolute economy of language in this parable, and the uncanny ability to present just the right details, and only them.

Gentle . . . and Stern

O NE THING about Jesus that must have puzzled people was that sometimes He talked as though His way of life was easy and pleasant, and at other times He presented it as something almost too rigorous to endure. He could shift from severity to gentleness and back again in a flash.

One day He was thinking of Chorazin (ko-RAY-zin) and Bethsaida (beth-SAY-ih-duh), two cities where He had done great deeds but found little response. Terrible words poured from His lips: "Woe to you, Chorazin! Woe to you, Bethsaida! If I had done the same deeds in Tyre (TIRE) and Sidon (SIGH-dun), they would long since have put on the sackcloth and ashes of repentance. On the day of the last judgment, they will fare better than you!"

Yet a moment later His tone changed and He turned to the people about Him and said simply, "Don't be afraid. Come to Me. All you who labor and are bowed down with burdens, come to Me. I will give you rest. Take My yoke upon you. It isn't heavy. Learn from Me. I am gentle. You will find rest for your souls. My yoke is easy, and the burden I put upon you isn't heavy to carry."

More often, we find Him making demands that seem to strain men to the breaking point. He could see into a man's heart and discover what his treasure really was, and when He discovered it, He insisted that it be given up in return for the only final treasure, God.

This happened in the case of the young man who came up to Jesus and earnestly asked, "What good deed must I do if I want to have eternal life?"

There was something appealing about the young man. He was not trying to ask a trick question. After a moment Jesus answered simply, "Keep the Commandments."

This was too general an answer to satisfy the inquirer. "Which ones?" he asked.

"You know them," Jesus replied. "Don't kill. Don't commit adultery. Don't steal. Don't lie about people. Treat your father and mother with respect. Love your neighbor the same way you love yourself."

A look of relief spread over the young man's face. "I've always kept all these Commandments. What else must I do?" He waited eagerly, perhaps hoping Jesus would say he had done all that was required.

"If you really want to lead a perfect life," Jesus replied slowly, "there is just one thing more. Sell everything you own and give it to the poor. Then come and follow Me."

The young man's face dropped. He was very rich. "That's pretty extreme," he mumbled. Shaking his head, he shuffled off into the crowd.

"Follow Me"

EXTREME as this demand was, Jesus made demands that were even more extreme. He did not confine Himself to saying, "Obey My teachings." He had a still more drastic demand: "Follow Me — without delay." He required personal loyalty as the center of the new way of life that He taught.

It was one of those times when Jesus and His disciples escaped from the great throngs and went off to a place by themselves. In the comparative tranquility and peace, a disciple came up to Him and said, "Master, I have a problem. I want to follow You, but my father has just died. Let me go home and bury him, and I'll hurry right back."

The group waited intently to hear what Jesus would say. They had all experienced His gentleness, His compassionate understanding. At last He spoke quietly, "Leave the dead to bury their own dead. Come, follow Me."

Such a demand wrenches ordinary human nature to the breaking point. But Jesus did not make demands of this sort in isolation. He coupled them with promises. We saw how He dealt with the rich young man, who went away sadder and wiser because he had discovered that his bank account was the real center of his life. At that time, Jesus turned to His disciples and sorrowfully said, "It's very hard for a rich man to enter the kingdom of God!"

A look of amazement passed over the faces that gazed at Him so intently. Many of them had a lingering idea that wealth was proof of God's favor, and poverty was an indication of His disapproval. Jesus knew what they were thinking. He went on, "Children, I tell you the truth, it's easier for a camel to crawl through the eye of a needle than for a rich man to squeeze into the kingdom of Heaven!"

"Then who *can* be saved?" a voice called out.

"Humanly speaking," Jesus replied, "the thing is impossible. But with God there is no such word as 'impossible.' "

Peter as usual had words to say. "Lord," he spoke up, "look at us. We've left everything behind to go with You."

Jesus smiled. He had a special affection for eager, bumbling Peter. "Don't worry," He said. "Whatever you've given up, you've gained more. Anyone who has left his home or his brothers or sisters or parents or children or property — left them for My sake and for My gospel — will get a double reward. He will have homes and property and brothers and sisters and parents and children a hundred times over in this life. And in the age to come, he'll have eternal life. But there will be some surprises. People at the top will find themselves down at the bottom, and those at the bottom will be on top."

Jesus' Purpose in Life

HOW CAN the gentleness and the severity of Jesus be reconciled? One moment He seems to be saying that His way of life is easy; the next minute He makes demands that tear our nature into shreds. The only way to fit the two things together is to understand the heart of His message. He did not come into the world merely to teach a lofty code of morality. *He came to make new beings out of quite run-of-the-mill people.* He knew that if they followed Him with unquestioning love and loyalty, God would enter into them, like a carpenter going into an old house that needs to be re-modeled from the inside. God would remake them. They would become citizens not just of the familiar world of time and space, but of the eternal world that has no beginning and no end. In short, they would truly become God's children, here and now.

Once that happened, the demands of the gospel — to love God and love one's neighbor — would be possible. They would move into a dimension of life in which things that are humanly impossible become everyday realities, thanks to the God who moved through the life and in the being of Jesus.

Something of this sort was what Jesus dramatized to people in His apparently contradictory demands and promises. He drove them hard, to make them see that only when they gave themselves completely into God's hands, through loyalty and faith in Himself, would it become possible for them to live the transformed life in which love spontaneously guides the decisions and acts of daily life. Once the transformation occurs, the impossible is the possible. This is what Jesus seemed to mean when He constantly affirmed that His "way" was both easy and hard.

As a part of His severity, one comes on many instances of blazing anger. These are a jolt to the reader who expects to find the "gentle Jesus" on every page. It takes some readjusting to recognize that He could be furiously indignant and speak words that burned and seared. We saw His anger at the cities that witnessed His great deeds but remained blind to their meaning. In general, His anger was directed against *wilful* spiritual blindness, especially when it was accompanied by self-righteousness and moral smugness. Sometime he used language that in modern times would bring a suit for slander.

The Pharisees were a particular target of His anger. Crossers of all the "i's" and dotters of all the "t's," they tried to make themselves strict examples of the moral life. Some were genuinely good people, and with them Jesus had no quarrel. But others were all surface. They went through the motions of loving God and obeying His law, but it was an external thing; within, their hearts were hard and unloving. It was against these that His wrath whipped like a tempest.

Strong Words

O NE DAY a mixed crowd was listening to Jesus preach. Some were His disciples, but scattered among them were also a number of Pharisees, fascinated by Him, unable to leave Him alone, but also unable or unwilling to believe in Him.

Jesus began the attack bluntly: "The religious scholars and the Pharisees are carrying on the tradition of Moses. So when they tell you what you ought to do, do it. But don't imitate their lives. They don't practice what they preach. Look at them. They impose all sorts of difficult religious requirements on other people, but do nothing to help them bear the burden. Everything they do is for public appearance. They scramble into the best seats in the synagogue, and love to have people call them 'rabbi' in the market place.

"Woe to you, scribes and Pharisees, hypocrites!"

They pray in public at the drop of a hat — when there's a big enough crowd looking on. They wear their piety on their sleeves."

The fire flashed in Jesus' eyes. It seemed to each Pharisee in the crowd that those eyes were fixed directly on him. "Woe to you, you hypocrites!" Jesus thundered directly at them. "You travel by land and sea to make a single convert, and when you succeed, look at him! You teach him to be twice as much a child of Hell as *you* are. You blind guides, you tell people that if they swear in the name of the Temple, it means nothing, but if they swear in the name of the Temple gold, they are bound by the oath. You blind fools, which is more important, the gold or the Temple? It's the Temple that makes the gold sacred, just as it's God who makes the Temple sacred.

"Woe to you, you hypocrites! You give a tenth of everything to the Temple, even trivial things like mint and other herbs. But you are too busy being 'religious' to worry about such things as justice and mercy and faith. You strain out a gnat from anything you drink, and swallow a camel! You are like people who wash the outside of a cup, but inside it is filthy. You are like whitewashed tombs. They look beautiful — from the outside. Inside there is nothing but decaying flesh and dead men's bones!"

It was as though each word was the lash of a whip. Some of the faces before Him were troubled and close to tears. But on the countenances of most of the Pharisees a hard look was settling, a fixed and frozen sneer. Jesus glanced around, slowly, and burst forth again: "I know you. You build tombs for the dead prophets, but you are kind who would kill a living prophet. Snakes that you are, you nest of squirming vipers, do you think you can escape the jaws of Hell?"

The Blind City

JESUS paused a long time. The fire in His eyes had subsided a little. Stony-hearted and stubborn though these men were, they were still precious in God's sight and in His own. If only there were some way He could break through to them, and open their eyes and hearts! When He spoke again, it was no longer to them in particular.

He intoned the words slowly, in an agony of brooding love: "O Jerusalem, Jerusalem, killing the prophets and stoning those who are sent to you! Time and again I would have gathered your children together as a hen gathers her little ones under her wings! But you would have none of this. Blind city, you will lie forsaken and desolate. I have come. I am going away; you will not see Me again until you say, 'Blessed is He who comes in the name of the Lord.' "

This was not the only time that Jesus' anger blazed forth in an intensity that bespoke His own inner agony of frustration. Several times He revealed a cold fury when people implied that literal obedience to every detail of the Mosaic Law must take precedence over the most obvious deeds of kindness and mercy.

One such instance took place in a synagogue. "Who is that?" Jesus asked a friend, as a shabby man by the wall silently held out his hand.

"Look at his hand," the friend said. "See how withered it is."

A little crowd, including several Pharisees, had gathered about. "Come here," said Jesus in a low voice. The man with the withered hand shuffled a little closer. Jesus showed his hand to the spectators. "Tell Me," He said, "is it proper to do good or to do harm on the Sabbath? Is it proper to save life, or to kill?"

He waited a long time for an answer. None came. His eye traveled from face to face. When He spoke again, there was a hard edge to His voice. He was furious at the cold-heartedness of men who would not simply say, "Every day is the right day to heal."

"Very well," He said brusquely. Then in a softer voice He spoke to the man. "Your hand will be all right," He said, and gently let go of it.

The man stared at his hand incredulously. "I can move my fingers now! See?" he shouted.

"Did I do something wrong?" Jesus asked the group. "This is the Sabbath, and the Sabbath is the Lord's Day. Tell Me, did I commit a sin?"

No one answered Him. The Pharisees, pale with anger, quickly slipped away, to meet with important friends of theirs and begin the plans that were to lead to the Cross.

Jesus knew what they had in mind. He watched them as they filed through the door. Once more the anger that had given an edge to His voice drained away. His heart ached for His enemies. If only there were some way He could make them hear, really hear!

At Jesus' command, the lame walked

Deeds Reinforce Words

ONE TIME, and one time only, we find Jesus supplementing words with violent action. It came about one day when He went to the Temple. This was the earthly home of His Father in Heaven, and He always felt a strong renewal of spirit whenever He stepped inside it. Heaven and earth seemed to come together there.

But this time the outer courtyard was particularly noisy. "Come and get your foreign money changed into Palestinian money for the offering!" half a dozen men were shouting, while doing a brisk business at their tables. Foreign money could not be used for making offerings in the Temple. Since there were always many Jewish visitors from abroad, the money-changers could make a handsome profit changing foreign money at a favorable rate — favorable to themselves.

"Unblemished cattle for sale," other voices were yelling. And for the poor people who could afford only a pigeon as their sacrifice, there were special booths and strident voices proclaiming, "First-rate pigeons, acceptable to the Lord! Come and get your pigeon while the supply lasts!" It was like the market place in a big city.

Jesus stood there, watching and listening. His ears caught scraps of conversation — broad jokes, anecdotes about questionable adventures the night before, plans for another "big night." A slow anger began to rise in Him. These men were treating God's house as though it were a market place.

"My house shall be called a house of prayer," He murmured. But there was no praying that His ears could catch, only the babble of business, intermingled with dirty jokes and boisterous yelling back and forth.

Fury seized Him. He looked about. Lying on the floor were several lengths of stout cord that had been used to tie up a box of pigeons. Quickly He picked the cords up, tied them together to make a whip, and swung it over His head.

"Take those things away!" Jesus shouted. He brought the whip down on the back of a money-changer, then wheeled sharply to his left to lash at a man who was selling pigeons. With a quick kick He overturned the pigeon cage. The birds escaped and fluttered out and disappeared.

"What's that fellow up to?" somebody shouted. It was a money-changer. Jesus turned on him and with a strong shove of His two hands overturned the table. The man got down on all fours, cursing in the name of both the Lord and the pagan gods, to scramble for the scattered coins.

"Out of here, all of you!" Jesus shouted. "This is the Temple, not a street market! The Bible says, 'My house shall be called a house of prayer,' but you've made it into a den of thieves. Out!"

He gave a kick at another money-changer's table, then swung his whip at a man who had three cattle to sell.

"Let's get out of here till they take care of this wild man," somebody said. The merchants, quickly gathering up their goods and equipment, beat a hasty retreat. Soon only Jesus was left — with one pigeon that somehow had chosen to fly back into the courtyard. It lighted on His shoulder and stayed there motionless for a long time, then finally flapped its wings and flew away.

Jesus was left totally alone, with His thoughts and His prayers.

Blessed Are the Humble

WE HAVE SEEN many ways in which Jesus revealed His character and personality by the things He said and did. But often you can learn as much about a man by observing, not him, but the reactions of other people to him. This is true of Jesus.

No one who came into close contact with Him was left the same. This does not mean that everyone turned to Him and became a follower. His enemies hated Him as vehemently as His followers loved Him. Proud and cold-hearted people could stand a while in His presence, and then that presence became unendurable. Their curiosity quickly changed to undying hatred, for He revealed to them — simply by the contrast between Himself and them — the hidden secrets of their souls.

Then these enemies would sneak off, spread stories about Jesus, and organize plots to get Him out of the way. His love and goodness, being more than they could endure, hardened their hearts still more and turned them inward upon their own flinty souls.

Many of the Pharisees who figure so prominently in the Gospels reacted in this way. There was enough good in the proudest to attract them to Jesus, out of curiosity if nothing else; but only a few of them were able to meet the test. After a while they drifted away, rejecting eternal life and love as though salvation depended on *denying* Him who was salvation itself.

There were many other people, however, who intuitively recognized goodness and love when it stood in their midst. These were most often humble people, with no great pretensions to virtue and religious merit. Sometimes they were downright sinners, or the kind of men and women one finds today living a half-underground, semi-criminal existence in the junglelike slums of great cities. The thing that made it possible for them to respond to Jesus was that they did not take themselves too seriously. They knew they weren't much to brag about. They wore no mask for public admiration. They had nothing to hide, no precious ego to protect. When love came their way, they could call it by its right name.

Sometimes the impact of a personality can be so overpowering that words are hardly needed for communication. Soon after Jesus had been baptized by John, at the very beginning of His mission, He happened to be by the Sea of Galilee. He saw two brothers, James and John, off a little distance in a boat, mending their nets. Their father, Zebedee (ZEB-uh-dee), was with them. Jesus called across the short stretch of water, "Leave your nets and follow Me."

Without a backward glance the two brothers clambered out of the boat and waded ashore, leaving their dumbfounded father alone in the boat.

A Foreign Woman

THIS KIND OF RESPONSE was not limited to Jews. People completely outside the Jewish circle of faith and life perceived that someone utterly different was among them. Sometimes Jesus tested their faith sternly, as one day when He was in the region of Tyre and Sidon. A Canaanite (KAY-nan-ite) woman suddenly ran across His path and knelt at His feet. "Have mercy on me, please, have pity, Master," she babbled. "My daughter — there's a devil in her — help her, Master!" She clutched at His knees imploringly.

Jesus seemed unaware of her. One of His disciples whispered in His ear, "Say the word, and I'll send her away. She's making a nuisance of herself."

With a slight start, Jesus glanced down at the woman. "Why are you turning to Me?" He asked a little sharply. "Don't you know that My mission is to the lost sheep of Israel?"

The woman clung to Him more desperately and continued babbling, "Master, Master, help me!"

He was still looking down at her. "Tell Me," He asked, "is it fair to take the children's bread and throw it to the dogs?"

The woman paused to think a moment. "No, Master," she replied, "but the dogs — even the dogs are allowed to eat the crumbs that fall from the master's table."

Jesus had the answer He was looking for. The woman was not coming to Him as one might visit a magician in the hope of special tricks. She trusted Him. She believed in Him — and proved it by meeting a test of faith that would have discouraged almost anyone.

In a gentle and reassuring voice He spoke to her, as He helped her to her feet. "Your faith is very great. Don't worry. You shall have your wish. Go home; you will find your daughter healed and well."

Sometimes the effect of Jesus' presence was to create a kind of fear. His goodness — but that is too tame a word — was actually God's holiness invading the ordinary world. In the presence of that holiness, the smallest sin became visible.

Peter was not a man much given to self-examination. He usually spoke or acted first and thought about it afterward — if at all. But one time he was overcome by an awareness of Jesus' holiness. This happened when Jesus was preaching to an immense crowd near the Sea of Galilee.

In their eagerness to be near Him, people were pushing Jesus closer and closer to the water. He noticed a couple of boats along the shore. "Row Me out a little way," He said to Peter as He climbed into the boat. Peter rowed Him out a few yards, where He could face the great throng and preach to them. After He had finished His sermon, and the people had begun to drift away, He turned to Peter and said, "Why don't you go farther out and see how the fish are biting?"

A Frightening Success

PETER LOOKED at Jesus almost helplessly. "We worked all night long, dropping the nets and hauling them in — and we didn't catch anything as big as my little finger! But if You say so, I'll give it a try." He seized the oars and rowed vigorously.

Soon they were at the deepest part of the lake. "Here goes," shouted Peter, feeding the nets over the side.

Suddenly the boat began to list toward the nets. "Hey!" Peter yelled. "The nets are full — they're going to sink the boat!" He turned toward the shore and called out in a thundering voice, "You fellows over there — bring your boat over and give us a hand."

The other boat came as swiftly as the men could row. Working together, both crews pulled in the nets and dumped the fish into the two boats. The load was so heavy that the boats sank down in the water until little waves were splashing over the sides.

"Row for all you're worth!" cried a man in the other boat.

Peter seemed not to hear Him. He had fallen on His knees before Jesus and was stammering incoherently. Finally Jesus was able to catch some of the words. "Go away," Peter was saying. "Go away. I'm a sinful man, Master. You shouldn't be with me. Go away."

It was as though, in this moment, Peter came to know the infinite distance between an ordinary, decent man, and the Man who shared the boat with him. But if that distance existed, it was a distance that Jesus knew how to bridge. "Don't be afraid," He said. "From now on, you'll be a fisher of *men*."

The Clear Sight of an Enemy

SOMETIMES an enemy can see a man more clearly than many of his friends do. Such an enemy was Caiaphas (KY-uh-fus), the high priest. He was an experienced politician as well as religious leader; he knew the art of keeping the nation on a more or less even keel and getting along with the Romans. He was no saint, but he was certainly a shrewd judge of men. He comes into the story after Jesus had raised Lazarus (LAZ-uh-rus) from the grave and proved that His power extended even to the dead. This miracle was, of course, talked about everywhere, and it led many people to believe in Jesus. But others, sure that He could not be genuine, took alarm and ran to Caiaphas to get his advice as to what should be done concerning this man who was disrupting their accustomed way of life.

The Sanhedrin (SAN-heh-drun) was in session — the Great Council at which important national affairs were decided. One of the Pharisees turned to the high priest. "What do you think we should do? There's no doubt about it, this man is performing many miracles. If we let Him go on this way, everybody will believe in Him. The first thing you know, there will be riots. Then the enemy legions will start marching, and the Romans will seize on the excuse to destroy the Temple and crush what little independence we have left."

Caiaphas smiled sardonically. "Isn't the answer obvious?" he drawled. "You have said that this man is stirring the people up, and it will inevitably lead to trouble with the Romans. Quite so. And war with the Romans would be suicide. So you have your answer."

"Yes?" another member of the Council asked.

"Quite simple," Caiaphas said, and flicked a speck of dust off his embroidered robe. "Quite elementary. It is better for one man to die than for a whole nation to perish."

"You mean we must get rid of Him?" an uncertain voice spoke up from somewhere in the council chamber.

"Yes," Caiaphas replied curtly. Fools made him impatient. "Yes, that's it precisely."

In all this, Caiaphas showed himself more discerning than some of Jesus' disciples. He knew that this man was no ordinary teacher. He knew that Jesus was not just a latter-day prophet, come to teach the people. He knew that something new — and dangerous — had come into the world. He knew, in short, that if Jesus were left alive and free to act, there was no way of telling what might happen. *Anything* could happen, with such a man in the world!

The Secret of Jesus

WHAT WAS THE SECRET of the effect Jesus had on friend and enemy both? The answer is that *God was acting through and in Jesus . . .* revealing Himself in this perfect human life — the life of His own divine Son. The men and women who stood in His presence somehow perceived the presence of God. If at heart they were lovers of God, they responded in one way. But if they hated God or wanted to keep Him at a "safe" distance, they responded in a different way and became the unrelenting foes of the man who made God real and inescapable to them.

Since this was the secret of His strange and disturbing power in the lives of everyone who met Him, the word *God* is also the key to the personal life of Jesus. We catch a glimpse of Him at the age of twelve, standing in the Temple and eagerly answering questions, no doubt about the nature and will of the God whose earthly home was the Temple. At around the age of thirty He reemerges, ready to begin His mission. What we see during that mission is a life absolutely centered in God. It was a life of complete trust. "My Father in Heaven" was not a distant and theoretical idea to Jesus; rather, a daily companion. Every word Jesus spoke, every deed He did, was in response to the will of His Father in Heaven. For this reason, His life had a stark directness about it. He aimed steadily at the goal set for Him by His Father — to serve as the One who would bridge the gap between God and man and reconcile mankind to its Creator and Father.

"Look at Me and See the Father"

THE AIR OF AUTHORITY in Jesus that either attracted or repelled people was there because, as He Himself put it, "I and the Father are one." This gave Him boldness in His preaching and teaching. He could cut through to the heart of question, instead of cautiously protecting Himself by a series of Biblical and rabbinical quotations. As He finished the Sermon on the Mount, the crowds were amazed — "He teaches like someone who has authority in His own right, not like one of our usual religious teachers."

Jesus praying to His Father

When Jesus taught, it was the final and ultimate Source of religious and moral truth speaking, not merely some scholar.

This was what set Jesus apart from every other teacher. When He talked, it was God teaching. This is why Jesus could say not merely, "Follow My teachings," but also "Follow Me." When He said, "Follow Me," it was the same as saying, "Follow God, who is made visible in Me."

At times, Jesus expressed this quite explicitly. In a conversation with Thomas, He said, "I am the way, and the truth, and the life"; and before Thomas — who is called the Doubter — could ask any questions, Jesus added, "The only way to come to the Father is by Me. If you had really known Me, you would have known My Father, too. If you know Me now, you know God and have seen Him."

Philip, like the other disciples, was frequently puzzled by Jesus' statements. What Jesus had just said did not seem to sink in. "Master," he pleaded, "show us the Father, and then we'll be satisfied."

Jesus spoke patiently: "Have I been with you all this long time, and you still don't know Me? Anybody who has seen Me *has* seen the Father. I am in the Father, and He is in Me."

These are the most daring words that human lips can speak. If they were false, the religious people of the time were justified in bringing charges of blasphemy against the man who spoke them. But if they were true, then the whole life and personality of Jesus stand illumined. His life is the very life of God Himself. His personality is that of the one perfect human being, illumined by the indwelling reality of God.

More Than Human, but Not Less

BUT THOUGH God moved uniquely through that life, it was still a human life. When Jesus had not eaten, He was hungry; when men closed their ears to His words, He could be hurt and angry. As a man He is one of us, sharing the common life of the human race, and knowing its joys and agonies from personal experience.

Sometimes a man's character and personality are most clearly revealed in the moments before His death. In the case of Jesus these were not moments, but the three hours He hung nailed to the Cross. While on the Cross, He spoke seven times — the "Seven Last Words" preserved by the Gospels.

The first of these utterances was spoken after the soldiers had nailed Him to the Cross and lifted it into place, between the two thieves. Looking down at the soldiers who had done their ghastly duty and were now casting lots for His outer clothing, and gazing beyond them at the little crowd, and beyond it to the gleaming roofs of Jerusalem, His first thought was not of Himself. A pain that was more than physical twisted through Him. It was pain at the blindness of the men who thought they were serving God or country by bringing Him to the Cross. "Father," He prayed softly, "forgive them. They do not really know what they are doing!"

Two Criminals at Odds

DURING the three hours on the Cross, the ministry of Jesus continued. He had two close companions, the two thieves. One of them was hardened and embittered, and, like many better citizens, was outraged by the very presence of Jesus. "So You're the Messiah, huh?" he snarled between groans. "All right, let's see what You can do. Come on down from that Cross and save us!"

But the other thief responded in the opposite way. He leaned as far as he could toward the first one and said, "Shut up! We're getting what's coming to us. But this fellow here — He's all right. What harm has He done to anyone? Leave Him alone." Then he turned his head toward Jesus and addressed Him in a softer tone. "I hope You'll remember me when you become a king."

Jesus did not seem surprised. "I promise you," He said. "Today you will be with Me in paradise."

Time passed. Below Him He could see His mother and His Aunt Mary, the wife of Clopas (KLO-pas). Mary Magdalene (MAG-duh-leen) was also there, and John was close by.

What would happen to His mother? There had been little time to be with her during the packed and turbulent months that lay behind Him. But He could not leave her helpless. "Mother," He called.

She looked up and tried to smile.

"There is your son," He said, nodding toward John.

Then He turned His head as much as He could toward John. "There is your mother," He said, now nodding toward Mary. With a sigh of relief, He saw that John had moved over to stand beside Mary; now He could brace Himself in some kind of peace for the minutes or hours that stretched ahead.

The fourth "word" was perhaps the most terrible of all. "My God, My God, why hast Thou forsaken Me?" He cried from the Cross. In an awful moment, the realization of God's nearness faded. One of our modern writers explains it thus: "He was without sin, yet He chose to take upon Himself the sins of mankind. He must experience the worst consequence of sin, namely, alienation from God."

This was not only an anguished personal cry from Jesus' own heart. He was reciting, too, the beginning of Psalm 22, which opens with this tragic question· "My God, My God, why hast Thou forsaken Me?" And we note that this Psalm moves from the initial question toward a triumphant affirmation of the victory of God over all enemies:

> All the ends of the earth shall remember
> and turn to the Lord;
> and all the families of the nations
> shall worship before Him.
> For dominion belongs to the Lord,
> and He rules over the nations.

The fifth utterance is simply "I am thirsty." It is a reminder that though Jesus was more than a mere man, He was not less. Nailed in the hot sun, hanging on the Cross hour after hour, He shared the physical nature of all human beings. He knew pain and thirst.

At last the merciful end drew near. "It is finished," He said. He bowed His head as though in assent, and prepared for death. His mission had been accomplished. It had been accomplished not merely by His life, but equally by His Cross and His approaching death. He had done what God had sent Him forth to do.

The Last Word

I T WAS now about mid-afternoon. The brightness had suddenly faded from the sky. One could no longer see the gleaming roofs of Jerusalem. The soldiers, bored with their long wait, fidgeted uneasily in the premature gloaming. Suddenly they leaped up as the Man on the Cross cried out in a loud voice, "Father, into Thy hands I commit My spirit!" By the time they reached Him He was silent, and when they touched Him He showed no sign of life.

The Roman captain who had supervised the Crucifixion spoke the last word. Thoughtfully looking up at the silent figure on the Cross, he slowly said, "There's no doubt about it, this man was innocent."

He said nothing more for a moment, but finally found the words he needed. He turned to the soldiers around him:

"This man," he said, and paused, "This man was indeed God's Son."

(continued from page 372)
because of these things. The mind of Christ is that which takes every reason for exaltation and transmutes it into a reason for selfless service. In essence His humility was His refusal to please Himself. He came not to be ministered unto but to minister.

Our Lord's character is crowned with perfection or *sinlessness*. This perfection was not simply the absence of sin, but the infusion of a heavenly holiness into all that He said and did. It may be objected that when Jesus gave way to anger and spoke out in bitter denunciation of the Pharisees (Matt. 23) that He revealed at least a trace of imperfection. But a character without the power of righteous indignation would be faulty. If Jesus had failed to expose these men He would not have done His full duty as the exponent of truth. He is the image of the Father, and God is angry with the wicked every day.

V. Influence. A life so brief, so confined in its geographical orbit, so little noticed by the world in His own time, has yet become the most potent force for good in all of human history. This is seen in the *Scriptures* of the NT. In every single book which goes to make up this collection, Jesus Christ is the inevitable point of reference. Even so brief and personal a writing as Philemon owes its inspiration to the Son of God who came to make men free. The Gospels picture Him in the flesh; the Epistles present Him in the Spirit. The Acts of the Apostles depicts the victories of His grace in the extension of His Church; the Revelation sets forth the triumph of His glory through His personal presence once more in history.

His influence upon the *saints* is so radical and comprehensive that nothing can describe it better than the assertion that Christ is their life. They were not truly living until they came to know Him by faith. Until He comes into the heart, self rules supreme. When He comes, He creates a new point of reference and a new set of values. To be Christ-centered is simply normal Christian experience.

What Christ can do in transforming a life may be seen to good advantage in the case of Saul of Tarsus. Apart from Christ the world might never have heard of him. Because in Christ he died to self and lived in the energy of the risen Christ to glorify God, his is a household name wherever Christians are found.

It is inevitable that *sinners* should feel the touch of Christ and never be the same afterward. Regarding the self-righteous leaders of His own time Jesus could say, "If I had not come and spoken unto them, they had not had sin; but now they have no cloke for their sin" (John 15:22). Christ is the conscience of the world. Because He is the light of the world, when men stand in that light then turn from it, they walk in deeper darkness and are without hope.

In a more general sense, Christ has mightily affected *society* in its organized state. He has taught the world the dignity of human life, the worth of the soul, the preciousness of personality. Because of this the status of women has steadily been improved under Christian influence, slavery has been abolished, and children, instead of being exposed as infants and neglected in formative years, are recognized as a primary responsibility for the lavishing of love and care. Human life, when weak or deformed or diseased, is no longer regarded as forfeiting a right to a place in society, but rather

entitled to help. The fact that governments and scientific groups are now engaged in social service on a large scale ought not to disguise the fact that the impulse for these works of mercy has been the Christian church acting in the name and spirit of Christ. The arts owe their sublimest achievements to the desire to honor the Son of God. Beethoven called Handel the greatest composer of all time, a man who could not complete his oratorio *The Messiah* without being moved repeatedly to tears as he thought upon the incarnation. Every cathedral spire that pierces the sky throughout Christendom bears its silent testimony to the loving outreach toward God that is induced through the knowledge of Christ the Lord. Moralists and philosophers, even when they lack faith in Him for the saving of the soul, nevertheless are often found acknowledging wistfully that they wish they had a personal inheritance in Him as they commend Him to others as the one great hope for mankind.   E.F.H.

CHRISTIAN (krĭs'chăn, krĭst'yăn, Gr. *Christianós*). The Biblical meaning is "adherent of Christ." The disciples were formally called Christians first in Antioch (Acts 11:26). Agrippa recognized that to believe what Paul preached would make him a Christian (Acts 26:28). Peter accepted the name as in itself basis for persecution (I Pet. 4:16). Thus gradually a name imposed by Gentiles was adopted by the disciples of Jesus. Some Jews had referred to them as "the sect of the Nazarenes" (Acts 24:5); and Paul, when a persecutor, as those "of the Way" (Acts 9:2). The Latin termination *ianós*, widely used throughout the empire, often designated the slaves of the one with whose name it was compounded. This implication occurs in the NT (e.g., Rom. 6:22; I Pet. 2:16). The apostles wrote of themselves as servants (slaves) of Christ (Rom. 1:1; James 1:1; II Pet. 1:1; Jude 1:1; Rev. 1:1). The NT calls the followers of Christ *brethren* (Acts 14:2); *disciples* (Acts 6:1,2); *saints* (Acts 9:13; Rom. 1:7; I Cor. 1:2); *believers* (I Tim. 4:12); *the church of God* (Acts 20:28); *those that call upon the name of the Lord* (Acts 9:14; Rom. 10:12,13); etc. To the first Christians, their own name mattered not at all: their concern was with the one Name of Jesus Christ (Acts 3:16; 4: 10,12; 5:28). Inevitably, the name which they invoked was given to them: Christians, Christ's men. Its NT meaning is alone adequate for us.   E.R.

CHRISTIANITY (krĭs'chĭ-ăn'ĭtē, krĭs'tĭ-ăn'ĭ-tē). The word does not occur in the Bible. Greek *Christianismós*, "Christianism," Christianity, was first used by Ignatius (*Ad Magnes* 10). Latin *Christianismus* occurs in Tertullian, *Against Marcion* 4, 33; in Augustine, *The City of God*, 19, 21, 1; and Jerome, on Galatians 6:4. Latin *Christianitas*, whence our word Christianity, occurs first in the *Codex Theodosianus* 16, 7, 7 and 12, 1, 112; and by metonymy for the Christian clergy, 12, 1, 123. The name was made by Christians to designate all that which Jesus Christ brought to them of faith, life and salvation. Its character is summed up in the words of Jesus, "I am the way, the truth, and the life: no man cometh unto the Father but by me" (John 14:6); "I am come that they might have life, and that they might have it more abundantly" (John 10:10). The classic summary of its doctrines is in the words of Paul in I Corinthians 15:1-4. It is all "according to the scriptures": OT and NT together form the authoritative revelation of what Christianity is. The resurrection of Jesus was the final proof to His disciples that He is the Messiah and Redeemer of men (Acts 2:22-36).

CHRISTMAS (krĭs'măs, krĭst'măs), the anniversary of the birth of Christ, and its observance; celebrated by most Protestants and by Roman Catholics on December 25; by Eastern Orthodox churches on January 6; and by the Armenian church on January 19. The first mention of its observance on December 25 is in the time of Constantine, about A.D. 325. The date of the birth of Christ is not known. The word Christmas is formed of Christ + Mass, meaning a mass of religious service in commemoration of the birth of Christ. Whether the early Christians thought of or observed Christmas is not clear. Once introduced, the observance spread throughout Christendom. Some Christian bodies disapprove of the festival. Many customs of pagan origin have become part of Christmas, e.g., the Christmas tree; but most of these no longer have a heathen connotation, but have acquired a Christian meaning (e.g., the Christmas tree points upward to God and reminds us of His gifts). A commemoration of the birth of Christ in harmonious keeping with the events surrounding that birth (Luke 2:1-20; Matt. 1:18-2:12) is a natural and normal expression of love and reverence for Jesus Christ.   E.R.

CHRONICLES, I and II, are called in Hebrew, *diverê ha-yāmîm*, "The words (affairs) of the days," meaning "The annals" (cf. I Chron. 27:24). Similar annals, now lost, are mentioned in I and II Kings (for example, I Kings 14:19,29); they cannot, however, consist of our present books, which were not written until a century later. The church father Jerome (A.D. 400) first entitled them, "Chronicles." Originally, they formed a single composition, but were divided into I and II Chronicles in the LXX, about 150 B.C. In the Hebrew, they stand as the last books of the OT canon. Christ (Luke 11:51) thus spoke of all the martyrs from Abel, in the first book (Gen. 4), to Zechariah, in the last (II Chron. 24).

Chronicles contains no statements about its own authorship or date. The last event it records is the decree of Cyrus in 538 B.C., which permitted the Jews to return from their Babylonian captivity (II Chron. 36:22); and its genealogies extend to approximately 500 B.C., as far, that is, as to Pelatiah and Jeshaiah (I Chron. 3:21), two grandsons of Zerubbabel, the prince who led in the return from exile. The language, however, and the contents of Chronicles closely parallel that of the book of Ezra, which continues the history of the Jews from the decree of Cyrus down to 457 B.C. Both documents are marked by lists and genealogies, by an interest in priestly ritual, and by devotion to the law of Moses. The closing verses, moreover, of Chronicles (II 36:22-23) are repeated as the opening verses of Ezra (1:1-3a). Ancient Hebrew tradition and the modern scholarship of Wm. F. Albright (JBL 40 [1921], pp. 104-124) therefore unite in suggesting that Ezra may have been the author of both volumes. His complete work would then have been finished some time around 450 B.C. (See CYRUS.)

Ezra's position as a "scribe" (Ezra 7:6) may also explain the care that Chronicles shows in acknowledging its written source materials. These include such records as those of Samuel (I Chron. 29:29) and Isaiah (II Chron. 32:32) and a number of other prophets (II 9:29; 12:15; 20:34; 33:

19) and, above all else, "The book of the kings of Judah and Israel" (16:11; 25:26; etc.). This latter work cannot be equated with our present-day I-II Kings, for verses such as I Chronicles 9:1 and II 27:7 refer to "The book of the kings" for further details on matters about which I-II Kings is silent. The author's source must have been a larger court record, now lost, from which both Kings and Chronicles subsequently drew much of their information.

The occasion for the writing of Chronicles appears to be that of Ezra's crusade to bring postexilic Judah back into conformity with the law of Moses (Ezra 7:10). From 458 B.C. and onward, Ezra sought to restore the temple worship (7:19-23,27; 8:33-34), to eliminate the mixed marriages of Jews with their pagan neighbors (9-10), and to strengthen Jerusalem by rebuilding its walls (4:8-16). Chronicles, accordingly, consists of these four parts: genealogies, to enable the Jews to establish their lines of family descent (I Chron. 1-9); the kingdom of David, as a pattern for the ideal theocratic state (I Chron. 10-29); the glory of Solomon, with an emphasis upon the temple and its worship (II Chron. 1-9); and the history of the southern kingdom, stressing in particular the religious reforms and military victories of Judah's more pious rulers (II Chron. 10-36).

As compared with the parallel histories in Samuel and Kings, the priestly annals of Chronicles lay a greater emphasis upon the structure of the temple (I Chron. 22) and upon Israel's ark, the Levites, and the singers (I Chron. 13, 15-16). They omit, however, certain individualistic, moral acts of the kings (II Sam. 9; I Kings 3:16-28), as well as detailed biographies of the prophets (I Kings 17-22:28; II Kings 1-8:15), features which account for the incorporation of Chronicles into the third (non-prophetic) section of the Hebrew canon, as distinguished from the location of the more homiletical books of Samuel and Kings in the second (prophetic) division. Finally, the chronicler foregoes discussion of David's disputed inauguration and later shame (II Sam. 1-4, 11-21), of Solomon's failures (I Kings 11), and of the whole inglorious history of Saul (I Sam. 8-30, except his death, 31) and of the northern kingdom of Israel: the disillusioned, impoverished Jews of 450 B.C. knew enough of sin and defeat; but they needed an encouraging reminder of their former, God-given victories (as II Chron. 13,14,20,25).

Because of these emphases, many modern critics have rejected Chronicles as being Levitical propaganda, a fiction of "what ought to have happened" (IB, III:341), with extensive (and conflicting) revisions as late as 250 B.C. (so Adam C. Welch, Robert F. Pfeiffer, and W. A. L. Elmslie). The book's high numeric totals (such as the 1,000,000 invading Ethiopians, II Chron. 14:9) are subject to particular ridicule, despite the elucidations that have been presented by believing scholars (see Edward J. Young, *An Introduction to the Old Testament*, Grand Rapids: Eerdmans, 1949, pp. 388-390). Liberal writers, however, with their prior repudiation of the Mosaic origin of OT religion, are simply unable to evaluate Chronicles in an objective fashion: its repeated validations of the ceremonies of the Pentateuch leave them no alternative but to deny its historicity. Yet excavations at Ugarit, a Canaanitish city of Moses' day, have confirmed the authenticity of just such religious practices (see J. W. Jack, *The Ras Shamra Tablets:*

their Bearings on the Old Testament, Edinburgh: T. & T. Clark, 1935, p. 29ff); and Albright observes that the reliability of many of the historical statements that are found only in Chronicles has been established by recent archaeological discovery (BASOR 100 [1945], p. 18). Furthermore, though Chronicles does stress the bright side of Hebrew history, it does not deny the defeats (cf. I Chron. 29:22 on the successful *second* anointing of Solomon and II Chron. 17:3 on the more exemplary *first* ways of David). The prophetic judgments of Kings and the priestly hopes of Chronicles are both true, and both are necessary. The morality of the former is invaluable, but the redemption of the latter constitutes the more distinctive feature of Christian faith.   J.B.P.

CHRONOLOGY, NEW TESTAMENT, the science of determining the dates of the NT books and the historical events mentioned therein. The subject is beset with serious difficulty since sufficient data are often lacking and the computations must be based upon ancient documents which did not record historical events under precise calendar dates like modern historical records. Neither sacred nor secular historians of that time were accustomed to record history under exact dates but felt that all demands were satisfied when some specific event was related to a well-known period, as, the reign of a noted ruler, or the time of some famous contemporary. Luke's method of dating the beginning of the ministry of John the Baptist (Luke 3:1,2) is typical of the historian's method of that day. Further, the use of different local chronologies and different ways of computing years often leave the results tentative. NT chronology naturally falls into two parts: the life of Christ, and the apostolic age.

Life of Christ. The erection of a chronology of the life of Christ turns around three points: His birth, baptism, and crucifixion. Luke's statement of the age of Jesus at His baptism (Luke 3:23) links the first two, while the problem of the length of the ministry links the second and third.

The Christian Era, now used almost exclusively in the Western World for civil chronology, was introduced at Rome by Abbot Dionysius Exiguus in the sixth century. It is now generally agreed that the beginning of the era should have been fixed at least four years earlier.

According to the Gospels Jesus was born some time before the death of Herod the Great. Josephus, the Jewish historian, who was born A.D. 37, affirms (*Ant.* XVII,6,4) that Herod died shortly after an eclipse of the moon, which is astronomically fixed at March 12-13, 4 B.C. His death occurred shortly before Passover, which that year fell on April 4. His death in 4 B.C. is also confirmed from the known commencement of the rule of his three sons in that year. The age of Jesus at Herod's death is not certain. The "two years" for the age of the children slain at Bethlehem (Matt. 2:16) offers no sure indication, since Herod would allow a liberal margin for safety, and since part of a year might be counted as a year. It does show that Jesus was born at least some months before Herod's death. Christ's presentation in the temple after He was 40 days old (Luke 2:22-24; Lev. 12:1-8) makes it certain that the wise men came at least six weeks after His birth. The time spent in Egypt is uncertain, but may have been several months. Thus the birth of Jesus should be placed in the latter part of the year 5 B.C.

Luke's statement (3:1,2) that Jesus was born in connection with the "first enrollment" when "Quirinius was governor of Syria" (ASV) was once fiercely assailed as erroneous, since Cyrenius (AV), or Quirinius, was known to be governor in connection with the census of A.D. 6. But it is now known that he was also connected with the Syrian government at some previous time. Papyrus evidence shows that Augustus inaugurated a periodic census every 14 years, from 8 B.C. onward. Herod's war with the king of Arabia, his troubles with Augustus, as well as the problem of the method of taking the census among the Jews, may have delayed the actual census in Palestine several years, bringing it down to the year 5 B.C.

Luke gives the age of Jesus at His baptism as "about thirty years" (3:23). Although the statement of age is not specific, it naturally implies that His age was just about 30, a few months under or over. Born in the latter part of 5 B.C., His baptism then occurred near the close of A.D. 26 or the beginning of 27. The 40-day period of the temptation, plus the events recorded in John 1:19-2:12 seem to require that the baptism occurred at least three months before the first Passover of His public ministry (John 2:13-22). Since Herod began the reconstruction of the temple in 20 B.C., the "forty and six years" mentioned by the Jews during this Passover, using the inclusive Jewish count, again brings us to A.D. 27 for this first Passover.

Apparently John began his ministry some six months before the baptism of Jesus. Luke dates that beginning as "in the fifteenth year of the reign of Tiberius Caesar" (3:1). Augustus died in August of A.D. 14, but 15 years added to that would be two years too late for our previous dates. Since Tiberius had been reigning jointly with Augustus in the provinces for two years before his death, it seems only natural that Luke would follow the provincial point of view and count the 15 years from the time of Tiberius' actual assumption of authority in the provinces. Thus counted, the date is in harmony with our other dates. The ministry of John, begun about six months before the baptism of Jesus, commenced about the middle of A.D. 26.

The time of the crucifixion will be determined by the length of the ministry of Jesus. Mark's Gospel seems to require at least two years: the plucking of the ears of grain (April-June) marks a first spring; the feeding of the 5,000 when the grass was fresh green (March-April), a second; the Passover of the crucifixion, a third. John's Gospel explicitly mentions three Passovers (2:23; 6:4; 11:55). If the feast of 5:1 is also a Passover, as seems probable, a view having the traditional backing of Irenaeus, then the length of the ministry of Jesus was full three years and a little over. This places the crucifixion at the Passover of A.D. 30.

Apostolic Age. Due to the uncertainties connected with the limited data for an apostolic chronology, authorities have arrived at varied dates. The Book of Acts with its many notes of time, mostly indefinite, offers but few points for the establishment of even relatively fixed dates. Even Paul's apparently precise chronological notes in Galatians 1:18 and 2:1 leave us in doubt as to whether "after three years" and "after the space of fourteen years" are to be regarded as consecutive or as both counting from his conversion. The death of Herod Agrippa I (Acts 12:23) and the proconsulship of

This hand tool was the kind used in the homes in Palestine to grind bread for daily use. The flour was ground between the two revolving stones.

This wooden bowl was used as a trough in which wheat flour was mixed with water and kneaded prior to baking on heated sand or flat stones.

This carpenter's shop in Palestine probably resembles the one in which Jesus worked for fifteen years. A carpenter in Jesus' time was responsible not only for all woodworking but cut the trees for the wood himself.

This street scene in the town of Cana, about two hours distance from Nazareth, shows the cube-shaped houses so typical of Palestine. In Cana Jesus performed his first miracle, changing water into wine at the wedding feast.

"And they that had laid hold on Jesus
led him away to Caiaphas the high
priest, where the scribes and the
elders were assembled."
(MATTHEW 26:57)

Jesus was taken prisoner in the Garden of Gethsemane, which
is approximately in the middle of the picture. He was led into
the Kidron Valley and then up the slope on the right, where
the palace of Caiaphas the high priest was supposed to have
stood among the group of houses at the right.

"And as they led him away, they laid hold upon one Simon, a Cyrenian, coming out of the country, and on him they laid the cross, that he might bear it after Jesus."
(LUKE 23:26)

This is a view into the old alley of the Old City in Jerusalem, the Via Dolorosa. This was the route along which Jesus was taken with His cross on the way to the hill called Calvary and the crucifixion.

Gallio (Acts 18:12) are important for the chronology of the period.

The death of Herod Agrippa I, one of the fixed dates of the New Testament, is known to have taken place in A.D. 44. It establishes the year of Peter's arrest and miraculous escape from prison. The proconsulship of Gallio is also strongly relied upon for an apostolic chronology. A fragmentary inscription found at Delphi associates his proconsulship with the 26th acclamation of Claudius as Imperator. This would place his proconsulship between May 51 and 52, or May 52 and 53. The latter date is more probable since Gallio would assume office in May and not in midsummer as some advocates of the earlier date assumed. Since apparently Paul had already been at Corinth a year and a half when Gallio arrived, his ministry at Corinth began in the latter part of A.D. 50. Efforts to determine the time of the accession of Festus as governor, under whom Paul was sent to Rome, have not resulted in agreement. From the inconclusive data advocates have argued for a date as early as A.D. 55 and as late as 60 or 61. The balance of the arguments seems to point to 60, or perhaps 59.

If the latter, the suggested dates should be adjusted accordingly.

Chronological Table. The dates for many NT events must remain tentative, but as indicated by Luke (3:1,2), they have a definite correlation with secular history. (See the accompanying diagram). The following chronological table is regarded as approximately correct. The dates for the NT literature assume a conservative viewpoint.

Birth of Jesus	5 B.C.
Baptism of Jesus	late A.D. 26 or early 27
First Passover of Ministry	27
Crucifixion of Jesus	30
Conversion of Saul	34 or 35
Death of Herod Agrippa I	44
Epistle of James	before 50
First Missionary journey	48-49
Jerusalem Conference	49 or 50
Second Missionary journey	begun spring 50
Paul at Corinth	50-52
I and II Thessalonians from Corinth	51
Galatians from Corinth (?)	early 52
Arrival of Gallio as Proconsul	May 52

Chronological Chart of the New Testament

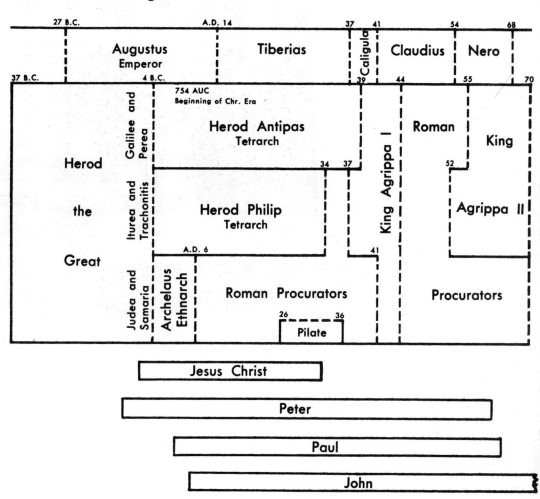

Third Missionary journey	begun 54
Paul at Ephesus	54-57
I Corinthians from Ephesus	spring 57
II Corinthians from Macedonia	fall 57
Romans from Corinth	winter 57-58
Paul's arrest at Jerusalem	Pentecost 58
Imprisonment at Caesarea	58-60
On Island of Malta	winter 60-61
Arrival at Rome	spring 61
Roman Imprisonment	61-63
Colossians, Philemon, Ephesians	summer 62
Philippians	spring 63
Paul's release and further work	63-65
I Timothy and Titus	63
Epistle to the Hebrews	64
Synoptic Gospels and Acts	before 64
I and II Peter from Rome	64-65
Peter's death at Rome	65
Paul's second Roman imprisonment	66
II Timothy	66
Death at Rome	late 66 or early 67
Epistle of Jude	67-68
Writings of John	before 100
Death of John	98-100
	D.E.H.

CHRONOLOGY, OLD TESTAMENT. The chronology of the Old Testament presents many complex and difficult problems. The data are not always adequate or clear, and at times are almost completely lacking. Because of insufficient data many of the problems are at present beyond solution. Even where the data are abundant the exact meaning is often not immediately apparent, leaving scope for considerable difference of opinion and giving rise to many variant chronological reconstructions. The chronological problem is thus one of the availability of evidence, of the correct evaluation and interpretation of that evidence, and of its proper application. Only the most careful study of all the data, both Biblical and extra-Biblical, can hope to provide a satisfactory solution.

FROM THE CREATION TO THE DELUGE. From the creation to the deluge the only Biblical data are the ages of the patriarchs in the genealogical tables of Genesis 5 and 7:11. The Masoretic text gives 1,656 years from Adam to the deluge; the Samaritan Pentateuch gives 1,307 years, and the Septuagint, 2,242. The numbers of the MT are in agreement with the Samaritan except in the cases of Jared, Methuselah, and Lamech, where the numbers of the MT are higher by 100 years, 120, and 129 respectively. For the eight patriarchs from Adam to Methuselah, the numbers of the LXX are a century higher in each instance than those of the Samaritan, while for Lamech the number is 135 years higher.

Extra-Biblical sources for this period are almost completely lacking. The early Sumerian king list names eight kings with a total of 241,200 years from the time when "the kingship was lowered from heaven" to the time when "the Flood swept" over the land and once more "the kingship was lowered from heaven." (Thorkild Jacobsen, *The Sumerian King List,* Chicago: The University of Chicago Press, 1939, pp. 71, 77). Such a statement, however, makes no practical contribution to the solution of this phase of OT chronology. Nor is modern science in a position to supply a detailed and final solution.

The Deluge to Abraham. For the period from the deluge to Abraham we are again dependent upon the genealogical data in the Greek and Hebrew texts, and the Samaritan Pentateuch. Reckoning the age of Terah at the birth of Abraham as 70 (Gen. 11:26), the years from the deluge to Abraham would be 292 according to the MT, 942 according to the Samaritan Pentateuch, and 1172 according to the LXX. But if the age of Terah at Abraham's birth is reckoned as 130 years (on the basis of Gen. 11:32; 12:4; and Acts 7:4), the above totals would be raised by 60 years. On this basis the Hebrew text would give 352 years from the deluge to Abraham, and the Greek, 1232.

In this area the testimony of the MT stands alone against the LXX and the Samaritan Pentateuch, where the numbers are 100 years higher than those of the MT for Arphaxad, Salah, Eber, Peleg, Reu, and Serug, while for Nahor, the grandfather of Abraham, the Samaritan is 50 years higher and LXX 150, than the MT.

Serious chronological difficulties are thus encountered in the period immediately beyond Abraham. Abraham was 86 years old at the birth of Ishmael (Gen. 16:16), and 100 at the birth of Isaac (Gen. 21:5). But how old was Terah at the birth of Abraham, 70, 130, or some number not revealed? And how old was Nahor at the birth of Terah, 29, 79, or 179? If Terah was 130 years old at the birth of Abraham, as seems to be indicated by the Biblical evidence, it must be admitted that the numbers of the Septuagint for this period (135, 130,130,134,130,132,130,179,130), are much more consistent with each other than the numbers of the Hebrew (35,30,34,30,32,30,29,130). But it will be noticed that in the case of nine patriarchs in the Septuagint, five of them were 130 years old when their sons were born, while in the Hebrew three out of eight were 30, one was 130, while the others were all in their thirties with the exception of Nahor who was 29—one year from 30. And if Terah was 130 years old when Abraham was born, why should it have been regarded as so very unusual for Abraham to have a son at the age of 100 (Gen. 17:17; 18:11; 21:2,5)?

An endeavor to assess the relative values of the three sources involved accomplishes little, for the indications are that none is altogether complete. Certainly the LXX had great weight in NT times, for in Luke's table of the ancestors of Christ, there is listed a second Cainan, son of Arphaxad (Luke 3:36), in harmony with the LXX of Gen. 11:12,13 —a name not found in the MT. If the LXX is here to be followed rather than the MT, another 130 years should be added to the years of the deluge and creation, for that is the age of Cainan in the LXX at the time of the birth of Salah.

The omission of the names of known individuals is frequent in Biblical genealogical records. Thus Matthew's table of the ancestors of Christ omits the names of three Judean kings—Ahaziah, Joash, and Amaziah—with the statement that "Joram begat Ozias" (Matt. 1:8), whereas Uzziah was actually the great-great-grandson of Joram. A comparison of Ezra 7:1-5 with I Chronicles 6:4-15 shows a block of six names missing in Ezra's tabulation.

Extra-Biblical materials from the deluge to Abraham are of little assistance in the establishment of an absolute chronology for this period, but there is sufficient evidence to show that the time involved is much greater than that indicated by the genealogical data of the MT. No exact synchronisms exist between Biblical and secular chronology of this period, and the exact chronology of Mesopotamia and Egypt has not yet been established.

Because of the difficulties involved, it must be admitted that the construction of an absolute chronology from Adam to Abraham is not now possible on the basis of the available data.

Abraham to Moses. From Abraham to Joseph the detailed patriarchal narratives provide more data than are available for the preceding periods, and we have the certainty that there are no missing links. There are, also, a number of correlations with later and better known periods. Since Abraham was 75 years old at the time of his entrance into Canaan (Gen. 12:4), and since he was 100 at the birth of Isaac (Gen. 21:5), there were 25 years from the entry into Canaan to Isaac. Isaac was 60 at the birth of Jacob (Gen. 25:26), and Jacob was 130 at his entrance into Egypt (Gen. 47:9,28), making 215 years from the beginning of the sojourn in Canaan to the beginning of the sojourn in Egypt. The total length of the sojourn was 430 years (Exod. 12:40). Did this involve only the sojourn in Egypt or did it include also the sojourn in Canaan? If Israel was in Egypt 430 years, there were 645 years from the entrance into Canaan to the Exodus. Otherwise there were 430 years from Abraham's entry into Canaan to Moses' departure from Egypt, and the length of the Egyptian sojourn would have been only 215 years.

According to I Kings 6:1 the temple was founded in the 480th year after the Exodus, which was the fourth year of Solomon's reign. On the basis of a 40-year reign for Solomon (I Kings 11:42) and in accord with the established chronology of the kings, that was 966 B.C. This would provide 1445 as the date of the Exodus and 1525 as the year of Moses' birth (Exod. 7:7). If the 430-year sojourn involved only the period in Egypt, Abraham entered Canaan in 2090. If it included the years in Canaan, the date was 1875. The answer depends on the meaning of the prophecy of Genesis 15:13-16 and the reconstruction of the details from Abraham to Moses. From Abraham to Joseph the details are known, but from Joseph to Moses there is only genealogical evidence.

Due to omissions, repetitions, and other variations in the genealogical lists, the endeavor to establish times by the evidence of such lists must be regarded as highly precarious. Compare, for instance, the line of descent of Samuel and his sons from Levi and Kohath as recorded in I Chronicles 6:22-28 and in verses 33-38, and see I Samuel 8:2 for the names of these sons. Compare also the various lists of the sons of Benjamin and their descendants as found in Genesis 46:21; Numbers 26:38-40; I Chronicles 7:6-12; and 8:1-40. The variations in existence here and in many other lists indicate the dangers involved in dogmatic reconstructions based only on genealogical evidence.

The ancestry of Moses from Jacob through Levi, Kohath, and Amram is repeatedly given (Num. 3:17-19; 26:57-59; I Chron. 6:1-3; 23:6, 12,13), including the ages of these patriarchs at the time of death (Exod. 6:16,18,20), but the ages at the time of their sons' births are not recorded. Jochebed, the wife of Amram and mother of Moses, is said to have been the sister of Kohath, son of Levi and father of Moses (Exod. 6: 16,18,20), and to have been born to Levi in Egypt

(Num. 26:59). This might appear to be conclusive evidence of a comparatively brief period in Egypt and to make a sojourn there of 430 years impossible. But there are difficulties. While four to five generations from Jacob to Moses may be indicated in the above line of descent, 11 generations may be counted from Jacob to Joshua (I Chron. 7:20-27). And that some considerable period was involved is clear from the fact that Joseph before his death saw the children of the third generation of both his sons (Gen. 50:23), and that at the time of the Exodus Amram and his brothers were already regarded as founders of clans (Num. 3:27).

Levi was the elder brother of Joseph and must have been born not more than ten years before Joseph (Gen. 29:30-34; 30:22-43; 31:41). Since Joseph was 30 when he stood before Pharaoh (Gen. 41:46), and since seven years of plenty and two years of famine had passed at the time of Jacob's entry into Egypt (Gen. 41:47,53; 45:6), Joseph would have been 39 when Jacob was 130 (Gen. 47:9,28), and would thus have been born when Jacob was 91. That, however, would have made Jacob an old man of about 80 at the time of his marriage and the birth of his firstborn. That is possible but hardly probable. In view of the frequency of the numbers of 30 or 130 in age lists of Biblical patriarchs, and in view of the significance of the number 30 in connection with the Sed Festival in Egypt honoring a ruler on the 30th anniversary of his appointment as heir to the crown, the question might well be raised as to whether 130 as the age of Jacob is employed in an absolute sense. If not, the chronological reckonings based upon it are only approximate and not absolute.

It should also be noticed that if the sojourn in Egypt was 215 years and if there were only four generations from Jacob to Moses, then Levi must have been about 100 at the birth of Jochebed, and Jochebed 84 at the birth of Moses. Since the birth of Isaac to Sarah when she was 90 and to Abraham when he was 100 was regarded as in the nature of a miracle (Gen. 17:17; 18:11-14; Rom. 4:19), these ages are hardly probable.

On the basis of the Old Testament data it is impossible to give a categorical answer as to exactly what was involved in the 430-year sojourn, nor is it possible to give an absolute date for Abraham's entry into Canaan. Paul regarded the 430 years as beginning at the time when the promises were made to Abraham (Gen. 12:1-4) and terminating with the giving of the law at Sinai (Gal. 3:16,17). On this basis the date of the entry into Canaan and the beginning of the sojourn was 1875.

An Exodus date of 1445 calls for 1405 as the beginning of the conquest (Num. 33:38; Deut. 1:3; Josh. 5:6). According to these dates the Exodus took place during the reigns of the famous rulers of Egypt's Eighteenth Dynasty, c. 1570-1325. This fits in well with the Habiru inroads of the Amarna period and with the evidence of Israel's presence in Palestine during the Nineteenth Dynasty, c. 1325-1200. In view of recent evidence of a sedentary occupation of Trans-Jordan from the end of the Middle Bronze Age, c. 1550 B.C., to the end of the Late Bronze Age, c. 1250 (see G. Lankester Harding, "Recent Discoveries in Jordan," *Palestine Exploration Quarterly,* Jan.-June, 1958, pp. 10-12), the view that non-occupation of that area from the 18th to the 13th centuries B.C. makes a 15th century date for the Exodus impossible, is no longer tenable.

The Conquest to the Kingdom. The establishment of absolute dates from Moses through Joshua and the judges to the setting up of the monarchy is again not possible with the available data. With the date 1405 for the beginning of the conquest, we secure 1399 as the year when Caleb received his inheritance, since he was 40 when he was sent as a spy from Kadesh-barnea (Josh. 14:7) in the second year after the departure from Egypt (Num. 10:11,12; Deut. 2:14), and he was 85 when he received his inheritance 45 years later (Josh. 14:10). The date of Joshua's death can not be given, for we do not know how old he was when he was sent as a spy, although he was 110 when he died (Josh. 24:29).

Many attempts have been made to set dates for the judges, but with the data now available an accurate chronology for this period is at present impossible. The data are as follows:

	Reference	Years
Oppression under Cushan-rishathaim	Judg. 3:8	8
Deliverance under Othniel; rest	Judg. 3:11	40
Oppression under Eglon of Moab	Judg. 3:14	18
Deliverance by Ehud; rest	Judg. 3:30	80
Oppression under Jabin of Hazor	Judg. 4:3	20
Deliverance under Deborah; rest	Judg. 5:31	40
Oppression under Midian	Judg. 6:1	7
Deliverance under Gideon; rest	Judg. 8:28	40
Reign of Abimelech	Judg. 9:22	3
Judgeship of Tola	Judg. 10:2	23
Judgeship of Jair	Judg. 10:3	22
Oppression of Gilead by Ammon	Judg. 10:8	18
Judgeship of Jephthah	Judg. 12:7	6
Judgeship of Ibzan	Judg. 12:9	7
Judgeship of Elon	Judg. 12:11	10
Judgeship of Abdon	Judg. 12:14	8
Oppression under the Philistines	Judg. 13:1	40
Judgeship of Samson	Judg. 15:20; 16:31	20
Judgeship of Eli	I Sam. 4:18	40

The sum of the above numbers is 450 years. But there is no evidence that that is the actual length of the judges' period. The judgeship of Samuel is not included in the above total because the years are not given. That these terms of judgeships and oppressions should be regarded as consecutive is mere conjecture. A number of the judges were unquestionably local rulers, exercising control over limited areas while others held office in other parts of the land. This was the case with Jephthah who ruled over Gilead (Judg. 10:18; 11:5-11; 12:4). Judgeships and oppressions at times overlapped as with Samson who "judged Israel in the days of the Philistines twenty years" (Judg. 15:20). Two oppressions might have been simultaneous in different parts of the land, as with the Ammonites in the NE and the Philistines in the SW (Judg. 10:6,7). The numerous 40's or multiples and submultiples of 40 (40,80,20,40,40,10,40,20,40) are no doubt to be taken as round rather than absolute numbers. Jephthah's 300 years after the conquest (Judg. 11:26) is almost certainly merely approximate. Due to the above uncertainties no detailed chronology of this period can be given with confidence.

The United Monarchy. Due to a number of\ uncertainties the absolute date for the establishment of the United Monarchy can not be given. The OT does not give the length of the reign of Saul, but Paul in a sermon at Antioch refers to it as 40 years (Acts 13:21). If Saul reigned a full 40 years, David was not born until ten years ·after Saul began his reign, for he was 30 when he took the throne (II Sam. 5:4). The battle with the Philistines at Michmash, with Jonathan in command of a large part of the. army, presumably took place early in Saul's reign, perhaps even in his second year (I Sam. 13:1,2). In such a case Jonathan would have been well advanced in years when David was a mere youth, which is out of harmony with the picture in the Biblical record. Other difficulties are also involved, all making it clear that Saul either did not reign a full 40 years, or that he must have been very young when he took the throne.

The reign of David, on the other hand, may be regarded as a full 40 years for he reigned seven years in Hebron and 33 in Jerusalem (II Sam. 5:4,5; I Kings 2:11; I Chron. 3:4), and one event is dated in the 40th year (I Chron. 26:31).

Solomon began his reign before the death of David (I Kings 1:32-48), but how long is not recorded. Presumably it was only a short time, but the indefiniteness of this period must be taken into consideration in any endeavor to establish an absolute chronology. And the 40 years of his reign (I Kings 11:42) might have been intended as a round number. Going back to the Exodus the recorded periods are as follows: 40,8,40,18,80,20,40, 7,40,3,23,22,18,6,7,10,8,40,20,40,40,40,40. Unless we can be certain that all these numbers are absolute, we cannot be certain of an absolute chronology for the periods involved.

The Divided Monarchy. For the period of the Divided Monarchy an entirely different situation is found. Here there are an abundance of data which may be checked against each other, and which are no longer round. Four Biblical yardsticks are here provided—the lengths of reign of the rulers of Judah and those of Israel, and the synchronisms of Judah with Israel and of Israel with Judah. Furthermore, a number of synchronisms with the fixed years of contemporary Assyria make possible a check with an exact chronological yardstick, and make possible the establishment of absolute years B.C. for the period of the kings.

Various methods were employed in the ancient East for reckoning the official years of kings. When Solomon's kingdom was first divided, Judah followed those nations where the year when a ruler took the throne was termed his "accession year." Israel, on the other hand, followed those nations where a king termed his initial year his "first year." According to this latter method the year when a king began to reign was always counted twice—as the last year of his predecessor and as his own first official year. Thus reigns reckoned according to this method were always one year longer in official length than those reckoned according to the former method, and there was always a gain of one year for every reign over absolute time. The following graphs will make these two methods of reckoning clear, and will show how the totals of Israel for this period increase by one year for every reign over those of Judah:

	Old king	New king					
	last year	accession year					
Accession-year reckoning	last year	accession year	1st year		2nd year		3rd year
Non-accession-year reckoning	last year	1st year	2nd year		3rd year		4th year
JUDAH, official years:	22	23	46	47	58	61	78	79
Rehoboam 17 Abijam 3 Asa	2nd	3rd	26th	27th	38th	41	Jehoshaphat 17th	18th
Jeroboam	22	Nadab 2	Baasha 24	Elah 2	Omri 12 Ahab 4th Zimri		22	Ahaziah 2 Jehoram
ISRAEL, official years:	22	24	48	50	62	66	84	86
Excess years for Israel	0	1	2	3	4	5	6	7

The following table shows how the totals of both nations from the disruption to the death of Ahaziah in Israel in the 18th year of Jehoshaphat in Judah (omitting the seven-day reign of Zimri) are identical and perfectly correct when correctly understood:

ISRAEL			JUDAH	
King	Official years	Actual years	King	Years
Jeroboam	22	21	Rehoboam	17
Nadab	2	1	Abijam	3
Baasha	24	23	Asa	41
Elah	2	1	Jehoshaphat	18
Omri	12	11		
Ahab	22	21		
Ahaziah	2	1		
Total	86	79		79

THE EXILE AND RETURN. The book of Kings closes with the notice of the release of Jehoiachin from capitvity on the 27th day of the 12th month, in the 37th year of his captivity and the accession year of Amel-Marduk (II Kings 25:27). That was April 2, 561 B.C.

Babylon fell to the Persians Oct.12,539 B.C., and Cyrus in the first year of his reign issued a decree permitting the Jews to return and rebuild the temple (II Chron. 36:22; Ezra 1:1). On the basis of Nisan regnal years this would have been 538 B.C. However, Nehemiah 1:1; 2:1 gives evidence that the author of Nehemiah reckoned the years of the Persian kings not from Nisan as was the Persian custom, but from Tishri, in accord with the Jewish custom. The Aramaic papyri from Elephantine in Egypt give evidence that the same custom was employed by the Jewish colony there in the fifth century B.C. (See S. H. Horn and L. H. Wood, "The Fifth-Century Jewish Calendar at Elephantine," Journal of Near Eastern Studies, XIII (January, 1954), pp. 1-20.) Inasmuch as Chronicles-Ezra-Nehemiah were originally one and came from the same author, the indications are that the first year of Cyrus referred to in Ezra 1:1 was reckoned on a Tishri basis, and that it was, therefore, in 537 that Cyrus issued his decree.

Haggai began his ministry on the first day of the sixth month in the second year of Darius (Hag. 1:1), Aug. 29, 520, and Zechariah commenced his work in the eighth month of the same year (Zech. 1:1), in October or November, 520. The temple was completed on the third of Adar, the sixth year of Darius (Ezra 6:15), March 12, 515.

The return of Ezra from Babylon was begun the first day of the first month, in the seventh year of Artaxerxes (Ezra 7:7,9). Artaxerxes came to the throne in December, 465, which would bring the first of Nisan his seventh year on April 8, 458, according to Persian reckoning, but on March 27, 457, according to Judean years. The evidence that this was the custom then employed has already been given above.

Word was brought to Nehemiah of the sad state of affairs at Jerusalem in the month Kislev of the 20th year of Artaxerxes (Neh. 1:1), and in Nisan of that same 20th year Nehemiah stood before the king and received permission to return to Jerusalem to rebuild the city (Neh. 2:1-8). That was April, 444. With Nehemiah's return to Babylon in the 32nd year of Artaxerxes (Neh. 13:6), 433/32, the chronology of the Old Testament proper comes to a close.　　　　　　　　　　　　　　　E.R.T.

The following are the conditions that make possible the construction of a chronological pattern of the kings based on the Biblical data which possess internal harmony and are in accord with the years of contemporary Assyria and Babylon: Tishri regnal years for Judah and Nisan years for Israel; accession-year reckoning for Judah except for Jehoram, Ahaziah, Athaliah, and Joash, who followed the non-accession-year system then employed in Israel; non-accession-year reckoning in Israel for the early period, and from Jehoash to the end, accession-year reckoning; synchronisms of each nation in accord with its own current system of reckoning; a number of co-regencies or of overlapping reigns when rival rulers exercised control; a double chronological pattern for both Israel and Judah involving the closing years of Israel's history.

The years of the kings based on the above principles are as follows:

ISRAEL

Ruler	Overlapping Reign	Reign
Jeroboam I		931/30-910/9
Nadab		910/9 -909/8
Baasha		909/8 -886/85
Elah		886/85-885/84
Zimri		885/84
Tibni		885/84-880
Omri	885/84-880	880 -874/73
Ahab		874/73-853
Ahaziah		853 -852
Joram		852 -841
Jehu		841 -814/13
Jehoahaz		814/13-798
Jehoash		798 -782/81
Jeroboam II	793/92-782/81	782/81-753
Zachariah		753 -752
Shallum		752
Menahem		752 -742/41
Pekahiah		742/41-740/39
Pekah	752 -740/39	740/39-732/31
Hoshea		732/31-723/22

JUDAH

Ruler	Overlapping Reign	Reign
Rehoboam		931/30-913
Abijam		913 -911/10
Asa		911/10-870/69
Jehoshaphat	873/72-870/69	870/69-848
Jehoram	853 -848	848 -841
Ahaziah		841
Athaliah		841 -835
Joash		835 -796
Amaziah		796 -767
Azariah	792/91-767	767 -740/39
Jotham	750 -740/39	740/39-732/31
Ahaz	735 -732/31	732/31-716/15
Hezekiah		716/15-687/86
Manasseh	697/96-687/86	687/86-643/42
Amon		643/42-641/40
Josiah		641/40-609
Jehoahaz		609
Jehoiakim		609 -598
Jehoiachin		598 -597
Zedekiah		597 -586